Olly Smith is the International Wine and Spirits Communicator of the Year 2009. He writes his weekly wine column for the *Mail on Sunday* and is a regular on *Saturday Kitchen* as well as *This Morning* and *Market Kitchen* and a popular host for food and drink festivals including Masterchef Live, Gordon Ramsay's Taste of Christmas, The F Word Live and Channel 4's Taste Festivals. He is also the main presenter on Channel 4's *Iron Chef UK*. When his heat-seeking nostrils and targeting taste buds are taking a break, he loves keeping pigs and bees, fishing, movies and roasting things on his home-made bar-b best of all.

Olly Smith
EAT & DRINK

Olly Smith
EAT & DRINK

GOOD FOOD THAT'S GREAT
TO DRINK WITH!

headline

First published in 2010
by HEADLINE PUBLISHING GROUP

1

Cataloguing in Publication Data is available from the British Library

ISBN 978 0 7553 6062 8

Design by Roland Codd
Illustrations by Olly Smith

Printed and bound in the UK by Butler Tanner and Dennis

All endpaper and introduction (pp 8–11) photographs courtesy of Olly Smith

All other photographs courtesy of Shutterstock: ampFotoStudio 72; a9photo 96, Angarato 79, anna1311 158,
172, AnnaTA 142, Robert Anthony 53; cenker atila 178, atilay 143, Awe Inspiring Images 63, barbaradudzinska
137, 177; BestPhoto1 110; Silvia Bogdanski 179; Bochkarev Photography 139; Bronwyn Photo 107, Chiyacat 196,
Perry Correll 226, crolique 17, Janaka Dharmasena 145, Willem Dijkstra 221, DJM-photo 33, Andreja Donko 217,
Drozdowski 116, Elena Elisseeva 43; Diane N. Ennis 24; Marie C. Fields 187; Susan Fox 82, Frances L Fruit 60,
21, ScottyH 21, 195, J. Helgason 185, Steve Holderfield 118, IDAL 127, idiz 48; inacio pires 160; Jaroslav74
100; jocicalek 153; Denise Kappa 75; Scott Karcich 64, Lasse Kristensen 138, Lana 78; lantapix 192, Karin
Hildebrand Lau 165, LianeM 84, Lilyana Vynogradova 49, lisasaadphotography 174, Alberto Loyo 117, Robyn
Mackenzie 105, 136, 189; Mona Makela 201, Cristi Matei 97; Mimohe 200; Kati Molin 18, 39, Monkey Business
Images 15, 30, 144, 146, 152, 181, 203; Luciano Mortula 13, Juriah Mosin 224; Mikhail Nekrasov 93, nito 162,
Ocean Image Photography 73, Nayashkova Olga 47, Payless Images 65, picamaniac 22, Pinkcandy 180, Denis
and Yulia Pogostins 136, Steven Poh 63, Quayside 45, Anna Sedneva 124, Torsten Schon 207, Shebeko 194,
Ekaterina Shlikhunova 151; Ralf Siemieniec 106; Sandra van der Steen 68; Ljupco Smokovski 131; sue120502
88; Jonathan Stokes / SelectPhoto 205; Maurizio Tome 215; UnaPhoto 176; Valentyn Volkov 199; Shane White
19, 95; willmetts 197, Kwong Yiing Woan 41; Dusan Zidar 128.

Headline's policy is to use papers that are natural, renewable and recyclable products and
made from wood grown in sustainable forests. The logging and manufacturing processes are expected to
conform to the environmental regulations of the country of origin.

HEADLINE PUBLISHING GROUP
An Hachette UK Company
338 Euston Road
London NW1 3BH

www.headline.co.uk
www.hachette.co.uk
www.ollysmith.com

CONTENTS

This book is dedicated to my gorgeous wife Sophie,
who I would eat if it wasn't illegal.

With special thanks to Granny Smokey and Granny Pip for inspiring
my endless love of eating and drinking.

FOREWORD

BY SIR ROGER MOORE

I enjoy many things in life – food and wine amongst them.

What better than a lunch or dinner with loved ones, over a bottle or two of delicious wine?

Though I have to warn, novices should beware: eating and drinking looks easy but, don't be fooled. It is, in fact, a skill to be honed over many years of practice. Hand and mouth coordination is all-important, as is hand grip around a bottle.

There are many wonderful chefs in the world who spend hours preparing and refining menus. I hasten to add that I am not a world-class chef, though I do enjoy dabbling in the kitchen. No, I am more of what you might call a world-class consumer – that is to say, quality and not quantity!

A world-class plate of food has to, in my opinion, be accompanied by a world-class glass of wine. That's where Olly Smith comes in.

He's one of those clever little devils who know which wine complements what food and which bottle will bring out the best of the flavours on the plate.

So, my advice to all you novices out there is to eat and drink this book, and then you, too, will be all-knowing.●

INTRODUCTION

My big brother Will was lucky enough to see *Moonraker* at the cinema. I was too young. But by the time *For Your Eyes Only* came out, I'd already seen and memorized most of the Bond movies on telly. Roger Moore was, and remains to this day, my hero. The first time I saw him on the big screen my jaw hit the floor. He was so warm, so smooth and so cool. I loved his Lotus Esprit Turbo, the little mole on his left cheek, his impeccable hair and the fact that he looked a tiny bit like my dad. I remember thinking in the cinema aged six, 'If he can do it, I can do it', and deciding there and then that one day I would meet Roger to thank him for bringing so much invention and adventure to my childhood. They say you should never meet your heroes but, take it from me, that is 100 per cent balderdash. You've got to deploy everything in your power to meet them – if they don't turn out to be who you thought they were, stuff 'em, but if they are . . . ! There was a moment on stage in New York a few years back when Roger collapsed. It terrified me. I hadn't met him yet – he had no right to conk out before I'd seized the opportunity to embrace him like a god! My pal Dan Chambers is a genius animation director and he created a small cartoon called 'Sir Roger Moore's Requiem'. It was more or less a fantasy of what would happen to Roger's soul in the afterlife, played out to the sounds of Verdi's *Requiem* and it was jolly funny. A hoot, in fact. Dan unleashed it on to the internet in a flurry of anticipation and a stampede of chutzpah. One way or another, it migrated to the bedside of Sir Roger Moore who emailed Dan to say he was 'tickled'. Dan still likes to think that it was his animation that nursed Roger back to health (rather than the small army of doctors and nurses who were determined, like me, that he would raise an eyebrow at them and illuminate the room with his warm-hearted hilarity again). Dan then brought me in on the Rog action – thanks, Dan! At the time I was working as an animation scriptwriter for *Charlie and Lola*, *Pingu* and even a single momentous day working on *Wallace & Gromit: Curse of the Were-Rabbit* (if you wait long enough during the credits I get a thank you, which is a huge buzz!). Together we approached Sir Roger's agent, the glorious and highly encouraging Gareth Owen, who has since become my dear chum, and suggested Dan and I make some animations to support Roger's work for UNICEF. I will never forget what happened next. Gareth said, 'Well, he's not in the UK for a while so unless you fancy going to Monte Carlo to meet him . . . ' Dan and I were on a plane next day.

We met His Rogesty in a suite at the Hotel de Paris and the reception guys couldn't believe that a couple of scruffy lads like us could possibly be there to meet Big Rog. But we were. And we did! He was wearing his resplendent white shirt, white trousers and white shoes. He looked like a god. He behaved like a king. He was funny, warm and, above all, extremely kind. I performed a voiceover opposite him and had to prevent myself from crying with joy. I felt so lucky that I had the chance to thank Roger for giving me so much fun as a boy sitting in the ABC cinema in Bournemouth and perched in front of our old black-and-white telly at home.

Yes, it was superb and deeply cool but, here's the thing, it wasn't just about hanging out with an iconic star and drooling over his impeccable degree of smoothness – though he is so charming it is hard not to start shrieking 'You're the coolest human!' into his face – Sir Roger also inspired me when we talked about UNICEF and the international work he undertakes. He had deeply impressive close knowledge of the problems faced by children the world over. His sincere, urgent concern was clear – he cares a great deal about the plight of kids who desperately need help on a series of fronts, from education to immunization, and from curing goitre to tackling AIDS. I decided there and then that I wanted to follow in his footsteps and do whatever I could to support his work and the work of UNICEF.

So, I say, meet your heroes if you can. Rog exceeded all my

expectations. He's now a good pal; we've been on *BBC Breakfast* together, and I even appear in his autobiography *My Word is My Bond* on page 286. What a gent. Thanks, Roger, and thanks to Granny Smokey for taking me to the cinema and cooking the world's greatest biscuits for me to eat there (see page 15). All I need now is to eat Granny's biscuits with Roger Moore and the circle will be complete. And that's what really counts when it comes to empowering and loading up a moment with potent energy so that it burns brightly in your memory – combinations. A film and a biscuit, a cuddle and a kiss, or, like my die-hard Welsh rugby-supporting friend Jimmy Garnon whose wife Sarah gave birth to their first son just as Wales won the Grand Slam in the Six Nations for the first time since 1978, a birth and a win. Now that's a memorable combination! And, for me, a genius food and drink combination can offer similarly potent imprints on the mind and unleash a stratum of pleasure that knows no end. It's all about great food that's good to drink with. When have you ever read that in a restaurant or food review? I, and many others like me, live for great food to drink with. Because of my job, I spend my life inventing recipes to match the wild cauldron of flavours that are busting to get out of my drinks cabinet. The recipes have to taste fantastic in their own right – with or without drink – or else my young daughters Ruby and Lily peer across their cutlery as though I'd just asked them to tuck into the dog. Raw.

Although CERN steals all the hype about particles colliding (mainly due to good publicity and semi-professional showing-off), the sort of molecular collisions that CERN rabbits on about occur every day on your plate, in your glass and across your tongue. As soon as you spread butter on to your toast you're effectively breaking and re-making a whole new world of texture, taste and bespoke sensual pleasure. Yes! You are a kinky headstrong maestro imbued with the power to penetrate a world of limitless invisible delight. To make your journey to Flavour Central a little simpler, I've divided my thinking into chapter headings dictated by flavour, instead of the traditional 'starters', 'mains' and 'puddings'. Let your mood and cravings decide whether to set sail across an ocean of smoky flavours, master a meaty feast or frolic with a fruity snack.

Recipes are the beginning of great days, the blueprints for a secret machine that will take you to an ever-changing dimension of pleasure, sharing and nourishment. The matrix of possible food combinations is endless – add wine and drinks into the mix as a fourth dimension and you're on the verge of extreme ecstasy (and in serious danger of plunging headlong into a whirl of multiple gastrogasms).

Any two distinct flavours can ignite a spark which blooms and multiplies into a richer dimension of dynamic stimulation. A bit like a horde of miniature carpet bombs firing pleasure and intrigue across your palate. The resulting sense of contrast and delight is capable of eliciting a far more resonant emotional response than the flavours might have done on their own. And, by engaging with place, provenance, newness and the spirit of playfulness, which chefs like Heston Blumenthal have deployed to such glorious effect, it only gets better. It's well known that memory is closely connected to aromas and tastes. Matching food to drink is, in part, about harnessing those memories and turning them into something new. A bit like re-mixing, re-energizing and composing a new soundtrack that will widen your sensory experience and engage more deeply with the fabric of your world. For me, pairing food with drink is the universe's most immediate and best-value vacation. And inventing fresh combinations, well, it's a bit like mining for jewels and discovering a hidden world of limitless horizons on the end of your shovel. When you combine two flavours that exponentially multiply the deliciousness of the dish, whether it's something as simple as a sip of Cognac with a frosty bite of Magnum for a DIY Baileys – TRY IT!, or eating a chunk of Stilton with a glass of chilled Hungarian Tokaji, you are making magic.

The point of all these matches, though, is to share them, delight in them and go to bed with a smile on your face that glows, warms and reflects back at you off your ceiling. Happy snoozing!●

SWEET

Sweet is a buzz. The tin of Golden Syrup in Mum's kitchen was, to me, a bit like the golden idol that Indiana Jones attempts to steal at the beginning of *Raiders of the Lost Ark*. Any price was worth paying. Scaling the kitchen units in my underpants was a favoured method for the mission. Sometimes I would wear my Zorro mask or tuck a plastic pistol into my pants. If you're going to go down, go down fighting. More often than not, though, I would succeed in my mission and snaffle the golden elixir of paradise but, even when the mission itself went undetected, Mum was highly adept at analyzing the threads, smudges and sticky trails that I inevitably left behind during my stealth attack for a sugar burst.

As the years went by, I discovered that something sweet by itself is actually less interesting than something sweet mingled with a gang of other flavours. Take caramel. It's good stuff. But add a pinch of salt and the intensifying effect on the entire mouthful is more thrilling than leaping from the top of the kitchen cabinets with no parachute. Take it from me. I've been there. Gradually, I learned to use sweetness in other dishes.

One of my first success stories, which I still make to this day, is my HOT CHOCOLATE SAUCE. It relies on salted butter to open a hidden dimension of sexual intensity. It is all done by feel and taste so it's up to you to try it, play with it and work out what is best for you. And if I can make it aged nine, then anyone can make it:

Melt a knob of salted butter in a pan over a medium heat. Add a generous, long drizzle of Golden Syrup. Add 1 or 2 tablespoons of cocoa powder. (You can add more butter and syrup to taste at this point – indulge yourself and try it straight from the spoon!) Add some full-fat milk and keep tasting, keep warming, adjust quantities, then serve immediately in a bowl around a knob of vanilla ice cream. Don't overdo the ice cream – this is all about the best chocolate sauce in the known universe.

After going hammer and tongs down Sweet Street a few times, I learned to use sweet as a linking device – sometimes in harmony with the dish (as with sweet custard over apple crumble) and sometimes as a contrast (honey in a zinging salad dressing). It's nothing new – think of a savoury croissant with chocolate, or the Mexican penchant for chocolatizing their meat, or, here in the UK, our love of fruity stuffings with a Sunday roast bird, or apple sauce with pork.●

Sweet does things to you and the key when matching a wine to a sweet dish is to make sure that the wine is as sweet as or sweeter than the dish. If your starting point is the sweet wine itself, though, then you don't have to go sweet with your food at all – a glass of Sauternes with a salty slice of Roquefort cheese is a joyful mouthful.

SWEET SPOT

These Sweet Spot recipes are all about their core of sweetness – their inherently sweet nature. It's up to you to take your sweet tooth in whichever direction you most fancy – right now!

As I got older, I moved away from raiding the tin of Golden Syrup and instead started delving into the adjacent tin of black treacle. Dark, burnt, sticky love juice – I still salivate just thinking about it. It's amazing added to meaty stews, is a key component of parkin (oooh you're going to love my parkin – see page 156!) and is generally a highly underrated ingredient. Use it sparingly, since it can be overpowering, and you will have a powerful ally in kitchen combat. My homage to that sticky tin of forbidden black goo is this recipe for TREACLE CARAMELS . . . Tickle with Treacle! This will make enough for a party:

200g treacle

150ml double cream

300g caster sugar

pinch of Maldon salt

→ Line a small baking tray with baking paper.

→ Place the treacle and cream into a saucepan over a medium heat and bring to the boil, whisking to combine.

→ Meanwhile, place the caster sugar into a separate pan over a medium heat and cook until a dark golden caramel colour, stirring occasionally.

→ Pour the hot treacle cream into the caramel saucepan and cook until thickened and a very dark caramel colour – if you have a sugar thermometer, it should read 128°C.

→ Remove from the heat, add a pinch of salt, and cool slightly before tasting.

→ Pour on to the lined baking tray and transfer to the fridge.

→ When it's just set, mark into bite-size squares. Allow to chill until completely hard and chewy before eating!

And, for a lighter bite, these SHORTCAKE CHERRY BISCUITS are the ones Granny brought with us to watch *For Your Eyes Only* at the cinema in Bournemouth when I first saw Roger Moore on the big screen. What a day! By the way, I remember one batch of these that came out flavoured with TCP thanks to Granny's overzealous cleaning of her mixing bowl. On a grey day, on the beach at Alum Chine, I remember her being very chirpy and insisting that the drizzle was just 'the midday gloom' (whatever that may be) while we ate TCP-flavoured biscuits. Nice.

Preheat the oven to 150°C/300°F/Gas 2 and lightly grease a baking tray. Beat **115g** butter with **55g** caster sugar until light and fluffy. Sift in **175g** plain flour. Mix with a wooden spoon and then finish off with your hands to form a ball of dough. Transfer to a board which has been lightly dusted with caster sugar. Roll out quickly to about 3mm thick and then cut into approximately 15 rounds. Place them on the prepared baking tray and cook for 30 minutes (watch they don't burn). When cool, decorate with half or quarter pieces of glacé cherries.

It's the crunch that I really love about Granny's shortcake – she always made them nice and thin so you could generate a decent amount of crumbs to scatter over the sofa. And GRANNY SMOKEY'S DIGESTIVE BISCUITS also had a spectacular crumbfall ratio:

Preheat the oven to 180°C/350°F/Gas 4 and lightly grease a baking tray. Rub 115g butter into 140g self-raising flour until it resembles breadcrumbs. Add 85g rolled oats or oatmeal, 2 tablespoons caster sugar and ¼ teaspoon salt. Using 1 beaten egg or 1½ tablespoons milk combine to form a firm dough. Roll this out to about 5mm thick, and then cut into approximately 28 rounds. Transfer to the prepared baking tray, prick all over with a fork and then bake for approximately 15–20 minutes. Remove from the oven and cool before eating.

For a classic British treat, match one of these digestive biscuits with a Cox's Orange Pippin apple and serve with a glass of vintage Port — the best you can find. It's an oddly satisfying moment in the world of eating and drinking when three entirely different things collide, like the Three Musketeers, to unify in a convincing and unexpected way. The sweet Port, the crunchy apple and crumbly biscuit interact with one another in a playful way and the apple is a superb palate cleanser. I can hear the sound in my head now of apple crunch, biscuit chomp and Port glug. All you'd need is an armchair and a chinwag to go with it and you'll have attained nirvana.

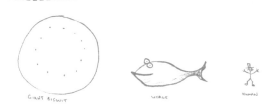

GIANT BISCUIT   WHALE   HUMAN

Biscuits are brilliant. No doubt about it. But ever since my dalliance with Golden Syrup and chocolate sauce, my fascination for chocolate has been acute. Mum and Dad were even persuaded to take me to a Swiss chocolate factory where I first learned about where cocoa comes from and the problems faced by its farmers. Fairtrade for chocolate and cocoa has got to be a good thing. I can still smell the factory now – there was a room where, if memory serves, they deployed something called 'conching', which I reckon was flopping the mix about and getting the air into it. The smell was heady, sweet and utterly intoxicating. Shortly after the trip to the Swiss chocolate factory, I got my first-ever holiday job while doing my GCSEs. It was working in a chocolate shop called The Chocolate Box in St Helier, Jersey. A lady known only as Mrs R ran it. I'm not sure where Mrs R was from, but she had an accent which also added to her mysterious and capable air. Her name sounded to me like that of a senior member of MI6 – someone who'd send James Bond on an impossible mission, probably to face significant peril. Mrs R was feared by one and all – customers and staff alike. But to me, she was just lovely. We cultivated an understanding: I worked hard for her; she turned a blind eye when I snaffled the odd fresh cream. From one holiday to another I slowly became educated in the world of Mrs R's outrageously luxuriant Belgian chocolate. I remember my favourites to this day – the white chocolate fresh creams with a delicate hint of praline – malty and sensational delicacies that I still dream about (as well as the dreams of giant tins of Golden Syrup being poured into my bathtub ready for me to be basted in).

My GREAT GRANNY'S CHOCOLATE BISCUITS are so easy to make that the kids cook them with me today and it is one of the first recipes I remember helping Mum with at home. To think she used to make them with her Granny, too! These quantities will make approximately 60 biscuits, so I usually halve it:

Preheat the oven to 170°C/325°F/Gas 3. Cream 225g butter and 115g caster sugar together in a bowl until light and fluffy. Sift 225g self-raising flour and 55g cocoa powder into the bowl and combine to form a dough. Roll into little balls the size of walnuts and place on a baking tray. Flatten with a wet fork, leaving grooves on the surface that will expand as the biscuits cook. Magic! Cook for 30 minutes but watch them in case they burn.

Chocolate in a biscuit is sublime but for a quicker hit of chocolate you should drink it. And if you're feeling like a double dose, dip your chocolate biscuit into your chocolate drink and I promise it will remain our little secret. I won't tell if you don't. The quantities of DADDY'S HOT CHOCOLATE given here serve me and my girls, who guzzle it whenever I make it:

Heat 3¹/₂ mugs full-fat milk in a saucepan over a medium heat. Stir in 1 teaspoon ground cinnamon and 3 teaspoons Fairtrade cocoa.

Dark chocolate is tangy, milk chocolate is rich, but the sweetest of all chocolates is white chocolate – which is generally just made of cocoa butter, sugar and milk. It can take an aromatic twist very well (try a square of white chocolate with a lime fruit gum) and here I've deployed the uniquely aromatic flavour of cardamom to offset the sweetness, which by itself is a bit one-dimensional. Harnessed here it develops a whole new layer of intrigue ... THE KING OF CAKES – WHITE CHOCOLATE AND CARDAMOM:

THE KING OF CAKES

200g white chocolate

6 medium eggs

250g caster sugar

8 cardamom pods, split and seeds crushed

150g ground almonds

For the topping

125g white chocolate

2 cardamom pods, split and seeds crushed

40g butter

→ Preheat the oven to 180°C/350°F/Gas 4 and line a 23cm loose-bottomed cake tin.

→ Melt the white chocolate in a heatproof bowl over a saucepan of barely simmering water, or in the microwave.

→ Meanwhile, separate 5 of the eggs. Add the final egg to the 5 egg yolks and whisk with the caster sugar until light, fluffy and thickened.

→ Add the crushed cardamom seeds to the egg mixture, and then stir in the ground almonds. Pour in the melted chocolate and beat well.

→ Whisk the egg whites in a separate bowl until they form soft peaks and then fold them into the cake mixture. Pour the batter into the prepared tin and smooth the top.

→ Place in the oven and bake for 45 minutes until risen and firm. Check the cake after 30 minutes – if it is looking a little brown, cover with a piece of tin foil and continue cooking. To check it is cooked, insert a skewer into the centre of the cake – if it comes out clean, the cake is ready. If not, return to the oven for another 5 minutes and check again. (The cake could take as long as 60 minutes to cook.) Remove from the oven and allow to cool in the tin before turning out on to a plate.

→ To make the topping, melt the white chocolate as above and then remove from the heat. Add the crushed cardamom seeds and butter and whisk to combine. Drizzle this over the cool cake, then leave to set for 5 minutes before serving.

I may sound like a wine pervert, but Italian Moscato D'Asti is the order of the day here. The sparkling fizzy elderflower fun of this wine brings a unique counterpoise to the richness of the dessert. And around a mere 8% alcohol it'll ensure your dinner guests don't slouch into an early booze-fuelled slumber. And, by a happy coincidence, a glass of sparkling Moscato is a rather superb way to start the day so if there's some left over then you can have a glass with your breakfast!

GRANNY SMOKEY'S BREAD AND BUTTER PUDDING

just less than 600ml milk

2 eggs

1 tablespoon caster sugar

1–3 slices white bread or brioche (depending on the thickness of the slice), buttered and cut into small triangles (you can also use croissant or panettone)

handful of sultanas

zest of 1 lemon

LONG LIVE THE LARDER!

Whereas Moscato is all about the flavour of fresh grapes, I'm also a huge fan of dried grapes, that is to say sultanas and raisins, which develop intense sweetness and a divinely squidgy texture that works superbly in cooking as in GRANNY SMOKEY'S BREAD AND BUTTER PUDDING. You can customize this bread and butter pudding with all sorts of spices (try a sprinkling of cinnamon):

→ Preheat the oven to 180°C/350°F/Gas 4 and grease a soufflé dish.

→ Beat together the milk, eggs and sugar, and set aside.

→ Layer the bread triangles with the sultanas and lemon zest in the soufflé dish, and then pour the egg mixture over the top.

→ Place in a bain-marie and into the oven until set (approximately 1 hour).

Sometimes, if we were especially lucky, my brother Will and I would get to raid the jam shelf in Granny Smokey's larder. Now, first of all, let me mourn the loss of the larder. I think every house should have one. A small room that isn't warm and that isn't refrigerated but that's perfect for storing cheese, cold meats, jam, veg, wine and for hiding in during games of hide-and-seek.

Granny Smokey's was not just a glorified food store, she kept cooking equipment and utensils in there, most of which I still can't fathom the purpose of. Exotic aromas of mountain greenery wafted into my freckly nose whenever I looked inside and, to my eight-year-old eye, she had an aqualung, ice skates and leather bellows roped together for bread-making, a tower of loose-leaf tea in tins that reached up the Buddha's Lair and a giant canvas book of recipes and cuttings that had the seal of the Lord Chamberlain on its cover.

Of course these images are entirely fanciful. But there was something magical about that larder. I think Granny had also managed to fit her spin-dryer in there as well, which breaks all the laws of architecture, physics and common decency. The woman was unstoppable. Actually Granny Smokey was literally unstoppable – a ball of energy, endlessly rustling plastic bags containing new delicacies, walking as much as she could, miles on miles from her house into Bournemouth city centre. A will of iron and the playful character of a scampering baby giraffe. One of her greatest legacies was her collection of jams. They lined the larder walls and Granny made everything from raspberry to damson and all sorts of different variations on sweet themes. She had not just one, but three different recipes for Strawberry Jam, all of which are excellent, but which all had differing levels of sweetness.

GRANNY SMOKEY'S VICTORIA SPONGE CAKE

This cake reminds me of Mr Baker. He was the man who came and painted Granny's fence with creosote every once in a while. I can picture him now in his blue overalls and flat cap; he was of similar shape and size to Alfred Hitchcock. He smoked Condor Ready Rubbed in his pipe and it was a highlight of my day to nip round to Reddell's the newsagent's to buy him his tobacco. I remember the plume of gentle blue smoke rising up through the leaves of the silver birch tree in Granny's garden as he sat with his mug of tea and slice of Granny's Victoria Sponge Cake. I never once remember him coming into the house, but I recall his impeccable manners, his gentle kindness and the grin on his face when we munched together on thick slices of this glorious cake.

Preheat the oven to 170°C/325°F/Gas 3 and line two cake tins. Cream 175G BUTTER with 175G CASTER SUGAR until light and fluffy. Measure out 175G SELF-RAISING FLOUR and then beat 3 EGGS into the butter and sugar mixture one at a time, adding a bit of flour after each egg. When all the ingredients have been combined, divide between the two cake tins. Bake in the preheated oven for 25-30 minutes. (Keep an eye on it!) When the cakes have cooled, spread with either RASPBERRY OR STRAWBERRY JAM and then sandwich together. Dust with ICING SUGAR and enjoy! (You can reduce the mixture to 115g butter/sugar/flour and 2 eggs if the cake tins are small.)

GRANNY SMOKEY'S JAM GENIUS

All these jams call for sterilized jars to store them in. Here's what you have to do:

Wash the jam jars in hot soapy water, then rinse well. Put them into a preheated oven at 170°C/325°F/Gas 3 until you are ready to use them.

All the recipes produce a weight in jam equal to their combined fruit and sugar weight, less a hundred grams or so. It varies quite a lot, though, depending on how long they've had to be boiled to set, how much liquid is in the fruit etc. And the number of jam jars you'll need depends entirely on the assortment of sizes that you've managed to collect! I always sterilize more than I think I'll need so there isn't a panic at the end of the potting process. (Although when that does happen, I use it as an excuse to eat some straight away on a bit of toast so none of it goes to waste.)

Strawberry Jam I

1.8kg strawberries (after hulling)

1.8kg sugar

Strawberry Jam II

450g strawberries (after hulling)

400g sugar

juice of 1 lemon

STRAWBERRY JAM I

→ Wipe the fruit with a cloth then put into a pan over a medium heat. Bring very slowly to the boil without adding water. Boil for 20 minutes.

→ Remove the pan from the heat and stir in the sugar until dissolved.

→ Bring back to the boil and boil for 10–15 minutes, until a little drop on a cold plate gels.

→ Pot in sterilized jars while the jam is still hot.

STRAWBERRY JAM II

→ Wipe the fruit with a cloth then put into a saucepan with the sugar and cook over a gentle heat until the sugar is dissolved, stirring all the time.

→ Add the lemon juice and bring to the boil. Boil steadily until set. (Cooking time should be approximately 15 minutes.)

→ Pot in sterilized jars while the jam is still hot.

STRAWBERRY JAM III
Method as Strawberry Jam II.

GOOSEBERRY JAM I
→ Simmer the fruit and water until soft.

→ Add the sugar and stir until dissolved.

→ Bring to the boil and boil rapidly until set. (Cooking time should be approximately 25–35 minutes.)

→ Pot in sterilized jars while the jam is still hot.

GOOSEBERRY JAM II
Method as above.

GOOSEBERRY AND STRAWBERRY JAM
→ Simmer the gooseberries in the water for about 10 minutes.

→ Add the strawberries and continue to cook until these are soft.

→ Add the sugar and stir until dissolved.

→ Bring to the boil and boil rapidly until set. (Cooking time should be approximately 25 minutes.)

→ Pot in sterilized jars while the jam is still hot.

Jam is magic – relying on the fruit component to provide the natural setting agent. Another very useful thing to have up your sleeve is SUGAR SYRUP, which often features in cocktails. It is worth making in bulk so you have a ready supply in the refrigerator. It couldn't be simpler:

Put equal parts white sugar and water (i.e. 3 cups of water to 3 cups of sugar) into a saucepan and heat until dissolved. Allow to cool and then unleash your inner cocktail! You can use sugar syrup in all sorts of other ways, too – desserts, dressings and cordials.

Strawberry Jam III

1.8kg strawberries (after hulling)

1.6kg sugar

juice of 4 lemons

Gooseberry Jam I

450g gooseberries

75ml water

450g sugar

(if the fruit is under-ripe use 550g sugar and 300ml water)

Gooseberry Jam II

2kg gooseberries

850ml water

2.7kg sugar

Gooseberry and Strawberry Jam

450g gooseberries

75ml water

450g strawberries (after hulling)

900g sugar

The same principle applies when it comes to making the rosewater syrup that is used in this ROSEWATER SHORTBREAD recipe:

Bring 2 parts sugar and 2 parts water to the simmer with a squirt of fresh lemon or lime juice, stirring occasionally for 10 minutes. If it's too runny add a sprinkle more sugar. Add ¼ part rosewater, and simmer for 10 more minutes. Remove from the heat, allow to cool and pour into a bottle.

Preheat the oven to 180°C/350°F/Gas 4. Place 100g icing sugar, 150g cornflour, 150g plain flour and 150g ground almonds into a food processor, and blitz for a couple of seconds. Add 250g unsalted butter and pulse until coarse breadcrumbs are formed. Pour in 3 tablespoons rosewater syrup and blitz once more until the mixture just starts to come together. Remove from the processor and knead the dough briefly on a work surface. Roll into 50p-sized balls and place them on to a non-stick baking tray, leaving a 3cm gap between each one. Flatten them slightly and then bake in the oven for 12–15 minutes until golden. Remove from the oven and cool before serving.

A brilliant match for these biscuits is LYCHEE AND LIME CHILL-OUT SORBET:

Place 2 x 400g tinned lychees in light syrup (1 drained and 1 liquid reserved) in a food blender with the juice of 1 lime and 3 tablespoons icing sugar. Blitz to a smooth purée. Pass through a fine sieve and put into an ice cream maker. Churn until nearly solid then add 1 egg white and continue to churn. Decant into a freeze-able container and freeze until solid – at least 1 hour. Remove from the freezer 10 minutes before serving to soften slightly.

Late Harvest Gewürztraminer from Alsace is more or less a tribute to rose Turkish delight and lychee so could mimic the flavours in this dish nicely. But for a bubbly contrast pour yourself a glass of sparkling Moscato from Australia; with its frothy grapey sweetness it is a gallon of fun.

SWEET SUPPORT

Keeping bees has been a recent revelation. I love the job that bees do of pollinating so much fruit and veg. I love the way they work together for the good of the colony's survival. I am constantly amazed by how far they can fly and the fact that they can 'waggledance' directions to other bees to find the flowers, pinch the nectar and build stores of honey. Along with the pigs I have started rearing, my bees make me a one-stop shop for honey-roast ham. For the greatest HONEY-ROAST HAM SANDWICH:

Add a touch of DINAH'S HOT PEPPER JELLY (see page 162), some sun-dried tomatoes, a few crunchy lettuce leaves and a scattering of Parmesan flakes to your basic ham and bread sandwich. The sweet/salt/spice balances with the fresh, crunchy lettuce and they elevate the ham to new heights.

It's a great example of sweetness in support of a dish rather than as the headline act. You see, sweetness doesn't have to come from the centre of a dish. It can be added to enhance an otherwise savoury dish – like a tiny sprinkle of sugar on your Special K in the morning, or the pinch of sugar that you add to a tomato pasta sauce, which boosts and brings out the flavour of the tomato. Sweetness can also come from other sources than sugar itself, such as dried fruit. Drying fruit is an excellent way of preserving the generous ripening powers of the summer so you can deploy them later during the colder months and they're mouthbombs of sweetness, too.

DEVILS ON HORSEBACK

I got this version of Devils on Horseback from my pal Lawrence Keogh while he was manning the Roast Stand at Taste of Christmas and it couldn't be simpler:

Cook a batch of COCKTAIL SAUSAGES. Wrap each sausage in STREAKY BACON (trim off any excess fat from the bacon first), spike with a cocktail stick, glaze with a light coating of MANGO CHUTNEY, and then grill for 2–3 minutes until the bacon is crispy. Delish.

PUMPKIN AND APRICOT TAGINE

2 tablespoons olive oil

1 onion, thickly sliced

3 garlic cloves, finely chopped

2 teaspoons *ras el hanout*

½ teaspoon ground cinnamon

½ teaspoon ground ginger

½ teaspoon smoked sweet paprika

1kg pumpkin or butternut squash, peeled and cut into 3cm chunks

400g tinned chopped tomatoes

½ teaspoon saffron threads, soaked in 1 tablespoon hot water

500ml vegetable stock

150g dried apricots, halved

2 tablespoons honey

50g flaked almonds, toasted

2 tablespoons coriander, roughly chopped

2 tablespoons flat-leaf parsley, roughly chopped

salt and freshly ground black pepper

I became fascinated by tagine cooking on a trip to Morocco. I feasted on the most tender lamb tagine in the town of Fez; it was so simple – cooked with apricots and served with saffron rice – but is beautifully vivid in my mind. In this PUMPKIN AND APRICOT TAGINE I've gone with the vivid colours of North Africa but given the dish an autumnal twist – perfect for Halloween! This serves 4:

→ Heat a large sauté pan until hot, add the olive oil, onion and garlic and cook for 2–3 minutes.

→ Add all the spices and cook for a further minute.

→ Add the pumpkin and fry for 2–3 minutes until slightly coloured on each side, then stir in the tomatoes.

→ Add the saffron, stock, apricots and honey and bring to the boil.

→ Turn the heat down, cover and simmer for 20–25 minutes until tender.

→ Add the flaked almonds, coriander and parsley and cook for a further 2 minutes.

→ Season with salt and pepper, and serve with some herby couscous.

Sweet flavours are glorious in their luxuriant life-affirming instant hit but there's a whole world of sweet flavours within wine itself! Sweet wines – also known as 'stickies' – are, in my view, massively underrated. If you're put off by the intensity or lusciousness of a sweet wine, experiment with less pricey examples by serving them over crushed ice as an aperitif or matching them with fruit salad to get your hand in, and then migrate to the serious kit.

Here are a few recommendations of sweet wine styles and some food matches to look out for from around the world. This is by no means exhaustive and, if any of these take your fancy, get in touch through www.hotbottle.co.uk and I will happily recommend some more!

GERMANY

Eiswein is made from grapes that have frozen on the vine and are usually picked at -8 degrees or colder! When the grapes are pressed, the frozen part leaves behind an amazingly sweet, pure and luscious elixir that has awesome tension between sweetness and acidity. Canada also produces some amazing Ice Wine that's well worth getting involved with — unwind in the bath with a very close friend and a glass or two and see what I mean.

Trockenbeerenauslese is pricey stuff but can be amazingly memorable. Made from grapes that have been infected with noble rot (*Botrytis cinerea,* which intensifies sweetness and zip) and shrivelled up to tiny raisins. Intense and sweet — Golden Syrup for grownups.

With their zip, these two styles of wine work magnificently with fruity puddings that have some acidity such as PLUM TATIN (see page 40) or apple strudel. Or you could serve them instead of pudding as a liquid sweetie!

FRANCE

Sauternes is a classic from Bordeaux, made using Semillon, Sauvignon and Muscadelle grapes with an intensity derived from noble rot. The best ones are aged in oak and develop a honey, lemon and vanilla-like aroma. They are expensive and the most famous of them is Château d'Yquem, which some would say is the world's finest sweet wine. Yields are so low that each vine produces just one glass of wine. Prices range from several hundred pounds per bottle to several thousand! Australia's answer to Sauternes is Botrytis Semillon which is often outstanding value and decent quality, too.

France also has some interesting and underrated fortified sweet wines from Rivesaltes, Banyuls and Maury in the Languedoc, which are made from fortified Grenache grapes and will appeal to lovers of Port. If you see the word Rancio on the label, it means it is particularly tangy and nutty thanks to deliberate oxidation. UNLEASH THE BEAST!

HUNGARY

My all-time favourite sweet wine is Hungarian Tokaji (pronounced Tock-aye) — I could bathe in it daily and never tire of its sheer awesomeness. It is the best drink to have with an orange pudding (match it with my TANGY ORANGE AND SQUIDGY ALMOND CAKE, see overleaf) and is increasingly easy to find. Made from local Hungarian grapes with amazing names that are so unlike anything we say in English that I often find myself incanting them in the shower like an old forgotten spell: Harslevelu (Harsh-lev-eh-loo), Furmint (For-mint), Zeta (as in Catherine Zeta-Jones). They all sound like varying degrees of contemplation. 'The patient finds herself in a state of fluctuating Harslevelu induced by a measured dose of sticky wine. Her Furmint levels are consistent and according to my spectrometer the patient's Zeta membrane is resonating like the sails of a Georgian warship on parade day. I commend the patient's health to the committee.' So the grapes may sound like obscure names of pre-war flu vaccinations but they taste like the milk of Zeus. (I have never tried to milk Zeus but I am sure if we harnessed him to a cow-machine he would yield sweet bounty.)

The sweet wines are produced thanks to mists that slide up the hillsides from the Bodrog and Tisza rivers (great names for twin puppies). The mists rot the grapes on the vines imbuing them with a noble rot (*Botrytis cinerea*), which desiccates the grapes like raisins, removing moisture and concentrating both sweetness and acidity. The resulting juice that gets squeezed out is unctuous and sticky. The true pleasure of Tokaji is in the balance of sugar to acidity, which is absolutely thrilling. When young, expect flavours of syrup and citrus peel, when it's aged it goes more nutty and savoury. Either way, it's a wine of great complexity to be sipped and lingered over. The sweetness of Tokaji is measured in Puttonyos: graded 1-6, with 6 the sweetest. This is topped only by the maximum glory of Essenzia, which is even sweeter and highly prize. If you want to go cheap to match my cake, try Australian Brown Brothers Orange Flora and Muscat for a fiver, which is nowhere near as complex as Tokaji but is rather good served in tumblers over crushed ice. Especially if your guests are too far gone to really appreciate the Tokaji!

SPAIN

PX stands for Pedro Ximenez — a treacle-black sweet sherry that is super-rich and concentrated, like liquidized figs and dates. Pour aged PX over vanilla ice cream and weep with joy. A real trophy and an underrated wine from Spain.

PORTUGAL

Portugal is rightly proud of its Port. I'm a big fan of Tawny Port, which is amber and less heavy than full-on red vintage Port. I'm especially partial to Tawny Port with an age on the label (this is an average age of the wine). They can be wonderfully concentrated with nutty, caramel and coffee flavours. Serve it chilled with salted almonds as an aperitif on a summery evening and feel the magic! It is also, in my view, the best style of Port to match with Stilton.

GREECE

Samos Sweet Wine is from the Greek island of the same name and production goes back beyond a thousand years BC! It is toffee-like and can be orangey, along with a luscious sweetness that is made from Muscat à Petit Grains. It works exceptionally well with gingery spice and cinnamon-infused puddings — with my PARKIN (see page 156) it's a stunner.

TANGY ORANGE AND
SQUIDGY ALMOND CAKE

Makes 1 x 30cm cake

4 Seville oranges

450g butter

450g caster sugar

6 eggs

650g ground almonds

For the syrup

125ml Seville orange juice

225g caster sugar

1 teaspoon orange blossom water

→ Preheat the oven to 180°C/350°F/Gas 4 and line a 30cm cake tin with baking paper.

→ Cut two of the oranges into thin slices, and then juice the remaining two.

→ Heat a frying pan until hot, add 25g of the butter and the orange slices and fry until just caramelized. Place the slices, caramelized side down, into the cake tin.

→ Place the remaining butter and the sugar into a bowl and whisk until light and fluffy.

→ Add the eggs, one at a time, mixing well.

→ Add the ground almonds and orange juice and stir to combine. Pour the mixture over the slices in the tin.

→ Place on a baking tray into the oven and bake for 25–30 minutes until just risen and golden.

→ Meanwhile, to make the syrup, place the Seville orange juice and sugar into a saucepan, bring to the boil and cook until it forms a thick syrup, but before it colours (about 10–12 minutes). Take off the heat and stir in the orange blossom water.

→ When the cake comes out of the oven, pour the syrup over it and allow to cool.

→ Turn the cake out so the orange slices are uppermost, slice and serve with a little whipped cream.

Of all the sweet things in my life I still have huge affection for Golden Syrup, even though I don't use it that much. Rather like looking forward to a pre-booked summer holiday, it's just good to know that my tin of Golden Syrup is there at the back of the cupboard – it's probably being raided by my daughters as I type. I just hope they leave enough for me!●

FR🍓ITY

Fruity is fun. Fruity is *Carry On* films, fruity is squidgy, fruity is vivid, fruity is generous. But before we do anything fruity, we must salute the most heroic fruit of all – the grape. Without the grape, there would be no wine. It is often said that wine is made in the vineyard, because you can't make good wine from bad grapes. It's a bit of a cliché, but it happens to be true. The winemakers always get the glory when a wine tastes great, but we ought also to congratulate the viticulturalists – the gardeners, the guardians, the guys who brave the elements tending to the grapes every day of the year to make sure they yield the best possible flavours. They are the team who are responsible for delivering the grapes in pristine condition to the winery. Some of the best wines in the world are made when there is a strong channel of communication between winemaker and viticulturalist. If they understand one another, the wine's quality often shoots through the roof and up to the stars.

But what makes wine and, therefore, the grape so special is that each fruit captures the characteristics of the place in which it is grown. Like a time capsule, a jewel, or a gem, the grapes are infused with the weather from the year they were grown, and the aspect of the land they grew on – if it's a sunny warm patch you're likely to get more sugar and ripeness; if it's a cooler patch you're more likely to get racier, zippier and zingier fruit. Harnessing the weather, the place, the rain, the sun and capturing the very essence of the spot where they were grown, after a bit of cheeky fermenting, grapes transform their secrets into a potion, an elixir, a magical drink that makes us happy! They are like prisms – crystals that capture and translate water, sunlight and their own personality (with a helping hand from us) into a drink that changes in the bottle with every passing day. I can get very carried away thinking about the poetic and whimsical nature of grapes and their potential to encapsulate, thrill and tell their own story. I remember once tasting a Cognac from 1805 and feeling enthralled not just because the drink still tasted amazingly fresh and full of life, but I swirled into a brain-migration deep down through the years, wondering what happened on the day those grapes were harvested. Was it rainy? Sunny? Who were the people who picked them? Where did the barrel get stored and what were the stories that wreathed around it over the years? Marriages, deaths, affairs, laughter, gluttony, theft, betrayal, ambition, poverty, wars – it was astonishing to think that the juice in my glass somehow came through all that, being infused for over two centuries and finally turning into a part of me as I sipped it with great reverence and a real sense of daring and thrill. It's a bit like eating a dinosaur – only more tasty and less impossible.●

FRUIT + TIME
= WINE

CHICKEN VERONIQUE

Wine is an awesome drink in its own right and can unlock multiple new textures and flavours within a dish – but sometimes a fruity wine can even form a part of the dish itself, as in the case of this recipe, which is great as a family dish or for informal entertaining.

Serves 4–6

1kg organic or free range chicken

50g butter

1 onion, roughly chopped

100g button mushrooms, sliced thinly

500ml fruity white wine

500ml chicken stock

300ml/½ pint double cream

200g white grapes, halved

salt and freshly ground black pepper

→ Preheat the oven to 180°C/350°F/Gas 4 and season the chicken with salt and pepper.

→ Heat an ovenproof casserole dish, big enough to fit the chicken snugly, until medium hot. Add the butter and heat until foaming, and then add the chicken and seal on each side for 1–1½ minutes until golden brown. Remove the chicken and set aside.

→ Add the onion to the dish and cook for 5 minutes until softened, then turn the heat up, add the mushrooms and cook for another 2 minutes.

→ Place the chicken back into the pan on top of the vegetables and pour in the white wine. Bring to the boil, then add the chicken stock and return to the boil.

→ Season with salt and pepper, cover and place in the oven for 1 hour until the chicken is tender and cooked through. Remove the chicken and set aside to cool.

→ Return the dish to the hob and bring to the boil. Add the cream and cook until the whole mixture has reduced by a third. Check the seasoning, add the grapes and then set aside.

→ Strip the chicken of all the meat and shred into 5cm strips (the carcass can be used to make stock). Add the chicken to the sauce and mix well.

→ Place back on the heat until bubbling, check the seasoning once more, then serve with some basmati rice.

Chicken provides an excellent opportunity to look both ways —
into glasses of red and glasses of white wine. My rule of
thumb is to pick out the dominant ingredient and match the
wine with that. Here, on first glimpse, it is quite tricky to
see where to go. Earthy mushrooms might make you think red,
but the creamy texture and white wine in the dish lead the
cheers for a rich white wine in your glass. With cream,
generally oaky white wines can be winning tickets and, in this
case with the more savoury mushrooms, I'd be peering into my
cyber-cellar for a dose of rich white wine. If you're a fan of
classics and you've got a bit of cash to waggle around,
Chardonnay from France's Burgundy region would be a good way
to go. They can come in a number of shapes and sizes but a
rich fleshy oaky choice such as Corton Charlemagne or
Meursault would work alongside the creamy texture, savoury
mushrooms and subtle chicken, instead of swamping the dish
which is what might happen with a more chunky and structured
red wine. But for value and quality you could look to some
world-class examples of Chardonnay from the New World, such as
Argentina or the Antipodes. New Zealand is worth considering —
particularly producers such as Kumeu River, Felton Road and
Mahi. Australia is producing some awesome Chardonnay — Western
Australia has some iconic gems from wineries such as Pierro
and Leeuwin Estate (both in Margaret River), or you might look
to Victoria's cool Mornington Peninsula to producers such as
Ten Minutes By Tractor Wine Company for an elegant vibrant
style of oaked Chardonnay (all their vineyards are ten minutes
away from one another). White Rioja from Spain or South
African Chenin Blanc are also worth considering as
alternatives but, wherever you go, remember you want an
oaked white wine to work with the rich creamy texture of
the dish.

THE JOY OF FRUIT

My love of fruit began with my admirable grannies and, in particular, their delight in the world of the raspberry. Both my grannies were seriously passionate about growing fruit and veg. Granny Pip (named after her senior and distinguished Jack Russell called Pip) had an enormous fruit cage in the garden of her old house, a former railway station called Kirkbank near Kelso in the Scottish Borders. My brother Will and I used to romp and roll around in the garden, re-enacting various movie battles from *Where Eagles Dare* and *The Wild Geese* until the quest for refreshment became too much to bear and we'd plead with Granny to unleash us in the fruit cage. Raspberries, tayberries, loganberries, blackcurrants, redcurrants – we would stuff ourselves on the spoils of war and then run off down the old railway track to hunt for wild gooseberries – the ultimate victor's spoils. Those gooseberries were hairy and tough with an awesome intensity – like biting into an explosive burst of free energy – but we also deployed them as miniature hand grenades during our military manoeuvres.

There was an old shack down the disused railway track, Peter's Cottage, which would be marooned and surrounded by some truly spectacular puddles during excessively drizzly weekends – perfectly designed to nearly dribble over the top of my wellies, but not quite. My pal Graham and I used to peer up at the mighty Giant Hogweed surrounding Peter's Cottage and regale each other with tales of the horrors it could do. It is toxic to the skin and we were careful not to touch it but I distinctly remember an over-enthusiastic child's voice exclaiming, 'Giant Hogweed is from outer space. If you look at it for more than a minute your eyeballs will blow up!'

They were great times, charging round Graham's farm on rickety rattly bikes. I remember seeing a calf being born, chasing rats with the dogs, climbing mountains of straw bales and paddling up the idling River Tweed where Grandpa would fly fish in his giant rubbery waders. Fantastic days fuelled on summery fruity flavours – the sort that don't just stain your clothes, but imprint deep on your palate. The freshness, the juiciness, the zippiness, the mouth-watering squish, the bitter tiny seeds with a satisfying tang that spend weeks trapped in your teeth. I'm sure I've still got several in there that will never be fully dislodged.

I was especially lucky to have not just Granny Pip's fruit
odyssey to get my chops into but my other granny, Granny
Smokey (so called due to her aged, highly gentle and respectable
cat Smokey – if Smokey were human, he'd have been everyone's
favourite uncle) was also a fruit fanatic. Now, Granny Smokey
had a town garden which was very different to Granny Pip's
rambling country spot. Will and I still used to run riot – Granny
had a detached house and ours at home was a terrace, so with no
neighbours except for some hard-of-hearing pensioners to worry
about, we went feral every time we visited. I distinctly remember
sliding down the banisters of Granny's house in my pants with a
rubber Tarzan knife in my teeth. Granny lived at 39 Sutton Road
in Charminster, Bournemouth, and we'd frequently pop round
the corner to the grocer's on Gresham Road, head off to Fiveways
for the butcher and out into the New Forest to forage and pick
our own. When it was too far to walk, we'd hop on buses
(sometimes strings of them linked in a row of impeccable timing
and planning on Granny's part) and always sit at the front on the
top of those striking, custard-coloured double-deckers. I
remember once rattling along to the beach at Le Hocq in Jersey
with a Thermos of tea, a fruit cake and some bamboo swords.
When we got there, Will and I re-enacted scenes from *The Black
Hole*. We shouted, 'Granny, you be Maximillian,' who is a sword-

handed robot villain. Granny rose to the challenge after a bit of encouragement and explanation about her character and motivation... and then she did exactly the same creeping, playful monster walk that she did when she was being The Pink Panther, Jaws from *Moonraker*, or indeed The Supreme Being from *Time Bandits*. Granny's adventures fired Will's and my imagination; she is directly responsible for me and my bro developing such a vivid sense of things. (Will is now a stand-up comedian, screenwriter and appears on telly as an actor, as well as being a full-time *Bergerac* obsessive.) Granny Smokey showed us the works and taught us about good things and bad things – how to interact with cats (stay still, be patient and let them come to you), Swingball (her fence smelt of creosote and now, whenever I smell creosote, it makes me want to play Swingball), how to dissolve fruit pastilles in your tea to hide them from Mum and Dad's prying eyes, Laurel and Hardy, Joan Hickson as Miss Marple, *Bergerac*, *The Empire Strikes Back*, *Raiders of the Lost Ark* . . . These and many more great TV shows and movies were thanks to Granny's penchant for an afternoon snooze in front of the telly or at the cinema. In fact, one time when Will and I were about to get up to leave the Odeon after *Condorman*, we noticed that Granny was still sleeping soundly, so – with a bit of a blind eye turned by a kindly usherette – we stayed in the cinema for the next showing. Heaven.

But, best of all, Granny Smokey grew the greatest raspberries in the world (and her roses were tip top, too, thanks – so she insisted – to their daily dose of tea leaves straight from the pot). Imagine me as a nipper, running around in a high octane buzz of enthusiasm for pretty much everything that wafted around Granny Smokey's house (riding bikes, Harold Lloyd, Swiss chocolate, cake, Johnny Weissmuller's black-and-white Tarzan, *Flash Gordon*, *Star Wars*, *Buck Rogers*, cups of tea, cars, swimming, stuntmen etc), imagine that chaotic whirl of excitement and then add into the mix the raspberry. I wanted to pick them and eat them all day, every day. But Granny Smokey taught me about patience. About waiting for the right moment. Waiting to get the perfect raspberry flavour and maximize the kick, the thrill, the buzz of an awesomely faultless capsule of sunlight, rain, summertime and fun. We waited. We looked. We sneaked an unripe green one and regretted

it. And then the day dawned when the raspberries were ready. Bowls and bowls of fresh raspberries, preserved raspberries, raspberry jam, raspberries smeared on to cake, dribbling down our chins, covering our hands with pinky-red blotches and our t-shirts with smudges to make Mum wince. Aaaah – top work all round.

Raspberries remain my favourite fruit to this day and, on my wedding day, Sophie and I had golden raspberries. They were my first-ever golden raspberries and looked amazing but, if I'm honest, didn't quite match the royal flavour of 39 Sutton Road's awesome crop.

The twin to early summer's raspberry treat is autumn's blackberry. The season seems to get longer every year, from late summer right through to Halloween, but I'm not complaining. Big, squishy, juicy blackberries are their most awesome at the moment of perfect ripeness, but if you do find you've inadvertently picked a few that are a touch under-ripe, do not despair – they can be doctored to provide blackberry nirvana by blending with apples and a touch of sugar to tone down their tang. To make GRANNY SMOKEY'S BLACKBERRY AND APPLE you need to:

Gather equal weights Bramley apples and blackberries. Peel the apples and add enough water to almost cover them. Simmer gently until the apples start to break up. Add the blackberries until they are cooked and then sugar to taste. Finally put the whole lot through a sieve. (If you're in a hurry, or like it lumpy, you can leave it unsieved – but watch out for the pips!)

My kids Ruby and Lily love this. Healthy fuel and a beautiful deep purple colour that I would love to dress up in. You can tuck straight in, adding a swirl of cream for an awesome pudding, or freeze it to deploy later as required.

Raspberries are the ULTIMATE FAST FOOD – you just pick 'em and eat 'em. But even the mighty raspberry can be a team player. A drizzle of Golden Syrup, a splodge of Greek yoghurt, mash with a fork and there you have a divinely simple and indulgent dish packed with texture and layers.

PLUM TATIN

280g butter

300g flour

250g caster sugar

4 egg yolks

10–12 large plums,
halved and stoned (or
enough to cover the
bottom of a 28cm pan)

Fruit is a unifying force in the world. Whenever I travel to wine producing regions, there are usually fruits lurking nearby and, without exception, everyone I have ever met can go misty eyed and swell with passion for one sort of fruit or another. We love the stuff! On a trip to South Africa, I was visiting the delightful Andrew and Rozy Gunn at Iona winery in Elgin – a region previously famous for apples but fast growing a new reputation for zingy wines. The orchards are still there, along with all sorts of other fruits, notably plums and a plethora of wildlife, including Sally the rat (sadly now in Ratty Heaven), Tiki the Jack Russell and a nest of wagtails all snuggled up overlooking the vineyards and fruit trees. Rozy made this PLUM TATIN for dinner for me and my dad and very kindly gave me the recipe for this book – it's an absolute rocker! I love the Gunns' kitchen – always awash with home-grown, brightly coloured fruit and veg, and always alive with warmth and creative conversation. Cheers guys! You can turn the recipe into an apple tatin by using about 10 eating apples instead of the plums. It is a big recipe and serves 8–10, but can easily be halved.

→ Preheat the oven to 200°C/400°F/Gas 6.

→ To make the pastry, rub 200g butter into the flour until it resembles crumbs. Add 50g sugar and the egg yolks and stir with a round tipped knife. Finally, press the dough together using your hands, wrap and chill in the fridge for at least half an hour.

→ Meanwhile, melt the remaining butter and caster sugar in a 28cm ovenproof pan over a medium heat until syrupy.

→ Place the plums carefully in the pan, cut side facing up. (Squash them in as they reduce in size during cooking.) Cook for 10 minutes until the fruit is bubbling nicely and the caramel has become syrupy again. Remove and set aside.

→ Roll the rested pastry out on a floured surface to form roughly a 28cm diameter circle. Place over the caramelized plums and try and tuck in any loose bits down the sides. Place in the oven and cook for 20 minutes, then reduce the heat to 150°C/300°F/Gas 2 and bake for a further 20 minutes.

→ Remove from the oven and prise the edges clear with a knife and turn out on to a plate. Serve with mascarpone or vanilla ice cream.

ALL PRAISE THE DURIAN!

During any journey into the world of all things fruity, you also need to delve into the tropical side of things. A year spent in Indonesia enhanced my fascination with fruit. The place for those tales of glory and adventure is in the Aromatic chapter where I describe my forays into Far Eastern street food but, while we're feeling fruity, I must mention the world's gloriously sweet and luscious papaya and the rambutan, which is a hairy little fruit the size of a conker and somewhere between a lychee and a grape in flavour and texture. But the mother of all tropical fruit is the notorious, stinking durian. The durian reeks. Honks. It's about the size of a melon, covered in rounded little thorny horns and I had it served in various milky sauces and puddings during my romp across the Indonesian archipelago. It may stink but its flavour is compelling. It's a Marmite moment – people love it or hate it. Think ripe cheese meets fruit. All I can say is, try it – if nothing else, it will be a memorably indescribable experiment.

SALUTE THE STRAWBERRY!

I think all Britons should proudly wear this slogan on badges, bumper stickers and tattoos throughout the land during the summer months. 'Salute the Strawberry' sums up the glory of eating something that flourishes in our climate during a precious window of seasonality. Nothing tastes better; nothing could be more British. Wimbledon is one of my favourite annual events and, in addition to John McEnroe's genius commentary, the one thing that makes the tournament more exciting than wondering whether a Brit will win once again is the thought that, wherever we are, at some point during Wimbledon, all of us will at least see, if not suckle on, the strawberry. Jams, compotes, puddings and cakes are all very well, but a naked strawberry is sexy, refreshing, juicy and unbelievably vivid, from its faintly hairy texture to the tiny pip crunches, and the final monster, juicy squish and bite of flavour explode in its eruption of outrageous freshness. I flipping love strawberries and have always grown them in pots, in gardens and if I could plant them in my belly button I would. When I was living in Brixton, I planted some small Alpine strawberries in a pot and used to love going out to gather them in late June to scatter on my cereal in the mornings. The unripe ones were a yellowy green and I remember once brushing one with my finger and was amazed when it disintegrated into a hundred particles — of baby spiders! Amazingly there are spiders that have evolved to cluster together as babies to look identical to an unripe strawberry, presumably to evade predators (although I like to think it is also to keep warm).

LONG LIVE THE STRAWBERRY!
GOD SAVE THE STRAWBERRY!

SEND THE STRAWBERRY VICTORIOUS,
HAPPY AND GLORIOUS
– RIGHT INTO OUR GOBS.

Like wine, fruit across the board is imbued with a variety of colours, flavours and textures. A kaleidoscope, a collage, a rainbow of freshness to delve into. The very essence of fruit, and arguably the most pure manner of extracting the central seam of flavour, is its juice. Crush it, pulp it, squeeze it, blend it or sample it as it comes – fruit juice is awesome.

We have some of the best apple juice in the world here in the UK – did I mention Granny Pip's cooking apples? Blimey, they were seriously tangy. We used to munch as much as we could just for the hit of terrific, acid, freak-out flavours – and, apart from the gorgeous purity of a simple glass of crushed Cox, Grenadier, Jonagold, Crispin or Howgate Wonder, apple juice can be infused with a wealth of different ingredients to titillate its fruity character to the max.

APPLE COR! is a genius non-alcoholic cocktail that works best with freshly pressed English apple juice. A terrific party drink for drivers, or you could add a kick of Somerset apple brandy for the designated passengers. Tip all the ingredients, except the ice and ginger ale, into a cocktail shaker and shake vigorously. Finally, pour into a Slim Jim glass over the ice and then add some ginger ale.

Apple juice is glorious but there are, of course, a billion other juices to slurp and you could even match them with food to bring out incredible untold depths of flavour.

APPLE COR!

100ml apple juice

½ teaspoon runny clear honey

½ small hot chilli, bashed or split to release heat

½ teaspoon elderflower cordial

½ vanilla pod

sprig of fresh mint

some ice cubes

75ml ginger ale (I recommend Fever Tree)

thin slice of apple (to garnish on the side of the glass – optional)

GREAT FRUIT TO EAT CHEESE WITH

Cheese and fresh fruit is generally a sublime combination – think of a hunk of Cheddar and a slice of apple.

If you're sipping the gooseberry-like Sauvignon Blanc get your teeth into some goat's cheese – it's an incredibly successful match that plays like with like. Think of the bright tang in soft goat's cheese – the crispness of Sauvignon Blanc is equally edgy, and the two share a similar intensity of zip that comes together with dazzling deftness. It's no surprise, therefore, that GOOSEBERRY AND GOAT'S CHEESE on cocktail sticks is an absolute winner. You need a fairly hard goat's cheese to cube roughly to the same proportions as a gooseberry and then skewer with a cocktail stick – goat's cheese beneath, gooseberry on top. Pinging mighty morsels! And guess what – they work a treat with Sauvignon Blanc.

FOR A NON-ALCOHOLIC MATCH, GOAT'S CHEESE AND GRAPEFRUIT JUICE IS THRILLING!

But preserved fruit is also a mine of glory for you to dig into. Behold the world of cheese and chutney! The principle is one of salty and sweet but also texture – hard cheese on its tod can be drying and gacky, but think of the glory of Manchego cheese with quince jelly. Suddenly there's a counterbalance of flavours and a more succulent texture to chew on. In fact, I urge you to experiment with all cheese and all jam – anything you've got in the cupboard. It won't always work, but when you hit a sweet spot, it's like a free holiday to Fruit Mountain.

If you're eating hard cheese with chutney, a tip-top wine match would be a late-harvest wine to double up on the fruity sweetness of the chutney — spread your wine wings and fly to the world of Malaga sweet wines or Australian Botrytis Semillon with its citrus-sweet verve. JOYFUL!

I'm a bit of a chutney fanatic. I love the sweet/sour tension and it can be anything from spicy to gingery, syrupy to tangy. It deserves a book in itself but, for me, texture plays a huge role – not runny but not solid either. This JAZZY MANGO CHUTNEY is a particular favourite thanks to its emphasis on fruity spice without being overly hot. It's a perfect all-rounder for a sandwich, curry or hunk of cheese. Have it! These quantities will make about 500g chutney.

→ If you plan to keep some of the chutney for a rainy day, you'll need some sterilized containers. Wash some jam jars in hot soapy water, then rinse well. Put them into a preheated oven at 170°C/325°F/Gas 3 until you are ready to use them.

→ Heat a frying pan until hot, then add the sunflower oil and red onion and fry for 2–3 minutes until just tender.

→ Add the chillies, mustard seeds, coriander, cumin and cinnamon and fry for a further 2 minutes.

→ Add the mango and cook for 1–2 minutes until just softened.

→ Add the brown sugar, apple juice and vinegar and bring to the boil. Cover and simmer for 5–8 minutes until the mango has broken down slightly and the juices have thickened.

→ Remove from the heat and allow to cool before serving or storing in the sterilized jam jars.

JAZZY MANGO CHUTNEY

1 tablespoon sunflower oil

1 red onion, finely diced

½ teaspoon crushed chillies

½ teaspoon mustard seeds

½ teaspoon ground coriander

½ teaspoon ground cumin

¼ teaspoon ground cinnamon

500g mango, peeled and cut into small chunks

65g light brown sugar

50ml apple juice

75ml cider vinegar

GREAT FRUIT TO EAT MEAT WITH

Mincemeat. You and I know it as the stuff that comes in mince pies. But in former ages, the Brits loved mixing meat and fruit. They are a great counterbalance – the density of the meat offset by the moisture of the fruit, and the zip of the fruit cutting through the texture of the savoury meat. Think of it like a window – all very well to cast some light, but with stained glass there are colours and enhanced illumination. Fruit adds vibrancy and stimulation to meat.

Granny Pip lived in Cyprus about six hundred years ago (sorry, Gran!) and her friend Zeeba gave her this Turkish recipe for stuffing. It's a fruity treat that is simple to do and brilliant with chicken, turkey or even pheasant. Cheers Zeeba! ZEEBA'S STUFFING goes like this:

ZEEBA'S STUFFING

1½ teacups rice

115g butter

115g (or more) whole almonds

1½ teaspoons cinnamon

55g raisins

salt and freshly ground black pepper

→ Cook the rice according to the packet instructions, drain and set aside.

→ Meanwhile, melt the butter in a saucepan and add the almonds. Toast until they are brown, then mix in the cinnamon and raisins and leave on a low heat for half an hour.

→ Finally, add the cooked rice and stir, making sure the mixture doesn't stick and burn.

→ Take it off the heat, let it cool and then stuff it in the back end of a tasty bird.

Birds give me great pleasure to match wine to because it's a chance to swing between red and white depending on the recipe. For turkey, it's all about the stuffing — bear this in mind at Christmas time. If you're deploying a fruity stuffing of dried fruits such as raisins or apricots, I prefer to go with an oaky white — Chardonnay can be sublime, and you don't have to pay through the nose to buy a posh white one from Burgundy such as Meursault or Puligny-Montrachet. Consider hunting for Chardonnay from the New World. Your money will go further and their cooler climate offerings (think coastal and high-altitude regions) tend to be seriously classy. Or you could experiment with white wines from the Rhône such as Condrieu made from the Viognier grape with its peachy apricot yum-hammer or, for a bargain version, buy Viognier from Chile. SCRUMMO!

If your turkey is packed with more savoury or meaty flavours, though, such as a sausage stuffing, it's got to be a red wine — and nothing too heavy or you'll swamp the bird. Think Pinot Noir (New Zealand is my tip for quality and value) or you could try lighter Italian reds, such as Cerasuolo di Vittoria from Sicily from producers such as Planeta. Fascinating booze — floral scented and can be served chilled. GRAB IT!

Talking of sausages, keeping pigs is awesome. Together with Sophie, Ruby, Lily and my passionate pig partners Chris and Jane Parkinson, I have fed, watered, housed, scrubbed and played with them – and been playfully nipped by them, too. Of course, eating them is the best part. Pork and fruit work extremely well together – our pigs loved eating the over-crop of plums, apples, greengages and acorns as summer played out and, matched with their meat, apple sauce from our own trees tastes fabulous. Here's how I make APPLE BUTTER:

Place 1.5kg cooking apples (peeled, cored and cut into chunks) into a pan with 500ml cider vinegar and 500ml water. Bring to the boil, then reduce the heat and simmer gently for 30 minutes until thickened. Place into a food processor, blitz to a purée, then pass through a sieve back into a bowl. Weigh the apple purée and add half as much caster sugar to the purée as there is purée (i.e. 1kg apple purée, add 500g sugar). Place back into a saucepan; add 2 teaspoons ground cinnamon, ¹/₂ teaspoon ground cloves, ¹/₂ teaspoon allspice and a squeeze of lemon juice. Cook over a gentle heat for 1–1½ hours until very thick and a spoon drawn through the centre leaves a clean line. Place into a sterilized jam jar (see page 22) to keep.

I've really enjoyed the experience of keeping pigs. When the first two went to slaughter, I felt a mixture of fondness for the animals and fondness for the feast they would provide. One of my sows didn't want to get out of the trailer at the abattoir; she was too happily stretched out for a nap. I took that to be a great sign – she was happy and relaxed at a time which could easily have been stressful and difficult. I love animals and wildlife and cannot abide unhappy animals. I believe we should give them a good quality of life and ensure their dispatch is as calm and quick as possible. This very morning at 5am I took the last two to slaughter. It's been a long journey for Sophie, me and the girls, and now we have seen them all off the planetary premises. In order to honour our animals, we should maximize the dishes that we make from their meat (find out how in the Meaty chapter). The first batch we slaughtered was some of the best meat I have ever tasted and I am looking forward to next year's weaners – we are going for Gloucester Old Spot this time. Watch this space!

TIP FOR APPLE SAUCE – USE TWO COOKERS TO ONE DESSERT APPLE FOR A TANGY, BRIGHT FLAVOUR.

FRUITY BRAISED RED CABBAGE

I love this alongside pork belly – it's piggylicious with all the fruit that contrasts with the savoury meat and it has the perfect texture to underpin the crunch of that rich crackling.

Serves 4–6

50g butter

1 red onion, finely sliced

1 garlic clove, finely diced

600g red cabbage, sliced very finely

100ml red wine

175ml orange juice

50g sultanas

75g dessert apples, peeled and cut into small cubes

1 cinnamon stick

½ teaspoon caraway seeds, ground

50g light soft brown sugar

3 tablespoons redcurrant jelly

salt and freshly ground black pepper

→ Heat a large saucepan until hot; add the butter, red onion, garlic and red cabbage and sauté for 1–2 minutes until just softened.

→ Add the red wine, bring to the boil and cook until reduced by half.

→ Add the orange juice, sultanas, apples, cinnamon stick, ground caraway, sugar and redcurrant jelly and bring to a simmer.

→ Cover and cook for 40–45 minutes, stirring occasionally, until tender.

→ Remove the lid and cook for a further 5–8 minutes over a high heat until the liquid has evaporated and the red cabbage is slightly sticky and glossy.

→ Season with plenty of salt and pepper, and serve alongside a hunk of freshly cooked pig.

PORK TENDERLOIN

STUFFED WITH APRICOTS, PISTACHIOS AND PARSLEY

The style of fruit you can use with pork is very wide. This is one of my favourites – like a giant piggy parcel filled with the exotic summery thrills of North Africa. A lamb tagine munched near the tanneries of Fez was the inspiration for this pig-tacular recipe. Although I was threatened with death and subsequently robbed within half an hour of my first-ever visit to Morocco, I also found it to be a country of immense culture, warmth and gastronomic excellence. The open pits of dye for the leather in the tannery were filled with bright colours, like giant paint pots glinting in the hot sun, and the food was magnificently fragrant and intensely coloured, too – bright yellow saffron rice, burnished apricots and purply green pistachio nuts. A feast for your eyes. Returning there always yields inventive ideas. I would love to see more quality wine produced in North Africa – it's had a fascinating heritage producing grapes for the French, the Romans and for fun.

Serves 4–6

125g dried apricots, stoned and chopped

50g pistachios, shelled and roughly chopped

2 tablespoons flat-leaf parsley, roughly chopped

2 tablespoons honey

2 x 300g pork tenderloin fillets, fully trimmed

2 tablespoons olive oil

25g butter

salt and freshly ground black pepper

→ Preheat the oven to 200°C/400°F/Gas 6.

→ Mix the apricots, pistachios, parsley and honey together in a bowl.

→ Slice the pork fillets lengthways three-quarters of the way through, and open them out to form a rectangle. Season with salt and pepper, then spoon the mixture lengthways on to the pork.

→ Roll the pork fillets into a pinwheel, starting at the longest side. Tie with string at intervals along the fillets to secure the filling.

→ Heat a frying pan until hot, add the olive oil, butter and pork fillets to the pan and sear on each side until golden brown.

→ Spoon the butter mixture over the pork fillets, and then transfer to the oven for 15 minutes, until cooked through.

→ Remove and rest for 5 minutes before carving into slices and serving with a green salad.

GINGER IS TO PORK
WHAT ANCHOVIES
ARE TO LAMB. YOU
CAN USE IT TO
MARINATE PORK,
SPIKE IT INTO THE
MEAT, OR MIX IT
WITH HONEY AS A
DRIZZLE FOR THE
PERFECT CRACKLING
TOWARDS THE END
OF THE ROASTING.

I love fruit. It is pure, vibrant, colourful, superbly diverse and often free in our British hedgerows. Red fruits, black fruits, tropical fruit, British apples, exotic kiwis, fruits with pips, fruits with seeds, fruits with flesh, melons, bananas, plums, elderberries, brambles, fruits served fresh and fruits doctored to deliver their best. I have a crab apple tree near me which has the most beautiful crop, but each year I have been beaten to the windfall by an unseen hand. This year I got in early, scooped the prize and made heroic Crab Apple Jelly with my mum. It felt better than saddling up Brian Blessed and riding him to victory at the Grand National. The colour made your eyeballs cheer; it was aglow with warmth and reddy-orange richness. Fruit is a nation populated with flavours, from over-ripe rustic and reeking, to fresh and pinging to the point of sharpness. But, perhaps, the greatest gift of all that fruit gives us is that of fermentation – the spell wrought in the midst of murk from which blossoms the greatest elixir known to man. Wine.●

CREAMY

Creamy is luxuriant, thick and rich. Creamy is a special treat, creamy is comforting, creamy is sexy. Creamy is a duvet wrapped around your flagging spirits on a drizzly dark Thursday in February. Creamy is the feeling of indulgent elevation that takes your taste buds on holiday. Creamy is a flavour but, more importantly, creamy offers a bonus dimension of texture that can range from glossy to fluffy, with everything in between. Like the actors who play James Bond, cream has an unmistakable character yet is strikingly dependent on the emphasis in its performance – from a drop to enrich savoury gravy to a splurge on a jammy scone, from carbonara to custard, from Moore to Connery, Brosnan to Lazenby, Dalton to Craig. And, while we're dealing with creamy, here's a word on butter. I remember at school when the dinners were truly mean, we used to attempt to gloss up the reedy thin gruel-like vegetable soup (which I remain convinced to this day contained leftover sugar puffs) by adding the little squares of butter in foil that we were given. It went some way to improve the texture and flavour with its creamy salty touch. Butter is itself 'creamy' in its simplest form. On toast, melted in a pan, folded into cake mix – butter rocks. Have you tasted Échiré butter? It's from a village in western France and dates back to 1208. They say that, rather than being down to the cows, like vineyards and their wine, it's the unique land and grass produced there that creates the subtlety, finesse and elegance of Beurre Échiré. Whatever the reason, get your face in it ASAP – it's a gastrogasm!●

THE JAMES BOND GUIDE TO CREAM

As a flavour, cream tends to round out and enrich a dish. It has an inherently glossy texture when poured and caps off acidity. Think of pure lemon juice and how it attacks your teeth. Now think of lemony cream – still bright, but mellowed like a sharp mountain capped in rounded snow. Cream is a key influence on texture and ought to be prized as a game-changing ingredient; a star with impact that can control the destiny of your dish, a bit like an actor controls the destiny and tone of a movie franchise. Yes. You know what's coming. The influence of cream in a recipe is a bit like the influence of the actors who each play James Bond…

WHIPPED CREAM is similar to Timothy Dalton. His Timness got a whipping from Bond fans for *Licence to Kill* but it's not as bad as you think you remember – there's a pock-marked Latino villain with an iguana living on his shoulder that wears a diamond necklace (the iguana, not the villain). That in itself is enough for me to fall in love with the collected Bond works of Dirty Dalton. The cream itself, aside from the whipping, is light, frothy and a fantastic accompaniment rather than headline ingredient – for example, dolloped on to a foaming cup of hot cocoa. To be clear, I am not saying tip-top Tim is light or frothy; merely that he got a whipping I think was unfair for his portrayal of Bond. Consider *The Living Daylights*, Tim's first outing. I admit that it does feature the unfortunate line, 'Are you calling me a horse's ass?', which is acutely un-Bond, but let's keep in mind that Bond crosses all seven continents to stop a villain with slicked-back hair called Georgi Koskov. What more do you need? Art Malik you say? Yep, he's in it, too. And a Stradivarius violin. I say hurrah for Timothy Dalton and hurrah for whipped cream. Unjustly whipped, but whipped Dalton remains.

The SOUR CREAM accolade goes to George Lazenby. Sour because Big George only played Bond once, his first was his only outing, something which I regret enormously. *On Her Majesty's Secret Service* is an awesome flick: Lord Lazenby is a spiffing Bond and *OHMSS* is the only Bond film that features his wife, Teresa, and her tragic assassination, which neatly sets up Bond's vendetta against Blofeld. This Bond has it all, including an Alpine Bond villain's lair on top of the Schilthorn (which I visited as a child – Mum and Dad said the revolving restaurant Piz Gloria was too expensive to sit in and have tea, which means that someday I have to go all the way back to the top of the Alps to check out that movie location in more detail. And, this time, I am definitely going dressed in a tuxedo, whatever my mum says). Sour cream itself, then, the clue is in the name – use it charged with the bite of chives to add stun-factor to a baked potato, or spoon it on a particularly spicy chilli to cool it down. It is refreshing, tangy and memorable and, therefore, the sour cream accolade goes to the underrated and rather sensational George Lazenby.

SINGLE CREAM is an icon in its own right – some say it is the original of the cream world and, therefore, I am singling out Sir Sean Connery for the award. Sir Sean is sexy, suave and ruthless in hand-to-hand combat. Just like single cream – which is perfect for pouring into drinks and on to desserts. Sir Sean, you are the ultimate ingredient. If only we could eat you. In fact, we can. Why is it illegal? WHY! LET US EAT SEAN CONNERY and serve our jail time with pride. Stop me.

600ml/1 pint hot water

200g creamed coconut

zest and juice of 2 limes

4 green chillies,
deseeded and chopped

4 garlic cloves, crushed
or chopped

1 pack fresh tarragon

2 level tablespoons
caster sugar

3 tablespoons light soy
sauce

2 level teaspoons
ground ginger

4 chicken breasts
(skin on)

DOUBLE CREAM is Sir Roger Moore, the smoothest and the most luxuriant Bond. Not only did Rog appear as Bond the most number of times (seven), but he also propelled his astonishing movie career outside the world of Bond and into my childhood eyeballs. Notable works in the canon of Moore include *The Wild Geese*, *The Cannonball Run* and *North Sea Hijack*, all of which unquestionably remain the three greatest films of all time. In fact, one rainy afternoon in north London my brother and I devised a menu to accompany *North Sea Hijack* which featured NORTH SEA CHICKEN IN A HIJACK SAUCE. I think Will got this from a supermarket recipe card. Wherever it came from, it tastes fantastic!

→ Add the hot water to the creamed coconut in a bowl to dissolve.

→ Put everything else, except the chicken, in a blender. Add the coconut water and blitz.

→ Make 3 diagonal cuts across each chicken breast and put them in a bowl. Pour over the marinade and leave them in the fridge for at least 30 minutes.

→ Remove the chicken from the marinade and grill on both sides for 10–15 minutes until cooked through. Meanwhile, heat up the marinade in a saucepan.

→ Serve the chicken with the warm marinade and some Thai fragrant rice.

Let me be the first to suggest that every Briton pays an extra penny on income tax to buy Roger a palace, a crown and a country to be declared the Double-O Kingdom of Smooth. Double cream is the best cream to pour over puddings, is easy to whip and pipe, and can be used in recipes where cream is heated since it is less likely to split than single cream. All hail His Rogesty and his indisputable double-creaminess.

CLOTTED CREAM is Pierce Brosnan. No, not because Pierce is a clot, but because it's easy to forget how awesome clotted cream can be! And it works in small doses as an accompaniment to jam and scones, for example. The later Brosnan outings tailed off, but the glory days of *GoldenEye* and *Tomorrow Never Dies* reinvigorated the Bond franchise, partly because Pierce is charming with twinkly eyes and has what I can only describe as the hypnotic 'Brosnanface'. It's when his eyes twinkle and his expression seems to say, 'You may not be aware, but I have the sexual prowess of a human meteorite. And I just stole your watch.' When was the last time you had a dose of clotted cream? Big up the Brosnan!

CRÈME FRAÎCHE is Daniel Craig – a dividing force that causes strong reactions. Crème fraîche is less thick than soured cream so a great one to deploy in lighter dishes or to finish off a sauce. The glory is in its tang. I rate Captain Craig's performance as Bond as excellent to god-like, but I am also aware that there are those who feel nothing but pure terror at the bowling ball shape of Daniel's shoulder muscles. And some say he has piggy eyes. I think he is a Lord of Humans: tangy and powerful, Craig is crème fraîche. Craig fraîche. Have it!

SOFTLY, MELLOWING, ENRICHMENT

Is there anything creamier than Greek yoghurt? Ever since I watched *Clash of the Titans* as a boy and saw Laurence Olivier hanging out on Mount Olympus with Ursula Andress, I knew in my heart that the gods lived off a diet of ambrosia, which bestows agelessness in much the same way as Greek yoghurt. OK I made that up, but if you've ever woken up on a hot day in the Greek islands, sniffed a *sketo* black coffee and tasted the thick creamy yoghurt with a drizzle of local honey, you know what it's like to feel immortal, if only for a split second. And let's get real here: stick with the full-fat, thick stuff, that's the ticket for a dose of Olympian ecstasy.

TOP TZATZIKI

Grate CUCUMBER and GARLIC into GREEK YOGHURT with LOTS OF CHOPPED FRESH MINT, salt, freshly ground black pepper and LEMON JUICE

Greek yoghurt in its own right is a kernel of creamy awesomeness but it can also be blended into dishes to give an unparalleled richness and subtle trademark tang. This FIGGY PUDDING recipe came from Mum through her pal Gabrielle and we're not 100 per cent sure where she got it – all we know is that it tastes great. It's not figgy pudding as you know it, but a creamy, indulgent and luxuriant dessert made with figs. It's simple to put together and very rich, sensual and utterly moreish:

Drain 1 tin green figs* and cut them into about 6 pieces each. Whip 175g double cream until thick and blend with 280g Greek yoghurt. Place alternate layers of figs and the yoghurt/cream mixture into a glass trifle bowl. Finish with a layer of the yoghurt/cream mixture and then sprinkle with brown sugar. Refrigerate (preferably overnight) and serve cold. If green

figs aren't available you can use tinned or fresh plums instead –
just chop them up and reduce them in some orange juice and
sugar over a medium heat until soft and squidgy.

If you're after a drink with the FIGGY PUDDING, the high
content of cream calls for a classic glass of Sauternes. It
has an unctuous texture, glorious sweetness and will manage
to cut through the texture of the thick cream thanks to its
brisk acidity. Class in a glass! If sweet wine is your
thing, please promise me you'll check out Muscat from the
Greek island of Samos — it is a gloriously sweet and rich
dessert wine with an orangey streak and is magnificent
around Christmas time with mince pies, fruit cake or
just as a kinky glass of Christmas cheer beside the fire
with a snuggle and a cuddle.

MEALS IN MASH

Mash is inherently creamy and fluffy – there are
endless opportunities to customize mash into a meal in
its own right. You can add doses of butter and cream to
enrich it, you can try blending potato mash with mashed
Jerusalem artichoke, swede or parsnip, or have a go at
sweet potato and roasted garlic mash, adding a drizzle
of extra virgin olive oil. Creamy texture and warming,
melting flavours – the ultimate comfort food!

OLYMPUS

I remember one weekend the whole family had convened in the Scottish Borders at my Granny Pip's house (my folks, Uncle Tom and Aunty Anne with their three lads James, Johnny and Olly) and after lunch Granny shuffled out of the dining room to grab the pud. Thanks to a gooseberry glut, Granny had thrown a gooseberry fool together for the whole family to dive into. I think the giggles kicked off when Uncle Tom and my dad saw the pinkish, salmony colour of the pud (thanks to some reddish gooseberries finding their way into the mix). The name Fool made us kids giggle and I'll never forget Granny's face – she must have thought her pudding was laced with laughing gas as the whole table fell about cackling, spooning out the pud with tears rolling down our faces! I call it QUICK AND GIGGLY GOOSEBERRY FOOL to this day.

Put 450-900g gooseberries into a saucepan with a tiny amount of water (you don't want the fruit to be too sloppy when you liquidize it with the cream). Bring to a bubble and simmer until they are stewed down to a lovely squidgy pulp. Add sugar to taste (they can sometimes be sharp). Liquidize with 300-600ml/½-1 pint whipping cream and a splash of elderflower cordial.

> Serve chilled with a fab-tastic glass of
> Sauternes or grab a top-value, quality
> Botrytis Semillon from Australia, from
> producers such as De Bortoli.

One summer holidays, we'd been staying at Granny Smokey's house in Bournemouth and I watched her make the best Baked Custards in the world over and over in her tiny kitchen. (Incidentally, as I typed up this recipe, because 'N' is next to 'B' on the keyboard, I kept typing 'Naked Custards', which is appropriate as that's all they are – simple custard, stripped down and bare!) These yummy, simple puddings were the first dish that I ever cooked from memory. When I came home and turned out my first batch aged eight, Mum and Dad were well impressed! Big up BAKED CUSTARD! Super-simple and an easy one for the whole family to master. You can, of course, customize it by adding dried fruit, jam, Golden Syrup, a dusting of cinnamon or nutmeg, or any other outrageous addition that takes your fancy.

Preheat the oven to 150°C/300°F/Gas 2. Beat together 2 large eggs and 1 tablespoon caster sugar. Add this to 600ml/1 pint milk and mix well. Lightly grease 4 ramekin dishes (or a dish that will hold over a pint of liquid) with butter and pour in the custard mix. Place the dishes in a bain-marie and whack into the oven for about an hour but check before the time's up to see if they are set. As soon as they are wobbly yet firm, serve instantly to a polite ripple of applause.

CUSTARD IS ONE OF LIFE'S GREAT GLORIES FROM CRÉME ANGLAISE TO CUSTARD TARTS AND EVEN THE LUMPY STUFF WE USED TO GET SERVED AT SCHOOL!

When I was eight, I remember being allowed to drink cups of sugary tea which seemed at the time to be an outrageous indulgent delicacy. Tea seems to run strong in my family — Granny Smokey always had a number of tins of different leaves, my parents' kettle is never cool, I have a large collection of loose-leaf tea which I adore and my youngest daughter Lily, aged two, can't keep away from the stuff! She rather sweetly calls it 'Some cuppa tea'. 'Please may I have some cuppa tea, Daddy?' 'Daddy, would you like some cuppa tea?' Adorable. Today, though, if I'm scoffing baked custard, I love a glass of Monbazillac, which is sometimes thought of as the poor relation of Sauternes. It has less acidity, aromas of brioche and a beautiful honey-like roundness that works a treat with baked custard. Cheers!

THE GLORY OF CHEESE

What could be creamier than cheese? And what to drink with this most creamy of ingredients? Wine, of course. Let's saddle up and ride the Bottle Rocket all the way to Cream City!

A general note that may surprise you is that I generally much prefer sipping a white wine than a red with cheese. Too often red swamps cheese and if I was selecting just one wine to go with a general cheese board it'd be white every time – refreshing on the palate and it gives the cheese a chance to flaunt its flavour, rather than be clobbered by a rich mouth-coating red which results in a CLASH OF THE TEXTURES.

SOFT CHEESE Generally, if you're dealing with a soft cheese that hasn't got a rind, a white unoaked wine is your target – a crisp English white would do it. If, however, you're a stickler for reds, then head for a lighter style, such as Beaujolais. The king of soft cheese is mozzarella. Too often it gets cooked and its creamy freshness and sensual chewy texture get hammered out. But it is an awesome cheese in its own right. The best mozzarella is like biting into a buttock. As far as wine goes, a glass of chilled prosecco is a sublime match (to the mozzarella, that is, rather than the buttock-biting, which I confess I have not yet tried with a glass of chilled prosecco – but rest assured, I will).

SQUIDGE -TASTIC!

CREAMY CHEESE With a soft rind cheese such as Camembert and Brie, go for oaky Chardonnay, South African Chenin Blanc or even experiment with Viognier, Marsanne and Roussanne. I am not a fan of reds with these bad boys but feel free to experiment. You might be able to push me to a rosé.

CREAMY, SMELLY CHEESE Cheeses such as Époisses, work with spicy rich whites such as Gewürztraminer. It is often worth experimenting with local wines from where the cheese is made, for example eating Époisses with mature red Burgundy (Pinot Noir that's spent a few years in a bottle to soften out its edges).

CREAMY, SQUIDGY, NOT-QUITE-HARD CHEESE Cheeses like Port Salut, Reblochon and Pont-l'Évêque, work with Pinot Gris, a massively underrated variety (same grape as Pinot Grigio but made in a richer style). Pinot Gris can be found in Alsace but some of my favourites are made in New Zealand, where they are fruity, pure and with a squidgy texture that picks up beautifully on the bouncy feel of Not-Quite-Hard Cheese.

HARD CHEESES The harder the cheese, the more chunky your wine choice can be. Eating Cheddar is the one time that red wine really comes into play for me. Cabernet Sauvignon or Bordeaux blends are generally a winning combo. Other chunky red grapes to consider might be Malbec, Syrah, Tannat (hefty), Nebbiolo (tannic) or you could hedge your bets and go with a more mellow red Rioja, which is a cracker if you're offering a range of hard cheeses with differing textures and intensity, from mild Cheddar through to Beaufort, Mimolette and Parmesan.

BLUE CHEESE The salty streak calls for a contrast of U-turn proportions to spank it into life. Sweeter flavours are the watchword – think Tokaji or Port with Stilton. Gorgonzola but especially Roquefort with Sauternes is also worth dosing yourself with. And, if you're up for it, bite into a dried apricot with your sliver of blue cheese.

> If there's one thing I want this book to encourage it is the opening of multiple bottles of wine during a meal, not consecutively but all at once so that people can take small sips of each one and come across unique flavour combos to scream about and encourage everyone at the table to indulge in. Every moment is potentially a cusp of gastronomic discovery and this is never more true than in the case of the cheese board. LET'S RIDE THE BOARD TO THE EDGE OF FLAVOUR!

THE DUVET OF DELIGHT

Cream as a texture is invaluable and enveloping, soft and lush with a sensual smoothness. It is luxuriant, it is a treat, it is sexy.

While I was shooting a TV series in Chile, my daily breakfast for four months was PALTA CON HUEVOS REVUELTOS. In my view, Chile is home to the tastiest, richest and creamiest avocados (*palta*) in the world. In fact, I have seen watchtowers towering over the avocado plants where – I am told, though I fully confess my leg may have been being pulled – snipers defend the crop against avocado rustlers. In this dish, scrambled eggs are served alongside mashed avocado and they would even sometimes be mixed together which, take it from me, really is a grizzly sight. Green eggs first thing in the morning are enough to curl your eyebrows into tight fuzz-balls of pinched, bristling shock and awe. My solution – which is dreamy:

Spread 1 ripe avocado, mashed, on buttered toast, and then spoon some well-seasoned scrambled eggs on top.

Rich and scrumptious, it's a true breakfast of champions!

> Match this with a cup of warm, malty Assam tea. I love tea — the tea gardens around the world where the plants are grown behave a lot like vineyards in the way they express the unique character of where they are made and this is coupled with the way that the tea is processed and interpreted to create the final brew. A current favourite of mine is loose-leaf Dejoo Tippy Golden Flowery Orange Pekoe which is properly malty Assam and a robust way to kick off the dawn alongside a creamy dish such as scrambled eggs.

And while we're talking breakfast, here's a top scrambled egg tip – stick your eggs in a bowl, whisk them and then place the bowl over a pan of boiling water. Add nothing! Keep stirring and after about ten minutes you see the most amazing deep orangey colour develop in your intensifying scrambled eggs and, when you finally feast, the dish is super-rich and unbelievably tasty. Big tip – use many more eggs than you think as they tend to reduce down during cooking. Six eggs are about right for three modest portions. And served with proper smoked salmon from the Hebridean Smokehouse (www.saleshebridean.co.uk) you just can't go wrong!

> To drink with this, it would have to be a champion glass of Champagne or a top glass of English sparkling wine from one of the top estates — Ridgeview, Hugh Hoath, Nyetimeher or Camel Valley. But make an effort to taste your local vineyard's fizz, rosé and white wine — they may be full of surprises and can be decent quality. My local vineyard is Breaky Bottom and they produce uniquely British fizz that I love to sip in the heart of Sussex.

Oooh and more egg tips: did you know their shells are permeable? If you're a fan of truffles and want to maximize the use of their uniquely curious flavour without even slicing into them, store them overnight in a jar of eggs and the eggs will become magically infused with the flavour. Awesome for a mushroom omelette or when adding another layer of flavour to scrambled eggs.

Before I reveal the recipe for another breakfast delight, my KICKING KIPPER KEDGEREE, I need you to think of the texture of kedgeree. It's as thick and creamy as the ultimate duvet and you need a white wine with a similar texture to squidge into it. Texture in white wine can come from a number of places: picking the grapes later, which gives them a more syrupy character and makes a sweeter wine, or plonking the wine into oak barrels. Oak staves (planks) and chips are also used and they tend to produce wines with less finesse – fine for a glug, not so fine to charm the in-laws, boss or for bribing corrupt border guards. The wine also needs to have enough flavour to cope with the kick of spice in the kedgeree. So, a later-harvested wine wouldn't work because the sweetness would overwhelm the savoury nature of the dish. The best option is to find a fleshy, oaked wine. And no white grape enjoys a romp in an oak barrel more than Chardonnay.

You've heard the phrase, 'I don't like Chardonnay, but I love Chablis.' Well, Chablis is made from Chardonnay (Chablis is the town where the wine is made). However, in Chablis they generally use the Chardonnay grape in an unoaked style. Chardonnay gets such a raw deal, mainly because oaky Australian Chardonnay was once so ubiquitous that it became a victim of its own success and popularity. You should give it another go! Some of the world's finest white wines are made from oaked Chardonnay in France's Burgundy region — Meursault, Puligny-Montrachet and Corton Charlemagne are all very famous places associated with producing fine, quality, oaked Chardonnay. But, equally, you can find some astonishing quality for between ten and twenty quid from Chile, in areas such as Limari (Maycas de Limari) or Malleco in the south (Aquitania's Sol de Sol); New Zealand has plenty on offer and Australia is worth peering back into, too. Argentina offers good kit from Catena (look for their Catena Alta featuring Chardonnay from the superb Adrianna Vineyard which I have romped around) and South Africa has some good stuff, too. Semillon from South Africa, especially when it ages in oak, develops a superb creamy texture and nutty flavour — world-class wine larks.

At the end of the day, a bit of oak in wine is immensely useful when matching it to food so don't write it off! Don't go cheap on oaked Chardonnay. Spend a bit more so you'll get a wine with a more subtle use of finer quality oak.

Wine fermented in stainless steel and then aged in oak barrels is likely to carry a more oaky (creamy and vanilla-like) flavour (especially if the oak barrels are new) than wine fermented in oak barrels. When it is fermented in oak barrels it gets a fleshy texture but the oak flavour tends not to be quite so in your face.

And so to the kedgeree, which serves 4:

→ Cook the butter and olive oil, onion, garlic and chilli in a frying pan over a high heat for 2–3 minutes until just softened.

→ Add the basmati rice, bay leaves and curry powder and stir-fry for 1 minute to coat the rice thoroughly.

→ Add the chicken stock, bring to the boil, then cover, reduce the heat to a gentle simmer and cook until the liquid is absorbed and the rice tender. It should take about 10 minutes.

→ Flake the kippers into the rice and cook for a further 2 minutes until the fish is cooked through.

→ Meanwhile, bring a pan of water to the boil, add the eggs and cook for 3 minutes. Drain and refresh under cold water, then roll gently on the work surface and peel. Cut into quarters and add to the rice with the parsley. Season the dish with salt and pepper and serve immediately.

With all the creaminess, richness, salty intensity, smoky and spicy touches in this Kicking Kedgeree, a fleshy white with rich texture is called for. Grape varieties that work well with cream and spice include Roussanne, Marsanne, Viognier, Chenin Blanc and Grenache Blanc, which can also work within a blend — these grapes all take well to oak and, thanks to their mellow fruity character, can take a light spank of spice. So they've all earned a ticket to ride the high road direct to Kedgeree City. Another great tip for a luxurious breakfast is to go for a richer style of Champagne — for example, Bollinger Special Cuvée which has a decent amount of flesh to its fizz.

KICKING KIPPER KEDGEREE

50g butter

1 tablespoon olive oil

1 onion, finely diced

2 garlic cloves, finely diced

1 red chilli, deseeded and diced

250g basmati rice

2 bay leaves

1 tablespoon curry powder (medium or hot, to your taste)

400ml chicken stock

600g kippers

4 eggs

4 tablespoons flat-leaf parsley, roughly chopped

salt and freshly ground black pepper

Risottos are famously creamy, and in Italy there's even a name for when you add the butter at the end for ultimate creaminess – *mantecatura*. My rule of thumb with risotto is to stick with Italian wines. If there are brighter, lighter flavours in the risotto, such as seafood, stick with white; if it is heavier, such as mushroom risotto, think red.

My most prominent risotto memory takes places in Georgio Locatelli's sublime Italian restaurant Locanda Locatelli. I had to review the restaurant undercover for the TV show *Food Uncut*. Knowing Georgio's talent for and delight in risottos, I ordered his *Risotto al Barolo e Castelmagno*, which the front of house always warns will take around 25 minutes. It's worth the wait. When it comes to the table it is finished with a spoonful of Barolo wine. My kind of dish. On the day I was filming undercover, the risotto was outstanding and I was just leaving the restaurant ready to review the experience with my piece to camera and thinking I had escaped unseen, when Georgio appeared and waved with a grin. He's a terrific chef and a great man – you should go to Locanda Locatelli and eat his *Risotto al Barolo e Castelmagno*!

PEA AND MINT RISOTTO

This is all about the spirit of spring, so a fresh Italian white is perfect. Gavi di Gavi is oft underrated but the top producers are nailing a renaissance and it's worth sampling some once more with its soft texture but refreshing character.

Serves 4

1 litre chicken or vegetable stock

1 onion, finely chopped

1 garlic clove, finely chopped

75g butter

250g Arborio rice

75ml dry white wine

125g frozen peas

2 tablespoons mascarpone

110g Parmesan cheese, grated

2 tablespoons mint leaves, roughly chopped

salt and freshly ground black pepper

→ Place the chicken or vegetable stock into a saucepan and bring to a gentle simmer.

→ Meanwhile, heat a saucepan until hot, then add the onion, garlic and half the butter and cook for a few minutes until softened but not coloured.

→ Add the rice and cook for a further minute, tossing to coat it in the butter.

→ Add the wine and reduce the liquid by half. Then start pouring in the warm stock, a ladleful at a time, stirring continuously. After each ladleful, stir until nearly all the stock has been absorbed and then add another. Keep going until the rice is just tender.

→ Add the remaining butter, the peas, mascarpone and Parmesan, and season well with salt and pepper.

→ Heat through, stirring all the time, before adding the mint. Serve immediately.

LILY'S SALAD

1 lettuce, chopped

2 eggs, hard boiled and chopped

15 black olives, roughly chopped

5 asparagus spears, cooked and chopped (3 minutes should do it – keep them nice and firm)

a finger's length of cucumber, peeled and chopped

For the dressing

3 tablespoons yoghurt

2 tablespoons mayonnaise

2 anchovies, finely chopped

1 garlic clove, crushed

handful of Parmesan cheese, freshly grated (plus extra shavings to garnish)

salt and freshly ground black pepper

YUM-TASTIC!

I invented LILY'S SALAD for my daughter when she had just turned two years old. It's all about the luxuriant creamy dressing and at the time I was going through a major Chicken Caesar Salad phase and I wanted to create a dish that was quick, seasonal, simple and fun. I love to make it when asparagus is marching across the landscape and on to the shelves. Outside of its season, you can replace the asparagus with a handful or two of lightly cooked frozen peas for a summery sweet buzz. Lily absolutely loved it and still laps it up to this very day! The quantities here will serve 4.

→ Combine all the salad ingredients in a bowl.

→ Whizz the dressing ingredients together and spoon over the salad. Serve garnished with Parmesan shavings.

Generally when it comes to salads, my advice is to pick out crisp white wines. If you think about the freshness and crunch of a salad, you want to mimic it with a light-bodied, crisp wine such as an Italian white — remember, it must be unoaked or the wine's texture will be too blocky. But, for this dish with its creamy dressing and salty, Parmesan tang, a white wine with some freshness balanced with a dose of oak will match up better. Think of the rich texture and salty/creamy flavours in the dish — you want something relatively subtle but with flesh on its bones. South African Chenin Blanc (Bruwer Raats and Ken Forrester are a couple of top names to look out for) would be good but if you want to splash out and feel like James Bond, try a rich style of Champagne such as Bollinger Special Cuvée.

GRIDDLED ASPARAGUS SOUP

My risotto was all about springtime and that wonderful *primavera* feeling that leads us straight into the asparagus season. I love that English asparagus is so outstanding, and I love that it only grows for a short season, from 1 May for six weeks. But look, I don't love that we call them spears. Spears are carried by Roman legionaries and are taller than a man. An asparagus is not a spear, nor is it a javelin. But if asparagus did grow taller than a Roman soldier . . . I would pioneer the world's first edible weapon – and there'd be more of it to chew on for those precious six weeks.

Serves 4–6

1 onion, finely chopped

4 tablespoons olive oil

550g asparagus spears, trimmed

1 tablespoon plain flour

550ml vegetable stock

50g Parmesan cheese, freshly grated

50ml crème fraîche

salt and freshly ground black pepper

→ Sauté the onion in half the olive oil over a medium heat until soft. Meanwhile, toss the asparagus with the remaining olive oil, some salt and black pepper, then place on a hot griddle pan until charred.

→ Remove the spears, roughly chop them and add to the onion. Stir in the flour and combine for 1 minute.

→ Add the vegetable stock, bring to the boil and simmer for 10 minutes until tender.

→ Place in a blender with the Parmesan and crème fraîche, and blitz to a smooth soup.

→ Season with plenty of pepper and serve.

The crème fraîche in this dish is a treat with its creamy texture and tang, and the asparagus goes well with Sauvignon Blanc — although Grüner Veltliner is the ultimate choice for me with its sensational skill at tackling tricky flavours (see Earthy for a fuller explanation). But for such a creamy soup, find a Grüner Veltliner that has been beefed up with oak — grab it and hurl your asparagus dart (yes, dart — a better sense of scale than spear, for sure), hurl your asparagus dart at the bull's-eye.

May I now pay homage to the creamiest, most shapely of fruit – the mighty banana. I reckon the making of the smoothest of smoothies comes down to the banana. Who would have thought such a hilariously shaped fruit would end up being popular not for its rather wonderful form, but because of its luxuriantly sweet, mellow flavour and thick texture? It is like nature's own squidgy moist cake. When I was teaching English in Sumatra, I discovered a whole new level of respect for the banana. The leaves were used to serve takeaway food in, the flesh itself went into *Pisang Goreng* (banana fritters – the batter base is made with rice flour and it's an awesome snack served hot with ice cream). But perhaps the simplest way to revere the banana is in a SMOOTHIE:

Blitz banana and ice and milk to taste and sugar, if you must. A terrific texture and a rather splendid way to spend half an hour slurping, chilling and nourishing. The cool mellow breakfast drink of champions.

While on my travels I encountered a whole stack of symphonic variations on the banana smoothie. They couldn't be easier to prepare – bung the ingredients in a blender with some ice and adjust quantities to taste. Here are four of the best and most playful:

THE CREAM SCHEME
Banana, avocado, blanched almonds, honey, full-fat milk and cinnamon powder.

THE CREAM TEAM
Banana, stoned dates, yoghurt and milk.

THE NUTS
Banana, Pistachio nuts, almonds, honey, cinnamon and rice milk.

SIR ROGER MOORE
Banana, runny honey, vanilla ice cream and full-fat milk. If you're feeling naughty, you could drizzle a jot of white rum into the proceedings… Now, let us drink Sir Roger Moore, taste and toast Sir Roger Moore – the Ultimate Smoothie!

Creamy is like a cuddle – you can't hold back and do half measures, you need to get in there and give it a proper squeeze. That's what cream is like – it's an ingredient that adds a dimension of flavour, texture and complexity, and the last thing in the world it can be described as is 'skimpy'. It's proper, full-on, joyful and celebratory. Creamy will always have a special place in my heart. I could secretly sip cream by the teaspoon – no wait, by the ladle – it's such a happy treat!●

BIG UP THE
BANANA!

FLORAL

I wish I was a bee. Bees get to sample nectar from the full catalogue of floral delights. I have an irresistible urge to eat every single flower I come across, which makes me think that perhaps I have an inner bee waiting to get out and pollinate for Britain. I am a butterfly fan, too. There is nothing more intoxicating than a warm, balmy, summery day with the heady scent of buddleia on the breeze and a pantheon of fluttering, flapping rags flittering from bush to bush in an extended dream sequence of their own concocting. Big up the butterfly! I almost wish I could eat them, as well.

Floral adds a unique dimension of flavour. You can't see creamy or salty or aromatic, but you can see, smell and taste floral – though extracting the flavour can be tricky. I wear flowery shirts, I plant my garden with flowers to attract bees and butterflies, I love scented flowers, gaudy flowers, subtle flowers, bulbs, tubers, seeds and fruit trees, and I yearn to eat every single one of them. Of course, some, like nasturtiums, you can eat and some floral flavours get infused through nature's links – acacia honey, for example. But it's the full-on fragrance of flowers that I would love to feast and gorge upon so that I could fully appreciate their subtle intoxicating diversity. And this is the thing. Flowers, in terms of flavour, are not that diverse. It's the smell of them that is like a massive cellar of wines all waiting to be uncorked and inhaled. In this chapter, my mission is to capture the invisible dimension of flowers – their scents. Scent is deeply linked to tasting – when you've got a cold, you can't taste anything. If you hold your nose and sip some red and white wine blindfolded, the difference is far less marked than with a fully functioning face-trumpet. A huge part of the pleasure I derive from wine is from smelling it – wine can smell intensely floral and you can even find fragrant notes in certain wines when you sip them. Aroma is a dimension that surrounds us, evoking powerful memories and powerful reactions – repulsion, attraction, arousal and disdain. Smell is also highly intuitive. We all have a unique signature 'scent' that plays a hugely important role in our courtship. I still remember now two girls called Amanda and Nicky at my primary school who were both intensely fragrant – I won't mention their surnames in case they get stealth-sniffed by their colleagues but it certainly had a marked impact on me at the time. And it sets up my Rule of Thumb #361, which is that it's generally harder – but not impossible – to kiss a person who reeks. Though, I remember once finding my girlfriend who'd returned from several days camping at the Glastonbury Festival irresistibly scented . . . I guess that's why some people find the earthy aroma of truffles so compelling. But to get back to the point in hand, the thing about flowers and floral as influence on flavour is that they are varied but all uniquely characterized by a fragrant roundness, which I find hugely inviting and very friendly! Of course, you can get notorious flowers like titan arum, the 'Corpse flower', which honk, but these are the exception to the rule. Flowers, generally, even when they are bright as in the case of lemon blossom, are rarely aggressive and almost always inviting. Flowers are the origin of flavour – without them enticing the bees, butterflies and insects, there'd be no blossom, no fruit, nothing!

I love lavender and it can be used in all sorts of recipes (most notably successful with lamb or infused at home into honey) but perhaps the flower I would most like to be able to taste is wisteria. I spent a few years growing up in Jersey in the Channel Islands and when my family first moved there from County Durham, I remember we stayed in a house at Le Hocq in St Clement called Belle Rive Villas (I think we lived at number 2). There was always an amazingly sweet scent wafting around the garden in early summer from the wisteria that curled up the walls. There were also stocks (*Matthiola*) which were deeply scented and sweetly intoxicating. I used to sit by the courgette plants that we grew, savouring the intensity of a packet of salt and vinegar crisps (in the days when the flavours properly chopped your palate off with their concentrated edges) and basking in the early summer sun, with the heady scents of the garden wreathing up from my ankles to my ears. I would dream endlessly of tasting wisteria. Tragically, it is poisonous, but that doesn't stop it possessing one of the sweetest, most sensual, sexily fragrant and alluring scents of all time. It is the smell I most love to have lingering around an open window on a summery morning. It seems its most intense then. It is honey-sweet, dreamy and transports like no other. You can wallow in a bath scented with wisteria oil and it is as if you're being devoured and absorbed by it. But, tantalizingly, you must never taste it. Oh, if only it was edible!

Help is at hand for all flower fans, though. Many wines have a floral quality, which is handy when it comes to matching them with aromatic flavours, when trying to complement a fruity edge, or to contrast with spice. Gewürztraminer is one of the most floral-scented wines in the world. Gewürztraminer from Alsace is famous for wines labelled Sélections de Grains Nobles which are syrupy and unctuous with some grapes affected by noble rot which intensifies and magnifies the flavour of the grapes.

Sparkling Italian prosecco is another wine style that can be floral – you can detect white flowers and sometimes a touch of something orange blossomy when you sniff it. Other whites to track and chase for their floral fragrance are sparkling Moscato, again from Italy, Riesling Spätlese from Germany, Pinot Gris from Alsace, Condrieu (Viognier from the appellation of Condrieu in

France which wafts honeysuckle), Viognier generally, and Argentinean Torrontes, which is super-heady and a floral escapade in a glass! If you're feeling patriotic, though, quite a lot of English white wine is scented with floral touches – think the hedgerow in springtime. Glorious!

Believe it or not, a fair number of reds can also honk like an English garden in full bloom. In Sicily there's a wine called Cerasuolo di Vittoria (the Planeta winery pumps out a reliably good one) which is partly made of the Frappato grape, which is super-floral and, such is its fragrance, it even reminds me of honey. Pinot Noir can have a perfumed twinge that ranges from incense-like to full-on floral. When Sophie and I first moved to Lewes, I joined a local wine club with a retired neighbour of mine, Brian. He not only has the coolest dog of all time, Jasper – who, for reasons I have never quite explained, I refer to as The Prince of Denmark – but he also has a fantastic cellar tucked under his house which is stacked with fine wine. A real gentleman's hideaway. I remember after a particular tasting where we'd been discussing scent and perfume in wine, Brian opened a bottle of fine, aged red Burgundy (it was a Clos Vougeot made by Anne Gros) and I will never forget the amazing niff of it. We sat there together marvelling at its complexity – touches of incense and spice, with floral echoes from when the wine was younger. Just magnificent and a real stand-out memory of the delights of smell!

Syrah (a.k.a. Shiraz) also has a floral dimension to it and you can sometimes pick it up in French wines such as Crozes-Hermitage or Côtes du Rhône, and even in bigger styles from South Africa and Chile. But for serious flower power in your red wine glass, check out Argentinean Malbec. The high altitude in Argentina is an awesome place to grow grapes – it's practically making wine in space! I often find a violet-like scent in the Malbec – intoxicating and inviting. FLORALICIOUS!●

FLOWER POWER

The simplest way to capture the power of the flower is physically to deploy it – leaves, petals, stems and seeds. When you eat flowers, though, they don't necessarily taste floral and you can sometimes find quite powerful flavours at work in their midst. Take nasturtiums. Climbing or trailing, wherever they unfurl themselves and set up their flat parasol-like leaves, it's never long before they set forth their red and golden trumpet-bell flowers and tootle merrily throughout the summer months, uplifting the garden with their upbeat jazzy persistence. You can eat the lot – leaves, flowers and seeds. Nasturtiums are awesome at surviving the entire winter and popping up in the most unexpected spots the following year. Watch out when eating the leaves, though, they're peppery – I adore the kick but they've got quite a bite to them! I scatter them through salads (similar to how you'd use rocket leaves) to add a layer of spice.

NASTURTIUM, CREAM CHEESE AND CUCUMBER OPEN SANDWICHES

Peel and finely slice 2 CUCUMBERS and place them in a bowl with 3 TABLESPOONS MALDON SEA SALT. Leave to soak for 20 minutes. Drain the cucumber and rinse thoroughly to remove any salt, and then pat dry. Roughly chop 15G EDIBLE NASTURTIUM FLOWERS and mix with 150G SOFT CREAM CHEESE and the fine ZEST OF ½ LEMON. Season with salt and freshly ground black pepper. Spread the flowery cheese over 4 SLICES DARK RYE BREAD, then top with the cucumber slices. Either cut into finger-sized strips or leave the bread whole. Sprinkle with some whole nasturtium flowers and serve.

Nasturtiums aren't the only common garden flower that you can deploy in your feasting. Look out for lavender. It's awesome! I remember driving in the back of Mum and Dad's clapped-out VW Golf across France with Will next to me. It must have been the early 1980s. Will always has been an avid reader and would perch in the back of the car ploughing through *The Animals of Duncton Wood*, *The Dogs of War*, *Watership Down* and various spin-off *Star Wars* books from *Splinter of the Mind's Eye* through to *Han Solo at Star's End*. I would generally be plugged into my Walkman listening to anything from Captain Beaky to Dire Straits – yeah, Will and I were cool kids. We endlessly chewed Hollywood chewing gum – thrilled at the kaleidoscope of flavours beyond the mint we were perpetually lumped with in the UK. Will was a huge fan of *citron*, my holiday treat was *fraise*. Around Grasse, where loads of perfume is made, we stopped at a lavender farm and it has never left my memory. Visually, it was a spectacle, thanks to the blue, purple and pinky tinges of all the different lavender plants, but the scent was intoxicating. And so was the activity from all the butterflies and bees – the place was alive with buzzing and flapping in colourful bursts that filled the golden day with the sound of innocent industry.

Today, my kids love peering across the garden at the lavender and the rosemary, and I get a kick out of the menthol darkness of rosemary compared with the mellow sweetness of lavender. Just as rosemary works a treat with sweet buttery lamb, so too can lavender add an extra surreptitious floral dimension to the meat and it's well worth experimenting with.

LAVENDER JELLY

2kg cooking apples

1.4 litres water

bunch of lavender with stems, leaves and flowers (maybe half a dozen stems)

approximately 1.3kg preserving sugar

LOVE IT!

LAVENDER JELLY is just one example given to me by the lovely Fiona Roberts-Miller. Basically this is lavender-flavoured apple jelly, so if you have a favourite recipe for that, just add the lavender to taste. You will need a large saucepan, a jelly bag, a large bowl or jug, and some clean, sterilized jars (see page 26):

→ Roughly chop the apples and tip them into a large saucepan with the water and half the lavender. Bring to the boil and simmer until the fruit has completely softened.

→ Strain the mixture through a jelly bag overnight, letting the juice drip into a large bowl or jug. As with all jellies, don't be tempted to squish it or it won't be clear!

→ Measure out the juice into a large saucepan and add 450g preserving sugar for every 600ml/1 pint of juice. Add the remaining lavender and bring to the boil slowly. Cook until the setting point is reached. (One way to test is to put a plate in the freezer for a few minutes, then drop some of the jelly on to it. If it wrinkles when you push it to the edge of the plate, it will set. If not, boil longer and test every few minutes.)

→ Remove the lavender sprigs carefully. I like to leave a few flower buds in there for effect. Pour into the prepared jars.

It's up to you how strong you make the lavender flavour – see how it tastes after the first stage of cooking, and if it's strong enough for you, don't add any lavender at the second stage. This method also works well with other herbs – you can add sage for eating with pork, thyme for chicken and so on.

LAVENDER-STUDDED

ROASTED LAMB RUMP

Another way to use the *stems* and the flowers, both of which are packed with fragrance (rub a lavender stem between your thumb and forefinger and smell for Britain!), is in this roast lamb.

→ Preheat the oven to 200°C/400°F/Gas 6.

→ Using a small knife make several deep slits into the rumps, about 4cm apart, and insert a small sprig of lavender in each one.

→ Heat an ovenproof frying pan until hot, add the olive oil and butter, and the lamb skin side down, and cook for 2–3 minutes, then turn and cook on the other side for 2 minutes. Place in the oven and cook for 12–15 minutes.

→ Remove from the oven and place the lamb on to a plate to rest. Return the pan to the heat, add the red wine, deglaze, scraping up any juicy bits, and cook until reduced by half.

→ Add the chicken stock and cook until reduced by half again. Season with salt and pepper.

→ Serve the lamb rump with a pile of Olive Oil Mash (see page 203) and spoon the sauce over the top.

Serves 4

4 x 225g boned rumps of lamb (ask your butcher to prepare them for you and keep the fatty skin on)

4 stems fresh lavender

50g butter

2 tablespoons olive oil

125ml red wine

150ml chicken stock

salt and freshly ground black pepper

Just as the lamb in this recipe is infused with a floral edge of lavender, other methods of infusion can also extract flowery delights for our delectation. Take tea, for example. High quality tea, such as loose-leaf white tea, should come from a bud and two leaves only – i.e. the very top of the plant and the very freshest leaves. I've recently spent many happy hours becoming a tea junkie and am taking great delight in discovering how different tea gardens produce different flavoured teas, rather like different vineyards produce unique wine. A great example is First Flush Darjeeling Tea from India. I've got some leaves from Margaret's Hope Tea Garden, which are aromatic, fragranced and almost strawberry-like in their aroma. Tukdah First Flush Darjeeling is more herby and Badamtam is crisp and refreshing. Wonderful! And that's just smelling them! You can add an extra layer to tea by using flowers themselves to impart their flavour. Jasmine tea is infused with the fragrant flavour of jasmine flowers and makes a great alternative to a pot of standard tea, but you can also use it when you make iced tea. Take your taste buds on tour and deploy it in summery cocktails for that special holiday feeling. For a FLOWER POWER ICED TEA COCKTAIL:

Combine equal measures Havana Club Añejo 7 Años, Cointreau and fresh orange juice, and ½ measure lime juice in a tall glass with crushed ice. Top up with several sloshes of jasmine tea and full-fat cola. Garnish with a slice of lime.

TIP – REPLACE THE JASMINE TEA WITH EARL GREY FOR A CITRUSY FLORAL BURST.

LASSOING THE INVISIBLE BEE

Bees get to taste flowers in a way that we just can't. For starters, have you ever tried shoving your head into a flower? Bees have a size advantage and they use it to the full. I wish that I could fully taste and explore the invisible fragrance of flowers. The closest I can get to lassoing the invisible stuff that bees get up close and personal with is through their honey. On my travels tasting wine I always try the local honey. Like wine *terroir*, it's amazing how honey tastes different depending on what flowers the honeybees have been working on and this changes with the seasons. We often talk about seasonality in the foodie world but the bees are right at the heart of it. We should follow their example! I tried a range of three honeys at a market in Provence once that all tasted wildly different – one from bees working beside a river, one from the forest and one from the mountains. I thought they were all magnificent – the forest honey had an odd, feral, savoury and rather funky taste to it. There are so many types of honey to experiment with:

Eucalyptus honey is dark and intense. Heather honey is orangey and floral. Chestnut honey is runny and a bit bonkers and has a tang but works in meaty glazes. Orange blossom honey can be found in Mediterranean countries and is wreathed in a joyful, fine orange-blossom flavour. Acacia honey is very popular because it stays runny and is so sweet it's usually a winner with kids. Active manuka honey is popular in New Zealand and thanks to the unique characteristics of the manuka bush has incredible antibacterial properties (for 'active' honey, you need to select manuka honey with a factor of ten or more, and this should be clearly indicated on the label).

My most memorable honey tasting, though, came in Cauquenes in southern Chile while on a wine-tasting mission to hunt Old Vine Carignan. I met a local priest who showed me some super old vines that looked like something out of *Lord of the Rings* and, on our way to see them, he revealed his passion for wild honey and let me taste some of his stash. It was the colour of fudge, almost aglow and very thick, shiny and rich. The flavour was somewhere between floral and citrus, with sweetness and refreshment, and it had a luxuriant, thick texture with very fine grains to keep your tongue tingling – enlivening! The priest and I got talking and when we parted company he gave me a tub of honey that was so big I could have done a Winnie-the-Pooh and got my head inside to lick every last morsel! It inspired me to learn more about bees and for the first time this year I started keeping bees with my bee-buddy Chris Parkinson. It has been a revelation. I've always enjoyed epics from *Star Wars* to *The Odyssey*, but never have I seen such battles and determination as when my bees defended their besieged hive from an invasion of wasps. Honey is worth fighting for! I've discovered, too, that one hive can produce many flavours – it changes through the seasons. In spring it is light, runny and floral, but the honey gets darker gradually through the months, depending on what nectar the bees are gathering. By late summer, when the ivy flowers, the honey is much more deeply coloured and aromatic, with a medicinal touch. Bees are connoisseurs of their precious art and, as we know, they are essential for pollinating a great deal of our fruit and veg. Whatever you can do for the bee, whether it's planting friendly flowers or putting a small hive on a wall somewhere (like the ones made out of sawn-off bamboo for solitary bees), you should do. LET'S BE FOR THE BEE!

If you're able to plant some or all of the plants listed opposite in your garden or window box, the bees will visit – and what could be more summery than watching their busy waggling and dipping in the floral kingdom on your doorstep? I love bird-watching but have you ever tried bee-watching through your binoculars? Find a lavender bush and get involved; it's joyful to see the bees so attentive and so rigorous! And they've got what I want – face-trumpets fully dunked in a flower.

Another way to lasso your flowers is by turning them into a cordial. Floral cordials are simple to make and usually involve dipping edible flower heads in boiling sugar syrup and enhancing this with citrus peel. Elderflower is the most common floral cordial and the flowers grow everywhere – in towns, the countryside and around parks and pitches. Google it, memorize it, smell it, cut it, use it. It's free!

I freeze this ELDERFLOWER CORDIAL recipe in ice-cube bags to deploy throughout the year in cocktails or just to make a gorgeous self-chilling elderflower drink:

→ Place the sugar in a large bowl, add the boiling water and stir until dissolved. Leave to cool until you can touch it.

→ Add the rest of the ingredients and leave covered with a tea-towel for 24 hours.

→ Strain through a muslin. Add sugar or lemon juice to adjust flavour. If you bottle it in sterilized bottles (see page 22), it will last for up to 3 weeks in the fridge.

ELDERFLOWER CORDIAL

900g sugar

3 litres boiling water

30 elderflower heads

50ml lemon juice

1 lemon, chopped

1 orange, chopped

1 lime, chopped

3 leaves fresh apple mint

Here's some insider intelligence on flowers that work brilliantly to attract our furry friends, garnered from the evening meetings I attended with my bee buddy Chris at the Sussex Beekeepers Association:

- WINTER ACONITE
- POACHED EGG PLANT
- WALLFLOWERS
- JUDD VIBURNUM
- PATTY'S PLUM (POPPY)
- MIGNONETTE
- HARDY GERANIUMS (MAVIS SIMPSON IS A GOOD ONE THAT SPREADS)
- COSMOS (KEEP CUTTING THE FLOWERS TO ENCOURAGE GROWTH)
- SNOWDROPS
- MICHAELMAS DAISY
- ASTERS (PINK CLOUD IS RECOMMENDED)
- CHRYSANTHEMUMS
- OXEYE DAISY
- ACACIA MIMOSA

NEVER WASH THE ELDERFLOWERS OR YOU WILL LOSE THE DELICATE FLAVOUR – REMOVE ANY INSECTS BY HAND!

SUNFLOWER HONEY

AND POLENTA CAKE

Sunflowers are super-easy and spectacular to grow. Mark them out and place your bets on which will grow tallest! Sunflower oil is magnificent stuff for pan-frying – with a high smoke point and a mild flavour. And some people swear by rubbing sunflower oil into their skin or dropping a few drips into a hot bath as a way to lock moisture into the skin. Sunflower honey tends to be rich and creamy and it works beautifully in this recipe.

200g sunflower honey

50g butter

50g caster sugar

zest of 1 lemon

200g quick-cook polenta

100g self-raising flour

50g ground almonds

1 teaspoon baking powder

150ml milk

1 egg, lightly beaten

100ml water

→ Preheat the oven to 180°C/350°F/Gas 4 and line a 20cm cake tin with baking paper.

→ Place 50g honey and the butter into a saucepan and heat until just melted, stirring to mix together.

→ Place the caster sugar, half the lemon zest, the polenta, flour, ground almonds and baking powder into a bowl, then add the melted honey and stir well.

→ Add the milk and egg, stirring all the time, to form a very thick, batter-like consistency. Pour into the baking tin, spreading evenly.

→ Place in the oven for 25–30 minutes until just risen slightly and golden.

→ Meanwhile, place the rest of the honey, the water and the remaining lemon zest into a saucepan, bring to the boil and simmer for 2 minutes.

→ Remove the cake from the oven and, using a fine skewer, make holes all over it. Slowly pour the honey syrup over the warm cake and leave to cool.

→ Cut into wedges and serve with a dollop of crème fraîche.

And pour yourself a chilled glass of Samos Muscat — gorgeous, fragrant sweet wine from the Greek island of Samos that is scented with orange and lusciously sweet. Or for a bargain you could look for Muscat St Jean de Minervois from France or Orange Muscat and Flora from Australia served fridge-cool. You could experiment by serving these last two over crushed ice to break up the texture and tone down the sweetness, if your guests are reticent!

4 large handfuls gorse flowers

600ml/1 pint cold water

250g caster sugar

juice of 1 lemon

zest of 1 orange

A less common but no less delicious cordial is GORSE FLOWER CORDIAL – I discovered the recipe on a brilliant website called www.eatweeds.co.uk – now that's an idea! (When on holiday in Greece during spring, you can find amazing *horta*, which is steamed greens sourced from local weeds, such as dandelion, wild spinach, nettles and beet ends. They are drizzled in olive oil with a squeeze of lemon, salt and pepper. Divine, simple and more or less free food.)

→ Bring the water and sugar to a rapid boil and keep boiling for 10 minutes. Remove the pan from the heat.

→ Add the lemon juice, orange zest, and gorse flowers to the sugar water (syrup). Stir in well and leave until cooled or overnight.

→ Strain the liquid through muslin or a jelly bag into a clean container such as a glass jug. You should end up with roughly 500ml of liquid.

→ Pour into a sterile bottle, cap and store. Refrigerate once you have given into temptation.

OLLY'S SHAM-PAGNE

For a cracking sparkling drink that is virtually non-alcoholic (save for the 3 drops of angostura bitters), combine 1 MEASURE LIME CORDIAL, 1 MEASURE ELDERFLOWER CORDIAL, 3 DROPS ANGOSTURA BITTERS and 250ML SODA WATER. Serve in Champagne flutes to blend in at a party. An awesome tipple and one I love to sip at lunchtime in the garden.

My favourite way of using floral cordials of any kind, though, is to add them to an otherwise unflowery pudding, like these ORANGE BLOSSOM RUM BABAS. Orange blossom water belongs in every store cupboard – you can boost a fruit salad with it, add a layer of complexity to marinades, stir it into drinks, deploy it in dressings and salads, and sniff it liberally for an uplifting nose tickle. These quantities make six babas:

→ Butter 6 individual baba moulds and preheat the oven to 200°C/400°F/Gas 6.

→ Put 2 tablespoons of the caster sugar, 1 teaspoon of the orange blossom water, the milk and orange zest into a bowl and whisk together.

→ Add the eggs and butter and beat until smooth.

→ Sift in the flour and yeast and continue mixing until the batter is thick and very smooth. Spoon the mixture into the buttered moulds, filling them about half way up.

→ Place in a warm place for about 20–30 minutes to prove, or until the mixture has doubled in size.

→ Place the moulds on to a baking tray and put in the oven for 10–15 minutes until golden, then remove and cool in the moulds.

→ Meanwhile, place the remaining orange blossom water and caster sugar with the water in a saucepan, bring to the boil and simmer for 2 minutes. Remove from the heat and add the rum.

→ Remove the cooled babas from their moulds and place in a deep tray. Pour the warm syrup over them and leave to soak for 30 minutes – spoon the syrup over the top a few times to make sure all of it is absorbed.

→ To serve, fill the centre of each baba with some whipped cream, and spoon over any extra syrup.

ORANGE BLOSSOM RUM BABAS

130g caster sugar

2½ teaspoons orange blossom water

60ml milk

zest of 1 orange

2 eggs

75g butter, melted, plus extra for greasing

125g plain flour

1 teaspoon quick action dried yeast

100ml water

75ml light rum

250ml double cream, lightly whipped

ICED ELDERFLOWER CUP CAKES

I've always found the delicate sweet floral flavour of elderflower to be perfumed, intoxicating and magical. But the flowers themselves are supremely delicate to admire up close. Whites and flecks of yellows with intricate little structures, like a mini royal festival of tents for tiny imaginary fairies to flit, dance and bubble about in. And these iced elderflower cup cakes are exactly what I imagine the fairies would be munching on to sustain their reveals.

Makes 12

175g butter, softened

175g vanilla sugar

3 eggs

80ml elderflower cordial

175g self-raising flour

3 tablespoons ground almonds

75g icing sugar

FOR A FINAL FLOURISH SPRINKLE ELDERFLOWERS ON TO THE CUP CAKES WHILE THE ICING IS WET.

→ Preheat the oven to 180°C/350°F/Gas 4 and line a 12-hole cup cake or muffin tray with paper baking cases.

→ Place the butter and vanilla sugar into a bowl and beat together until light in colour and very soft.

→ Add the eggs, one at a time, beating well between each.

→ Add 50ml of the elderflower cordial and beat once more.

→ Carefully sieve the self-raising flour into the bowl and fold in. Add the ground almonds and mix carefully once more – the mixture should now drop off the spoon quite easily.

→ Spoon into the baking cases and then place in the oven and bake for 20 minutes until golden and risen. Press lightly on the centre to see if they are cooked – if they spring back they are ready. If not, return to the oven for another 2–3 minutes.

→ Remove from the oven and cool before removing from the bun tin.

→ Meanwhile, to make the icing, sieve the icing sugar into a bowl and then add the remaining elderflower cordial. Mix to a thick paste. Spread over the top of the cold cup cakes. Allow to set before serving, if you can . . .

Rose syrup is flower cordial royalty and I created this cocktail for my old flatmate Sean. The rose syrup adds a floral touch to an otherwise bitter drink. I call it THE SNIPER because it does tend to creep up on you and get you right between the eyes:

Combine 1 measure gin, 1 measure vodka, ½ measure rose syrup, ½ measure grenadine and 1 measure Campari. Shake over ice. Fill a Slim Jim glass with ice and a lemon slice. Pour halfway up with the mix and top up with Fever-Tree tonic water. Unleash The Sniper!

Extracting the floral essence in a sweet cordial is one thing, but capturing a flowery note in a bitter form is even more cunning and will make you feel like a kinky wizard! Make some ROSE VINEGAR by placing 1 cup rose petals into 500ml white vinegar and leave to infuse for at least 1 week. Strain and use as you would normal vinegar. I like to give summery salad dressings a flowery punch with mine.

DOSE BARGAIN BUBBLY WITH FLORAL CORDIALS TO UPLIFT THE DRINK. TRY ELDERFLOWER OR ROSE CORDIAL, OR EVEN LYCHEE SYRUP WILL DO.

TASTE EXPERIMENT

Make two salad dressings:

1) 1 TABLESPOON ROSE VINEGAR, 3 TABLESPOONS RAPESEED OIL and A PINCH OF SUGAR
2) 2 TABLESPOONS ROSE SYRUP, 1 TABLESPOON CHARDONNAY VINEGAR and 3 TABLESPOONS RAPESEED OIL

Dress some salad leaves and see which is more rosy!

ASPARAGUS AND POACHED DUCK EGG SALAD

Another way to deploy your rose vinegar is to dress a light, warm dish in it... Try this Asparagus and Poached Duck Egg Salad.

Serves 4

2 tablespoons rose syrup

1 tablespoon Chardonnay vinegar

3 tablespoons rapeseed oil

16 spears asparagus, trimmed

1 tablespoon light olive oil

4 duck eggs

1 small bag pea tops

salt and freshly ground black pepper

YOU CAN USE ROSE VINEGAR IN THE RECIPE INSTEAD OF ROSE SYRUP AND CHARDONNAY VINEGAR, BUT ADD A PINCH OF SUGAR TO COMPENSATE.

→ Place the rose syrup, vinegar and rapeseed oil into a jar, close tightly, and shake to combine. Season to taste with a little pinch of sugar, salt and pepper.

→ Toss the asparagus with the olive oil and some salt and pepper.

→ Heat a griddle pan until hot, add the asparagus and char on each side for 1–2 minutes until slightly blackened and tender.

→ Bring a small pan of water to just simmering. Swirl the centre of the pan to create a vortex then carefully drop the eggs in, two at a time. Cook gently for 2–3 minutes, depending on how you like your eggs done.

→ Remove and drain on kitchen paper.

→ Toss the pea tops with a little of the rose dressing and pile in the centre of 4 individual plates. Top each pile with 4 stems of asparagus and a poached egg. Drizzle over the remaining dressing and serve with some crusty bread.

Floral is an unseen dimension in our lives thanks to the fragrance from flowers wreathed in the power to set your nostrils and taste buds on a course hitherto known only by the bees – now that's what I call a real buzz. I am surrounded by it in my life, whether I'm catching a subtle waft of the blossom from the apple trees in my garden, visiting my family Camilla, Mike and Puka in Dingle and snooting the wild honeysuckle in the lanes around Ballyferriter, scenting the sweet peas in Granny Pip's garden (her favourite flower), or simply enjoying the smell of a wild rose on a summery stroll. The trick is using a bit of know-how to convert the secret gems of the floral kingdom to enhance your feasting. Somehow smelling flowers always makes me feel as though I am floating. I would love to ride their wafting streams up into the skies on giant perfumed invisible currents, like trails that lure us all home.●

NUTTY

Nuttiness is also a wonderful, enriching and comforting dimension in a dish. It can offer texture, crunch, creaminess and even a bitter tang – think walnuts and Gorgonzola, an awesome combination that starts like clash of the Titans but always ends up in a giant smooch. Get in there and feel the love! But I am addicted to peanuts. There. I've said it. I'll dabble in salted peanuts, unsalted, even salt and vinegar which sort of worked but have disappeared from our shelves along with Tangy Twiglets. For me, though, the supreme gastro-hit packed with umami (see page 205) and salty enchantment is the dry-roasted peanut. I crave them, I secretly worship them and if I cannot get my hands on them during a moment of intense craving, I actually see armies of peanuts marching across the work surface towards me in a cruel, nut-fuelled reverie of untold desire. But the dry-roasted peanut is also my arch nemesis. Peanuts generally don't do too many favours for wine, muting the flavours and coating the mouth. I always opt for a pint of Harveys Best Bitter – rich enough and tangy enough to cope with the texture, flavour and saltiness of the peanut. If you are a fan of other nuts, unsalted almonds work with Champagne, salted almonds with a glass of chilled Tawny Port and a glass of oloroso sherry can be sublime with a rustling punnet of walnuts.

Styles of wine, such as oloroso sherry, are often described as having a nutty character thanks to their long ageing in a solera system. The solera system is an ingenious way of maintaining a constant style by fractionally blending wines from many different barrels for anything up to 25 years or more. You can also find nutty notes in Tawny Port, which are labelled with an age (10, 20, 30 or 40 years old), representing the average of what's inside the bottle. The nuttiness comes from ageing in barrels – the wine oxidizes, making it go brown and develop a complex, nutty character. Nutty aromas in younger wines are thanks to the use of oak, for example in certain styles of Champagne and also in oaked white wines such as white Burgundy (made from Chardonnay).

Another drink that gives off, among other niffs, a nutty character is coffee. Coffee beans are fascinating to me. Like wine, coffee tastes different depending on where the beans are grown in the world. Not only that, but just as in winemaking when decisions are made about technique and which tools to use to bring out the character of a wine so, too, in the production of coffee, decisions such as how long to roast the beans have a profound effect on the flavour of the resulting coffee. The big difference between the two, though, is that coffee relies on us to create the final drink. We need to do justice to the careful growing and roasting and not cock it up. With wine, it's simpler – we just have to pour. That said, when we do pour it, it's important to unleash the wine at a temperature that can show it off in its best light and we should also serve it alongside a dish that will bring out the best in the food and the vino.

Nuts can have a transformative effect on a dish. I remember once having lunch with James Winter, the producer of *Saturday Kitchen*, in Arbutus restaurant in London's Soho. The chef there, Anthony Demetre, produced some superbly inventive dishes and we were thrilled by his work. One of them was a cold soup with toasted hazelnuts, grapefruit segments, carrot and green olives which I will never forget – the perfect balance between creamy, mellow and zingy with saline moments and the glorious nutty edge of the hazelnuts. Simple yet complex, I loved it. ●

NUTS IN THE RAW

Before nuts are cooked, they can be found in three different states – their virgin state, coarsely ground for their woody crunch and blitzed to emphasize their creaminess. And the magic doesn't stop there – they can also be processed for their oil. Groundnut oil is superb for stir-fries and has a higher smoke point than many other oils which means it can withstand a fair whack of heat before it burns. Toasted sesame oil is the nuts with stir-fries and for adding an eastern twist to a dressing. Unleash the nut!

When puréed, blitzed and blended, all nuts give rich base textures and flavours to build on – and you can even spread them on toast. Oh yes, there is life beyond mere peanut butter… behold – NUT BUTTERS!

To serve 4, place 200g whatever (unsalted) roasted nuts you fancy – mixed or one type – into a food processor and blitz to a purée. Keep blitzing while you add 3–4 tablespoons light olive oil, or water or a flavoured oil to match your nuts. Keep going until the nuts turn to a thick purée. (Add more water if you fancy a softer texture.) Season to taste with Maldon sea salt and a little freshly ground black pepper.

And, here we are, dealing in the savoury dimension of the nut, but of course we all remember the days when King Cone adverts were proudly belted out across the nation's cinema screens with a cascade of chopped nuts falling into the perfectly sculpted ice cream (sadly, they always looked rather squished whenever I bought one from an obliging usherette). The point is that nuts can, of course, adorn our desserts, from pecan pie to Christmas pudding. Here's a super-simple sweet nut recipe for HAZELNUT BRITTLE that works as a fun snack on its own, or crunched and sprinkled over vanilla ice cream:

To serve 4, place 300g caster sugar into a saucepan and cook over a medium heat until the sugar turns to a dark caramel colour. Add 100g skinned, toasted and roughly chopped hazelnuts and stir well. Tip out on to a baking-paper-lined tray, tilting the tray to get an even layer. Set aside for 20–30 minutes until hardened, and then break into medium-sized pieces.

This brittle recipe will work with any kind of nut. But there are some massive nuts in the world – consider the coconut! It's often treated like a fruit but the coconut is, in fact, a giant seed and, as such, works extremely well with the other seeds and nuts in this chapter. One of the most memorable tastes of my childhood is CHOCOLATE COCONUT. It's a Granny Smokey special and she always had a tin of it lurking in her larder. In fact, she seems to be able to produce it just about anywhere: in Tupperware at the beach, from greaseproof paper in the New Forest, from a rustling plastic bag in the cinema . . . Wherever she was, Granny Smokey always took chocolate coconut with her. My mum also makes it today and I make it for my girls. It's a huge family favourite, and so easy to make the kids can do it themselves:

Preheat the oven to 170°C/325°F/Gas 3. Beat 115g butter with 55g caster sugar until light and creamy. Stir in 80g desiccated coconut (or you could try 40g desiccated coconut and 40g ground hazelnuts) and 115g self-raising flour. Tip into a 15cm lightly buttered square tin, smooth the surface and bake for 30–40 minutes. Leave to cool in the tin. When cold, cover with a thin layer of melted milk chocolate (melt cubes of chocolate in a heatproof bowl over a saucepan of barely simmering water, or in the microwave). Leave to set and then cut into small squares. Store in an airtight tin and then hide it from me or I will smell it out, bust into your larder and scoff the lot. You have been warned.

THE COCONUT TOWERS

2 egg whites

150g caster sugar

150g desiccated coconut

Another great way to use desiccated coconut is to build architectural temples to its glory. Behold THE COCONUT TOWERS! These serve a tea party of six grown ups or twelve hungry nippers!

→ Preheat the oven to 170°C/325°F/Gas 3 and grease and line a baking tray.

→ Place the egg whites into a bowl and whisk until soft peaks are formed.

→ Add the caster sugar a third at a time and whisk until firm shiny peaks are formed.

→ Add the coconut and fold in carefully.

→ Spoon on to the baking tray twelve little towers. Place in the oven and bake for 15–20 minutes until just golden. Allow to cool on the tray before serving.

This is great as a snack or as a pudding served with sweet wine made from Chenin Blanc such as a South African Straw Wine — look out for iconic Vin de Constance, which was enjoyed by Napoleon. Good enough for Boney, good enough for us. I've always found richly textured Chenin Blanc works well with the oily richness in coconut — Cape Malay cooking in South Africa deploys a fair amount of coconut and their local Chenin has the right proportions of texture and acidity to complement it and cut through.

CASHEW NUT, TOFU AND CARROT STIR-FRY

I've mentioned that nuts and nutty sauces can slay the subtle flavours in wine – but if you must have nuts, unsalted cashews can work with Champagne. With their uniquely sweet, creamy, mellow flavour, I love them and particularly so in this stir-fry.

Serves 4

2 tablespoons vegetable oil

125g cashew nuts

2 tablespoons sesame seeds

250g firm tofu, cut into 1cm cubes

1 small onion, finely sliced

2 garlic cloves, finely chopped

3cm piece ginger, peeled and finely chopped

3 carrots, peeled then sliced finely using a potato peeler

2 tablespoons sesame oil

2 tablespoons soy sauce

2 tablespoons oyster sauce

2 tablespoons water

2 tablespoons coriander leaves, roughly chopped

→ Heat a wok until smoking hot, then add the vegetable oil and cashew nuts and cook for 1–2 minutes until golden brown and toasted.

→ Add the sesame seeds and cook for 45 seconds more until they are golden, too. Remove from the pan with a slotted spoon and drain on to kitchen paper.

→ Add the tofu to the pan and stir-fry for 3–4 minutes until golden brown and hot through. Remove and place with the nuts.

→ Add the onion to the pan and stir-fry for 2 minutes then add the garlic and ginger and stir-fry for a further 1 minute.

→ Add the carrots and stir-fry for 2 minutes until just softened, then add the toasted cashew nuts, sesame seed and tofu to the pan and fry for 1 minute.

→ Add the sesame oil, soy sauce, oyster sauce and water, and cook for 1 minute. Taste and adjust the seasoning if necessary.

→ Serve with some noodles tossed in sesame oil and chopped coriander leaves.

Nuts in the Raw are a great headline flavour but they can also be great in a more supporting role. For example, you can vamp up simple bread mixes, like this one from Granny Smokey, by adding a handful of mixed crushed nuts or seeds to Gran-ary it up. Geddit? Granny… Granary…

GRANNY SMOKEY'S BASIC BREAD RECIPE

Bizarrely when I was typing up this recipe, I noticed that Granny Smokey had included a 25mg vitamin C tablet. Can't work out why – flavour or health reasons? Answers on a postcard please! Mix 2kg plain flour, 1 level dessertspoon salt, 1 teaspoon sugar and 15g lard in a bowl. Stir in 30g yeast and 400ml warm water. Knead for 10 minutes. Put the dough in a polythene bag in a warm place for 30 minutes to rise. Once it has risen, divide the dough to form 2 loaves and leave to rise for a further 40 minutes in loaf tins. Meanwhile, preheat the oven to 245°C/475°F/Gas 8. When the loaves have risen, place in the oven and bake for 30 minutes.

NUTS. THEY'RE NOT JUST FOR SQUIRRELS.

CUSTOMIZE AND TANTALIZE

Nuts in their own right are awesome. But a little bit of ingenuity can bring out new aspects to their flavour and texture with some customized preparation. Here in the UK, we've got great nuts, from hazelnuts and chestnuts to walnuts. I feel I ought to confess here that in addition to my addiction to dry-roasted peanuts, my favourite snack is toasted pine nuts. I love them! (Super-simple to make – just toss them in a dry frying pan, but be careful not to burn them.) As a general rule, the toasted pine nut thrown into a cheesy pasta dish or alongside pancetta adds a superb dimension. Praise the pine nut! They are one of the key ingredients of fresh PESTO – red or green – and it couldn't be easier to make:

Blitz toasted pine nuts with Parmesan or pecorino cheese, garlic, extra virgin olive oil, fresh basil leaves or sun-dried tomatoes, salt and freshly ground black pepper – be creative with quantities! If you can't find pine nuts, you can use all sorts of other nuts – try walnuts. Or hazelnuts.

Nuts are responsible for many gastro-moments. Take tahini, we never really talk about it, but we all rely on that sesame smoothness for our daily dose of hummus (don't pretend, we're all addicted to hummus, and the sooner we admit it the better). Hummus is one of those moments in cooking that, like pesto, offers a classic base with a million opportunities to customize – there's nothing to stop you blending it with smoked paprika, cumin, garlic, flavoured oils and spices. Try this HAPPY HUMMUS AND PERFECT PITTA:

To make the pitta, mix 300ml warm water, 7g dried yeast sachet, 1 teaspoon sugar and 1 tablespoon olive oil together in a bowl and then leave to one side for 5–10 minutes. In a separate bowl, place 450g granary flour, 1 teaspoon salt and 1 teaspoon ground cumin and then add the yeast mixture. Mix well with a wooden spoon then transfer to a lightly floured surface and knead until it forms a dough. Knead for a further 5–8 minutes. Cover and put in a warm place to rise for at least 1–1½ hours, until nearly doubled in size. Punch the dough back and knead once more, then divide into 8. Roll each bit of dough into an oval about 5mm thick and

PESTO CAN BE TRICKY TO MATCH WINE TO. WITH GREEN PESTO I STICK WITH CRIPS LIGHT ITALIAN WHITES SUCH AS VERDICCHIO – A BRIGHT WINE FOR A VIVID DISH!

place on to an oiled baking tray. Rest for 5 minutes while the oven heats up (the oven needs to be quite high – about 240°C/475°G/Gas 9). Place the tray in the oven and cook for 5–6 minutes until they just begin to go golden brown and puff up. Remove from the oven, serve immediately or wrap in a tea towel or napkin for 5 minutes to steam slightly – this gives a more characteristic chewy texture.

To make the hummus, blitz **400g tinned chick peas**, drained and rinsed, **2 tablespoons lemon juice**, **3 tablespoons tahini**, **2 small or 1 large garlic clove**, **1 teaspoon ground cumin**, **1 teaspoon ground coriander**, **90ml water** and **1 tablespoon extra virgin olive oil** in a food processor until smooth. Season with salt and freshly ground black pepper and add a little more lemon juice or a pinch of paprika, if desired. Serve with a drizzle of extra virgin olive oil over the top.

Serve the hummus and pitta together.

Staying with sesame for one moment, I urge you to create this NUT SMOOTHIE:

NUTS! THEY'RE ALMOST AS SMOOTH AS SIR ROGER MOORE!

> Greek wine is massively underrated, partly because it's hard to find in the UK and due to the small supplies it's pricey, but it is fabulous. For this dish, hunt for peachy and mildly aromatic Malagousia — a Jurassic Park of a grape brought back from the brink of extinction by intrepid wineologist Evangelos Gerovassiliou. If you can't find Malagousia, Viognier will do fine — opt for a Chilean bargain or try some from Victoria in Australia or sample some super-posh Condrieu from France.

Blitz **1 banana**, **1-2 teaspoons tahini**, a drizzle of **runny honey** and some **full-fat milk**. It is luxuriant and richly sexy with a glorious nutty texture.

And it's not just tahini that can bring a sesame element to your dishes. I love cooking with sesame oil – using it in stir-fries and creating dressings with it, too. And I could munch prawn toast until the cows come home. And my adoration of the sesame doesn't stop there. Check out OPEN SESAME QUAIL:

Cut the quail down the back bone to open it out. Brush the skin with honey and then coat it with sesame seeds. Roast at 220°C/425°F/Gas 7 for 20–25 minutes. And serve with some wilted pak choi dressed with toasted sesame oil.

Granny Pip is also a big fan of the nut and she picked up a brilliant GROUNDNUT STEW recipe when she lived in West Africa. I'm awe-struck hearing her stories of months at sea travelling to West Africa during the war, terrified that she was going to be torpedoed as she clutched her recipe books and family photographs. Granny's stories of entertaining and adapting her cooking to suit the West African ingredients are also great fun. This recipe came about as homage to the surplus of nuts she once gathered in the kitchen garden. With a civil banquet to cater for and a bit of ingenuity, Granny came up with this stew. I've modified it to add a bit more texture and, though Granny swears by a cold, crisp glass of lager with it, I'm a fan of rich South African Chenin Blanc – preferably with a syrupy texture and some serious oak to bring out a big wedge of nutty oomph:

SHE'S A TOUGH BIRD MY GRANNY, HEART OF IRON AND WILL OF STEEL. GRANNY TELLS ME HER STRENGTH COMES FROM HER MUM WHO WAS A HARDY SHETLAND ISLANDER. NOW THOSE ARE SOME GENES I'M REALLY HOPING I'VE MANAGED TO INHERIT!

Fry some chicken (I like to use legs, wings and thighs – to serve 4 use eight thighs or six legs) in a casserole dish with 1 large chopped onion. Pour in 300ml/½ pint chicken stock and cook covered for half an hour. Add a generous squirt of tomato purée, 300ml/½ pint coconut milk and ¾ jar smooth peanut butter, and cook uncovered for a further half an hour. Finely dice 1 hard-boiled egg (optional) and stir in before serving. Garnish with OLLY'S ONIONS (crispy spring onions, finely chopped and fried in groundnut oil) and serve to four hungry chums with boiled rice and side dishes of chopped tomato, banana and raw onion.

GADO-GADO

100ml boiling water

250g raw spinach, baby leaf

½ cucumber, chopped into batons

250g bean curd, chopped into cubes and then fried until golden in toasted sesame oil

3 eggs, hard boiled, peeled and sliced

60g bean sprouts

1–2 tablespoons spring onion, finely chopped and then fried in toasted sesame oil

handful of prawn crackers, either crumbled over the salad or served in a separate bowl alongside

For the sauce

200g unsalted peanuts, toasted in a hot frying pan until gorgeously golden on all sides (keep stirring or they'll burn!)

1 or 2 red chillies, deseeded and finely chopped (1 for spicy, 2 for hot!)

½ teaspoon salt

½ teaspoon shrimp paste

1 teaspoon caster sugar

1 x 250ml tin coconut milk (give it a stir before pouring)

And it's not just African cooking that revels in the peanut. Thai, Malay and Indonesian cuisines all embrace the princely peanut and give it a leg-up to the stars. I remember quite vividly one morning in Indonesia, when I was feeling a touch rough in the cheek after indulging in one too many Bintang beers the night before, I strolled (or should that be weaved) into a roadside shack to embrace the day and begin anew. GADO-GADO was the dish that I ordered and my palate felt like the phoenix rising from the ashes when it tasted the mixture of nutty nourishment, fresh crunchy lettuce and penitent spice. I marched onward, led my class of English students through their morning lessons and spent the afternoon playing badminton in – what I think was – a court room. Don't ask. The quantities here will serve 4:

→ Grind or blitz all the sauce ingredients into a paste. When ground, add to a saucepan and warm through, stirring all the time. Add the boiling water and then reduce until the sauce is rich but not too runny – it should fall slowly but easily off the back of a spoon. Take off the heat.

→ Toss the spinach in a salad bowl with the cucumber, bean curd, sliced hard-boiled eggs and bean sprouts. Pour over most of the sauce (keeping some aside) and toss so the salad is coated in nutty glory.

→ Garnish with the fried onion and prawn crackers and serve as a centrepiece for your guests to dive into, with the extra sauce in a bowl for dipping and drizzling.

For a quick version of the GADO-GADO sauce, stir ¾ JAR CRUNCHY PEANUT BUTTER, 200ML COCONUT MILK, some DRIED FLAKED CHILLIES and salt to taste into a saucepan. Heat and reduce. Add a splash of water if it looks too thick but keep tasting to make sure you don't make it too dilute.

SATE is another sauce that I found tremendously useful in Indonesia. You can splurge it on most meats, from chicken to pork, beef or even goat. Skewer the marinated chunks and then cook them on charcoal. It's great for barbie season! At its simplest, sate is merely a question of blitzing the following ingredients in a blender (this'll make enough sauce to coat 4 chopped chicken breasts):

→ Heat the sauce in a pan until it bubbles. Add a drop or two of water to stop it getting too thick, but you want the sauce to remain rich and unctuous, not runny. As soon as it starts bubbling, take it off the heat and immediately spoon over cubes of meat. Traditionally the meat is served on wooden skewers (griddled over charcoal burners on street stalls) but you can serve as it comes in a centrepiece, garnished with slices of fried spring onion and lime wedges for guests to help themselves to. Serve it with rice and extra sauce spooned over the top. Yummo!

→ You can customize the sate to make it more complex by adding one or more of these ingredients: turmeric, coriander, cumin, red curry paste and fresh ginger.

Back to my dry-roasted peanut fetish. They may knacker wine but with a pint of British beer, get licking! And, just in case I have offended the mighty peanut, I have another taste sensation to share. Earlier in this Nutty chapter, I mentioned that pine nuts and pancetta make a rather splendid combo when tossed into pasta or salads. But have you ever tried a crispy bacon sandwich lined with butter AND peanut butter? Oh my dear, I wish I was with you to experience your first bite. Sublime – the salt of the bacon, the creamy nut, the squidge of warm butter and the crunch of toast. A breakfast treat that'll do your nut.

SATE

2 tablespoons crunchy peanut butter

½ tablespoon soy sauce

juice of 1 lime

2 garlic cloves, peeled

2g fresh chilli, deseeded (4g for a spice burst)

1 tablespoon palm sugar

1 tablespoon groundnut oil

GRANNY PIP'S CHESTNUT PUDDING

115g bitter cooking chocolate, broken into small pieces

115g caster sugar

55g butter

1 can chestnut purée

2 egg whites

whipped cream, to decorate (optional)

Granny Pip often made an amazing chestnut pudding around Christmas time, and it's true that it offers a nutty dose of festive cheer. But I also loved scooping up heaps of it during the summer months after rampaging around Granny's garden. Trust me – if you're refuelling for another bout of cowboys and Indians, GRANNY PIP'S CHESTNUT PUDDING is your ticket to a successful campaign:

→ Line a loaf tin with foil.

→ Melt the chocolate in a heatproof bowl over a saucepan of barely simmering water, or in the microwave.

→ Meanwhile, cream the sugar and butter in a mixing bowl until light and fluffy. Pour in the melted chocolate while it's still soft and stir.

→ Add the chestnut purée and beat well.

→ Whisk the egg whites in a separate bowl until fluffy and then fold with a metal spoon into the chocolate and chestnut mixture.

→ Spoon this into the loaf tin, cover with foil and leave in the fridge overnight.

→ When you are ready to serve, turn the pudding out on to a plate and cover with whipped cream.

You can also decorate the pudding by browning 2 TABLESPOONS FLAKED ALMONDS in a KNOB OF BUTTER in a frying pan. Sprinkle over 2 TABLESPOONS SUGAR and continue to cook until the sugar and almonds are a bit like toffee! Tip out on to some greaseproof paper and allow to cool before breaking up and sprinkling over the pudding. Very good and very rich!

Nutty is a flavour that, to me, is summed up by its mellowness and roundness. I adore nuts! They are nutritious in the raw, full of fibre and oils, and are massively customizable into a creamy blitz, a dry crunch or a toasty edge. Roasting chestnuts in cold weather is fun and delicious, and cracking nuts at home slows you down, brings you closer in touch with the food you're eating and makes you feel like a monkey. In my book, they're the greatest snack of all time. Think about the generous texture of marzipan, the unique fragrance of frangipane – both these almondy treats would be nothing without the nut. The colour of a hazelnut is so deeply beautiful and darkly glowing, and their flavour is so sweetly creamy – contrast that with walnuts which taste as tangy as licking the varnish off a mahogany piano. There are so many different aspects to nuts and so many different ways in which to combine them with other flavours that it makes my adoration of the humble dry-roasted peanut all the more perplexing. What can I say, I just love 'em.●

NUTS. THEY'RE NOT JUST FOR CHRISTMAS.

Citrus is a world of brightness, of uplifting triumphant flavours and sunny thrills. If you're ever feeling blue, in the nicest possible way, go suck on a lemon! I love the variety of flavours in the citrus family; they are all bound by a spine of acidity and it's that raciness which I've captured and worshipped in these dishes. The point of citrus is the power of its ping. It's all about the acidity, the freshness and invigoration. Think about when you deglaze a pan, that's what the citrus flavour does to your palate – it polishes it! It's mouthwatering and it gets your saliva going in readiness for a feast.

Citrus fruits generally come from evergreen trees or shrubs that originated in Southeast Asia. They usually have a leathery skin which is rather bitter and highly tangy, and a more juicy, zippy, sweeter fruit flavour in the pulp. Although all citrus fruits have similarities, i.e. they're pingy; there are some more defined fruit families to consider. Take the awesome orange, from that simple starting point we can tap into an entire world of orangey deliciousness – Valencia orange, blood orange, satsuma, mandarin, tangerine, clementine and the tangelo (a cross between an orange, a grapefruit/pomelo, and a tangerine).

Citrus is a window on to a world of wine styles – usually white – that straddle different grapes, regions and winemaking techniques. Think of the diversity in citrus – bright lemons, aromatic limes, juicy oranges and zippy grapefruit. There's a world of subtle diversity to infuse into a realm of brightly tinged recipes and wine matches.

Let us surge forth and ride the great citrus rocket all the way to Planet Ping. Cheers!●

In wine terms, whether you're dealing with lime, lemon, grapefruit or kumquat, the key point to bear in mind is the intense zip of citrus flavour. The most similar grape variety is Sauvignon Blanc with its grapefruity tang — you can find shrill and elegant Sauvignon Blanc in the Loire Valley from Sancerre, for example. New Zealand Sauvignon Blanc has become famous for its passion-fruit verve, especially the examples from the sunny South Island region of Marlborough. South African Sauvignon Blanc has crisp, appley characteristics from cooler areas such as Elgin, and even a smoky quality from other plots round the Cape. How the citrus is deployed in the recipe (for example, whether it is in combination with salty or sweet flavours, rich or fine textures) will have a great impact on the wine style to match it up with. When citrus lurks in a creamy, sweet pudding, it's usually time to call upon the services of Sauternes — sweet wine from France featuring the Semillon, Sauvignon Blanc and Muscadelle grapes, which have been dried out and intensified by noble rot. The texture of Sauternes is rich and creamy, the acidity is dazzling but there is also a luscious amount of sweetness to balance. Citrus-pud-tastic! And yet, if there is a citrus streak lurking in a more salty dish, for example something with the briny tang of a green olive, then the nutty and fleshy texture of a crisp, zippy fino sherry is called into play.

THE POWER OF PING AND THE EDGE OF REASON

The Power of Ping is what I think about the zip, freshness and acidity of citrus juice and pulp. Meanwhile, citrus peel inhabits a whole other dimension that is more bitter and aromatic. It is a challenging and dividing flavour group, hence the Edge of Reason. Have you ever tasted Campari? It's all about the Edge of Reason, with a spanking tangy flavour that I adore. One of the exceptions to the PoP and EoR rule is the kumquat. It's one of the few citrus fruits that you can eat whole, rind included. I first came across them while performing in a theatrical production of *The Fantasticks* – I played a character called El Gallo which means The Cock. They featured in the script. There is a whole bundle of juicy sourness to kumquats that I adore. You can create preserves, add them to salads, or macerate them whole in spirits such as vodka with a dash or two of sugar to harness their vim. All hail the kumquat!

Now, in addition to food and drink, I am the world's biggest film fan. In fact, I'm such a movie lover that I appeared not once but twice on Channel 4's *Moviewatch* when I was a student. I worked at the Cameo Cinema in Edinburgh selling popcorn and I have even created various recipes over the years in homage to my favourite films, notably HARRY POTTER CHICKEN IN A CHAMBER OF SECRETS SAUCE which makes my daughters Ruby and Lily whoop and feast like cubs on a zebra carcass. Couldn't be simpler:

Stuff the halves of 1 lemon up a whole chicken, smother the bird in butter and thyme, season with salt and freshly ground black pepper and then roast at 190°C/375°F/Gas 5 until done. Serve it with the juices drizzled over.

The idea is that Harry Potter is the lemon and the chicken is the Chamber of Secrets. And you really have to be four years old to get it. (It has to be said that some of my film cooking creations have been less successful – I am thinking particularly of my Hoth Cake which attempted to recreate the ice planet from *The Empire Strikes Back* and melted in my dad's favourite chair.)

The FROSTYSECCO is more of a classic than my movie-related recipes – it is a variant on a classic Venetian Bellini. Venice is a marvellous movie maze of locations from box office hits. *Don't Look Now*, *Moonraker* (ah yes, the glory days when Roger Moore was king of the box office) and even *Indiana Jones and the Last Crusade* were both filmed there. I adore the city for its romance, its outrageous ambition (only the Italians would build the world's most beautiful city on a sinking island) and Harry's Bar, where the Bellini was born. Sipping Bellinis in Venice and cuddling on the Bridge of Sighs is a rite of passage and always the start of a high-kicking, razzle-dazzle evening of glorious indulgence. The FrostySecco works magnificently as an aperitif to light up the palate like a disco glitter ball, but it's also a triumphant palate cleanser between courses. It even works after a meal to cool and soothe your stretching tummy:

In my house, the FrostySecco is usually a racy blend of lemon sorbet, grappa and prosecco but you can customize it in seconds by replacing the grappa with vodka or gin, adding a fruit purée (peach is a classic but I love it with mango) or even whizzing fresh basil leaves into the sorbet for a buckaroo herbal kick. The most inventive twist I have yet devised is to add a slosh of elderflower cordial to a few scoops of lemon sorbet, blitz them in a blender with a sprinkling of dried chillies and blast off!

For a seriously bright start to any celebration, I have just one word for you: *pisco*. Pisco is a clear spirit distilled from grape juice that is produced in Peru and Chile. It has a clean, bright hit like no other spirit, which makes it the perfect citrus partner. The PISCO SOUR is probably the most famous way to sip it and it's a turbo-charged face-lifter of a drink. The best pisco sour I ever tasted was made for me by Chilean movie director Silvio Caiozzi – a mighty man whose beard would put Stanley Kubrick's face fuzz to shame. After several pisco sours we made a pact to work together and then we hit the road for a four-month filming extravaganza that gave me the opportunity to scale the Andes, surf a moving tractor and have my hair eaten by a hungry alpaca. Good times. In fact, they were so good that on my way across a glacier with a very dodgy wi-fi connection I bought the domain name piscodisco.com which I still own to this day.

SIP-TASTIC!

Take **4 shots pisco** (pisco made from Quebranta grapes is favoured by Silvio), **1 egg white, 5 teaspoons sugar syrup** (as mentioned before, easy to make – equal parts sugar and water, heated until the sugar dissolves, then cooled to serve) and the **juice of 2 lemons** (ideally Peruvian Pica lemon, or blend half and half lemon and lime juice) and blitz in a blender with **ice**. Serve in a Champagne glass with **a drop of angostura bitters** in the centre of the foaming mousse.

I savoured a variation on the pisco sour theme when visiting Madame Alexandra Marnier-Lapostolle in her winery/Bond villain's lair at Casa Lapostolle in Chile's baking Colchagua Valley. Colchagua is roasting in the day but chilly at night – in fact, while filming a night harvest in just a t-shirt, my nipples froze as hard as limpets and scuttled off my body in search of a warmer host. I digress. One hot afternoon, I was on the cusp of sipping a glass of cool beer, when Madame Alexandra stayed my hand. Alexandra's great grandfather invented Grand Marnier and she is a formidable lady and, as it happens, a magnificent rider. The horse she gave me to ride tried to bite me while we were out for a gallop but, fortified with a MARNIER SOUR, my bravery enabled me to dismount swiftly and run for the hills to escape the horsey gnashers and prove, beyond doubt, what an absolute wimp I really am. The Marnier Sour is simple to recreate:

Take **2 measures pisco, 1 measure Grand Marnier, the juice of 1 Pica lemon** (or use a mix of half lemon, half lime), **$^3/_4$ measure sugar syrup, a pinch of salt, $^1/_4$ measure egg white and stacks of ice** and shake together like crazy. Strain and serve in Champagne flutes and remember never to drink in the vicinity of a hungry, flesh-eating horse.

During my four months in Chile filming the TV series, I learned all about the flavours of that magnificent land. Being in South America was a truly soul-shaking experience. The first thing that hits you is the light. Whether you're balancing on the peak of an Ande, crunching your way across a glacier, sheltering in the shade of a giant rock from the searing desert sun or pounding the streets of Valparaiso hunting for the world's finest ceviche, the light pours from the sky like a kaleidoscope melting into focus. Somehow the passion of the locals infuses deep inside you and marinates your core into a more upbeat, jiggly and winking frame of mind. The film crew I was travelling with began referring to me as 'The Albino Latino' thanks to the spring in my step which became more like a leap the longer I spent there.

My first taste of ceviche was up north – remember, the further north you go in the southern hemisphere the hotter it gets. I was on a wine-tasting trip on my way to Limari and Elqui Valley. On the way, La Serena (The Mermaid) beckoned. It's a beach-side resort with a similar vibe to Brighton – fun loving, laid back and mobbed in the summer (though it has to be said, La Serena has far fewer stag and hen parties clad in rubber devil's horns roaming the streets braying at one another like hooting zombies). The seaside is glorious and, to me, the Pacific has a particularly intense briny character on the breeze. I don't know if the smell is reinforced because the ocean is so massive or whether it's something about that stretch of coast, but I can tell you it smells fresher than any advert for detergent, washing powder or liquid softener. It's real, it's unleashed, it's free and it produces some of the most sublime shellfish in the world. If you find yourself in Chile, fall to your knees on the beach and give praise to the Humboldt Current which flows up from Antarctica in a chilled blast and keeps the fish and shellfish up the Chilean coastline impeccably fresh. I have seen bivalves the size of my head thanks to Harry Humboldt and, for that, I hi-five the gods of gastronomy.

The great thing about C E V I C H E is its versatility. Once you've sourced some fresh fish, you can customize it any which way you like and serve it for brunch, lunch, a snack, a starter or even as a light main dish. The principle of ceviche is to pickle and cure fish or shellfish in the zing of a citrus fruit. You can deploy lemon juice, lime, orange, grapefruit and I've even tasted a ceviche made with passion fruit. The fish you use depends entirely on what is freshest. I have made it with sea bass, salmon, squid, prawns, halibut, tuna, mackerel, huss and gurnard, finely sliced or chopped into morsels. In Chile, you pour over enough citrus juice to cover but not have the fish swimming in it, and then you wreath the dish in chopped deseeded chillies (red or green), chopped fresh mint or coriander leaves, finely sliced onion, sea salt and freshly ground pepper. You can boost the dish by serving chunky side dishes – in Peru it is often served with

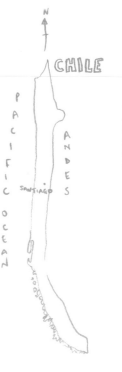

corn on the cob or chunks of sweet potato. Preparation could not be simpler:

Chop your raw fish into bite-sized pieces, toss it in your own customized blend of citrus juices, add chopped red chillies, finely sliced red onions, chopped fresh mint, leave for a few minutes and serve. If you're feeling brave, the *leche de tigre*, or tiger's milk, is supposedly an A-grade hangover cure and involves drinking any leftover spicy marinade from shot glasses. Now that's what I call firewater!

```
Wine with ceviche should complement rather
than contrast the dish. We're hunting zing
and freshness, so look for white wines
produced from cooler climates (think coastal,
mountainous, or just downright chilly). Wines
from France, Muscadet, Sancerre and Picpoul
de Pinet are all worth a shout. In terms of
grape varieties, Sauvignon Blanc is a cracker
(go New Zealand for tropical pungency or
South Africa for appley freshness), Greek
Assyrtiko is a winner, Verdelho or dry
Riesling from Australia — look for Clare
Valley or Tasmania. But, for me, because I
associate this dish so strongly with Chile,
it's got to be a Chilean Sauvignon Blanc —
and there are many regions to choose
from: Limari, Casablanca, San Antonio
and Leyda are my top Chilean regions,
producing just the right level of thrust
for lift-off with this dish.
```

I am a passionate fisherman. I love spinning for mackerel out at sea or on the pier at Newhaven with my buddy Sean, or hunting bass in Bosham with my old mate Digby. Whether you get a nibble or a full-blown catch, there are few days that rival a session at the rod. Watching Sussex or England play cricket perhaps . . . And rugby – the Six Nations is the pinnacle of human achievement. But back to the point, fresh fish rules! However, when you have a surfeit, it is always a bit of a dilemma how not to waste them. Sure you can freeze them, but where fresh fish is concerned there's a simple citrusy preserving recipe that will let you keep them for several days. I took the basis for my CITRUS MARINADE from a traditional Spanish anchovy marinade and it works with most white fish:

Combine lots of olive oil, garlic cloves, salt, fresh or dried thyme leaves, and a mixture of orange and lemon juice and their zests. Vary the quantities according to how zingy you want the marinade to be. Make enough to almost cover the fish. Cover with cling film and keep refrigerated.

This combination also works as a marinade for shrimps, prawns and langoustine before pan-frying or tossing them on the barbecue. Or, of course, you could add it to almost any white fish to give it a kick of citrus flavour before cooking.

ALMOND SOUP

WITH PINK AND WHITE GRAPEFRUIT AND GREEN OLIVES

A slice of grapefruit is extremely tart and a serious wake-up call during any breakfast spread. Pink grapefruit has more depth of flavour and makes for an amazing drink – intense, piercing and superbly refreshing.

Serves 4

250g sourdough or country bread, crusts removed

750ml vegetable stock

1 pink grapefruit

1 white grapefruit

250g good quality blanched skinless almonds, preferably Marcona

3 garlic cloves, peeled

125ml extra virgin olive oil (plus extra to garnish)

3 tablespoons sherry vinegar

2 teaspoons salt

90g large Spanish green olives, stoned and cut into slivers

freshly ground black pepper

→ Place the bread in a bowl with 500ml of the stock and leave to absorb for 5–10 minutes.

→ Segment the grapefruit over a bowl, reserving any juices, and then set the segments aside.

→ Place the soaked bread into a food processor with the almonds and garlic cloves and blitz to a purée.

→ Add the reserved grapefruit juices, olive oil, vinegar and salt, and continue to blitz.

→ Pour into a large bowl and add enough stock to form a thick soup. Season with more salt and pepper, to taste.

→ Chill slightly before ladling into serving bowls. Top with the grapefruit segments, olive slivers and a drizzle of extra virgin olive oil.

This dish reeks of Spain — it's served chilled and makes an inventive alternative to the perpetual presence of Gazpacho . . . The creamy almond combined with the zingy grapefruit makes for a wine-combining challenge and this dish offers an awesome opportunity to rummage through Spain's up-and-coming white wines. Have you tried Albariño from Galicia? Dry with an aromatic twist — like Chablis sipped in a Thai street market. And whites from Rocking Rueda? Prestigious Priorat? Both regions are worth exploring for whites — crisp dry and fruity from Rueda and rich, classy, complex and sometimes oaked from Priorat. But for this dish, I'm heading to the classic region of Rioja. Rioja is like a greatest hits compilation of Spain's wine styles. Rioja isn't just about red wine — they make rosé and a whole range of whites, too, ranging from dry and zingy to more creamy and nutty. For this soup, I'm hunting a white wine with enough rich texture to work with the richness of the almond, the right zing to cope with the grapefruit and sufficient depth of flavour to stand up to the spice. What you need is a white Rioja with a touch of oak to flesh out the mix. Muga make a decent Rioja Blanco that will work a treat.

CHEERS!

HOMAGE TO THE LEMON

POWER ZING!

Lemon is the original citrus. If the lemon was James Bond, it would be Sean Connery because you never quite forget the original incarnation. A potent lemon moment came for me while visiting my old flatmate Krisna who had taken a teaching job in Greece. I arrived in Sitia via a dusty bus that rumbled past the blue Aegean, through olive groves, past vineyards, monasteries and whitewashed tavernas. I finally stepped out into the dazzling Cretan sunshine to the sound of cicadas, a murmuring of local gents rattling their backgammon dice and… no Krisna. My first instinct was that I had arrived in the wrong town, at the wrong time, on the wrong day. But after a chat with the girl behind the counter in the bus station, she nodded and giggled, 'Aaaah, Krisna, we call him Fisherman, he is always fishing. Yes, you can find him at the school. And remind him he is to come olive picking with me, please.' Off I trotted around the deserted midday streets, too hot for sightseeing and far too roasting for work. I strode up a side street and there was Krisna. He was Buddha-like, teaching a bunch of grinning primary school children English under a lemon tree. I have never forgotten quite how happy he looked at that moment. After dismissing his class for break, he lived up to his name and took me fishing. And nearly got us arrested by the Greek army. But that's another story (see page 138).

If you're really after a citrus explosion, Assyrtiko (you say it ass-ear-tea-ko) is a unique grape variety from the Greek island of Santorini and it gets my vote as one of the best on the planet. It is bone dry and can be packed with the intensity of a lemon harnessed to the thrust of an F-16 fighter jet. Racy, zesty and with a curious salty-smoky tang thanks to the local volcanic soil and the sea mist that creeps over the vines and leaves a little crust of salt on the grape skins. Genius. One sip usually makes me thirsty for the next. If you're a fan of intense citrus-salty flavours, grab a bottle from Gaia, Hatzidakis or Domaine Sigalas — all excellent winemakers.

GREAT GRANNY LENNARD'S

CRUNCHIE PIE

This recipe is as written down by Granny Lennard on a bit of paper for my mum. We don't know where she got the recipe from, but she was a very inventive cook. I love that this recipe has come to me as the fourth generation in my family to cook and taste it. Amazing to think it's more than a hundred years old and still tastes great.

115g digestive biscuits

55g butter, melted

150ml double cream

1 x 200ml can sweetened condensed milk

6 tablespoons lemon juice

zest of 1 lemon

→ Crush the biscuits and put them in a bowl. Pour over the melted butter and stir. Line a pie plate or flan ring with this crumb mixture to form a shell with a good edge.

→ Whip the cream, and then fold in the condensed milk, lemon juice and zest. Pour this into the biscuit shell and chill overnight.

→ Decorate as you like with toasted nuts, grated chocolate or cherries.

Lemons are iconic, awesome and, particularly when they come from Amalfi in Italy, deeply fragrant. You can use the zest, the juice, slices, wedges; add them to salads, marinades, puddings, teas, cocktails, even use the juice to cure fish to save you the job of cooking it! Without lemons, I would be in perpetual mourning. We salute the lemon!

PINGING LEMON POSSET is a simple and delicious pudding that can be made in any quantities and tailored to your taste. Have fun with it. All you need is some plums, butter, cinnamon, brandy, double cream, sugar and, last but not least, lemons. And if you ain't got plums, you could make it with peaches, nectarines, cherries, or just about any soft and squidgy fruit you like. And you can vary the flavour of the cream by using lime juice and zest or orange juice and zest. Get involved!

Quarter the plums and then pan-fry them in a little bit of butter. Add a sprinkle of sugar, a pinch of ground cinnamon and flambé with a splosh of brandy. Set aside and leave to cool. Meanwhile, boil some double cream with sugar for a few minutes, until the sugar has dissolved. Remove from the heat and add the juice and zest of as many lemons as you dare, stirring like mad, until it tastes awesome. Spoon the cooled plums into individual glasses, about a third of the way up, and then pour the lemon cream over the top. Place in the fridge until set. Genius!

THE ROBUST SKIN OF CITRUS FRUIT IS A GOLDMINE OF INTENSELY FLAVOURED OILS TO FINELY GRATE OVER SALADS, DRESSINGS, STIR-FRIES, ROAST LAMB, FRESH PASTA OR EVEN INTO YOUR BATH! JUST BEWARE NOT TO GRATE TOO FAR INTO THE WHITE BITTER PITH . . .

Get stuck into a dose of POWER PORRIDGE – a whole lemon squeezed into your porridge with honey, milk and a sprinkle of nutmeg... I'm considering adding a few dried chilli flakes... It's the breakfast of champions if you've got a snuffle... and whisky... add whisky... yes, whisky... lots of whisky...

Scoop up a bottle of Sauternes to pop with your posset — it's lemon and cream in a glass. The wine is named after the place where the wine comes from — Sauternes is in Bordeaux, southwest France, near the river Garonne. It's made from a blend of Semillon, Sauvignon and Muscadelle grapes infected with noble rot (posh fungus that dries out the grapes and magnifies sweetness). Delicious — it has a creamy texture and is sweetly intense with a streak of zing to balance. This vino can be pricey so if you're after a cheaper alternative, check out wines from nearby Monbazillac — same grape, similar wine, less prestigious. (The difference is a bit like the Dimblebys. I love them both but if I had to choose I'd go for the sheer blinding excellence of David.) However, it has to be said that Australia is the place to look for the ultimate alternative to Sauternes — peer in the Aussie section at your supermarket and look for 'Botrytis Semillon' (you say it bot-right-iss sem-ee-yon). The quality of Aussie sticky wine is generally fab and good value, and at this price you could even be a wine pervert and serve it over crushed ice in shot glasses as an outrageous aperitif. YUMMO!

I'VE ALWAYS LOVED SHERBET LEMONS — IF YOU'RE A FAN TOO, GET YOUR CHOPS ROUND A BOTTLE OF CHILLED GERMAN SPÄTLESE RIESLING — STARTS OUT SWEET AND ENDS UP WITH A SHERBET-LIKE ZING.

You can harness your love of lemon flavours not just to sweet dishes but also to more savoury, salty dishes. It's a U-turn in flavour that demonstrates how versatile and exciting this citrus champion truly is. I invented PRESERVED LEMON PASTA for a dinner party with some old mates. I wanted to serve *Biblia Chora Sauvignon Blanc-Assyrtiko* from Greece – a pingy, zingy, crisp white with a unique salty, herby tang – and I wanted to find the perfect dish to match. Inspiration struck during a stroll with my dog Barney (he's an absolute legend – the face of a teddy bear, the manners of a gentleman and the loyalty of a brother). I needed zingy and salty so preserved lemons leapt to mind. Salty feta and thyme both loop up neatly with the provenance of the vino and the Greeks have been making pasta for years – they call it *zymarika* but just in case your local supermarket doesn't sell Greek pasta, I've suggested an Italian alternative.

To serve 6 people, cook 1kg fresh trompetti pasta in plenty of lightly salted boiling water until *al dente*. Drain and jumble together with 200g finely chopped preserved lemons, 200g crumbled feta, masses of fresh thyme leaves stripped from the stem, salt and freshly ground black pepper.

> The dish works just as well with Sauvignon Blanc (hunt a bottle with the dazzle and energy of a shooting star) or, at a pinch, use a crisp, Italian dry white from grape varieties such as Greco di Tufo (also the name of the place where the grape comes from), Grecanico from Sicily or, for a more aromatic fruity twist, try Falaghina from Campania. YAMAS!

Lemons can also be deployed in more meatylicious dishes and I find they work supremely well with pork. SOLOMILLO IBERICO is my take on an amazing pork steak I munched in a tapas bar in Tarifa, with the kite-surfers hurtling round the bay just outside and the shores of Africa gleaming in the distance. Even though I keep pigs where I live in Sussex, I hadn't tasted pork as good as this for ages – top pigmanship! I dreamt about the dish for days afterwards and recreated it as soon as I got back to Blighty. It's a great dinner party dish for everyone to dive into from the centre of the table, or it makes a quick weeknight supper:

Marinate some juicy pork chops in fresh oregano, salt, a couple of cardamom pods, lemon juice and shredded lemon peel – preferably overnight but if it's a weeknight and you're in a hurry, 20 minutes will do. Pan-fry in olive oil and serve ready-sliced on a wooden board surrounded with fried potatoes and onions sautéed with smoked paprika and salt.

The dish is a treat on its own, but serve it with a fino sherry and it enters another dimension. Forget the stuff your granny drinks, fino sherry is light, dry and pinging with energy; it's like surfing a crisp wave of outrageous power right up the beach and into the pub for a night of revels and ecstasy. I love fino as an aperitif with slices of jamón ibérico (*pata negra* is the one my kids and I love to share; the pigs are fed on acorns to give the meat an amazing texture and richness). You could sip it while munching on a bowl of almonds or salted nuts, or just have it on its tod — but remember to serve it well chilled and keep it in an ice bucket or cooling jacket and serve in small glasses to keep that refreshing chill. With this dish, fino has a rich enough body to work with the pork-tastic meat, and enough zip to love that lemony tang in the dish. The subtle nutty character of fino will pole-dance with the paprika and the overall combo is so well poised it makes Torvill and Dean look like Little and Large. Genius wine, stonking recipe, piggy snorts!

HOMAGE TO THE LIME

The flavour of limes is unmistakable. They have a sense of aromatic depth and a rounder, fuller flavour than lemons and complete the perfect gin and tonic – you can even freeze lime juice in ice cube trays to add an even zippier dimension to your G&T. A simple combination of lime juice, soy, garlic, ginger and chilli is enough to tart any meat up into a funkier feast. Limes helped the British Navy combat scurvy – and Brits are still referred to as Limeys to this very day!

MAKE HOMEMADE LIMEADE BY INFUSING FRESH PEEL IN WATER.

My mum is not a trout but this is her recipe so I thought I'd name it after her – TROUT MARY-CLARE. We'll see what she has to say about it!

Zest and juice 1 lime. Melt a large knob of butter in a frying pan and add the lime juice. Add 2 (or more if there are more of you) fresh trout fillets and sprinkle the zest on top. Cook over a gentle heat until the trout is opaque, pearly and obviously cooked – roughly 20 minutes. Remember it keeps cooking when you take it off the heat so, if in doubt, slightly undercook. Serve with mashed potato, asparagus or finely sliced runner beans.

After taking the kids to the cinema one summer bank holiday, I needed something quick and fun to cook. I came up with COINTREAU PRAWNS. It is the perfect dish – entertaining with the flambé fireworks, it's got zingy lime, a sweet citrus lift from the orangey Cointreau, some heat from the chilli and the mouth-coating umami in the juice from the prawns – irresistible! You'll be dipping your fingers in any leftover juices and scrabbling for the last drop. The trick is in the timing of the reduction once you've added the lime juice – you don't want it too runny but you don't want to wait for it to burn. When it really starts to boil, pour the lot on to a big plate – it makes an awesome dinner party starter in the centre of a table. Get stuck in! This will serve 2:

Pour 1 tablespoon olive oil in a hot frying pan, toss in 100g raw tiger prawns, 1 finely sliced garlic clove and a fingernail piece of chopped red chilli. Cook the prawns for 1–2 minutes on each side. Add a capful of Cointreau – it will flambé if you tip the pan. Stir in the juice of 1 lime and reduce for 3 minutes. Tip on to a warm plate, sprinkle with sea salt and freshly ground black pepper and serve with a lime wedge.

Viognier is a white grape that makes dry wine with a subtle fruity character that reminds me of apricots. It tastes peachy and there are some real bargains coming out of rural France and Chile. It's a great wine to unwind with whether you're jiggling in a disco, snoozing in the garden or cuddling on the sofa. And it's the nadgers with tiger prawns — on the barbie or here in this recipe with some ping and spice. Condrieu is the poshest place that makes Viognier in France's Rhône Valley and if you're out at a restaurant it's worth choosing as an alternative to Chardonnay as it can offer better value than top, posh French Chardonnay from Burgundy. You say it 'con-dree-er' and it's well worth a squirt.

BE ADVENTUROUS AND SWITCH A LEMON FOR A LIME. CHOP FRESH MINT, SQUEEZE IN LIME JUICE, CHOP A FEW CAPERS, AND SOME CASTER SUGAR AND MIX IT ALL UP.

Prawns and lime juice are an awesome combo for party food, and the lime is also king of party drinks – refreshing, crisp and gorgeous. Think of the traditional margaritas and mojitos. Limes rule! And anyone who says otherwise is a brawn-headed moon-fairy…

I invented the MR AND MRS BYRNE for the wedding of my dear friends Sean and Cath Byrne. It's a cocktail that works in two parts from the same root, just like a marriage! It serves one, twice:

Combine 1 measure Tanqueray 10 or Beefeater 24 gin, 1/2 measure ginger wine and 1 teaspoon lime marmalade. Shake over lots of ice and serve this delicious Mr Byrne in a martini glass.

As you draw near the end of the drink, a little pool of richly infused lime marmalade joy will gather in the bottom of your glass. Top up at once with Champagne or prosecco to create the awesome Champagne cocktail called… Mrs Byrne!

It's a two-part aperitif which, if you're attentive and serve your guests promptly, will be guaranteed to get your party swinging. Cheers!

CHICKEN AND LIME LEAF KEBABS
WITH CHILLI LIME DIP

This dreamy Thai dish is all about lime freshness and chilli kick – it's easy and informal.

Serves 2

4 chicken breasts, boneless and skinless, cut into 3cm chunks

10–12 lime leaves, torn in half

4 wooden skewers, soaked in cold water for 1 hour

1–2 tablespoons vegetable oil

1–2 limes, cut into wedges

salt and freshly ground black pepper

Chilli dip

75ml lime juice

75ml rice wine vinegar

150g caster sugar

2 red chillies, finely chopped

3 tablespoons fresh coriander, finely chopped

→ Thread the chicken on to the skewers, alternating with pieces of lime leaf. Ideally, place in the fridge for 1 hour to infuse.

→ Meanwhile, make the chilli dip: place the lime juice, vinegar and sugar into a small saucepan and cook until dissolved.

→ Add the chillies and cook for 2–3 minutes until just thickened. Remove from the heat and allow to cool slightly before adding the coriander.

→ Brush the chicken with some of the vegetable oil, then season with salt and pepper. Place on a hot griddle and cook on each side for 2 minutes until golden brown and cooked all the way through.

→ To serve, pour the dip into a bowl and pile the skewers on to a plate alongside. Finish with a couple of wedges of lime.

I love Pinot Gris with mild spicy dishes — Alsace makes syrupy textured Pinot Gris with just a touch of sweetness that will be toned down by the spice, so it'll seem like you're sipping a dry wine. Or, for a more aromatic flourish, you could try a floral Torrontes from Argentina — a genius dry white wine that tastes floral and aromatic, a bit like lemon Turkish delight, but usually manages to stay dry and zippy at the same time. DELISH DELOSH DELIGHT!

HOMAGE TO THE ORANGE

Aaaah the orange. The streets of Seville are lined with them. My mum and dad make marmalade from them every year. And my kids eat them by the bucket. Has there ever been a more perfect circle of sunshine. It's the flavour most of us start the day with and it often arrives in chunky wedges at half time during a rugby match. Nothing quite says 'sunshine' like the orange does. Sicilian blood orange juice has an extra squirt of intensity about it that takes mere orange juice into the gym and sends it out leaping and glistening like Rocky Balboa. I love the juicy sweetness of the orange – more than any other citrus fruit, if you get it freshly squeezed on your fingers, it's super-sticky and that means it is packed with natural sugars. A genius balance of sweet and sour!

For a long time, orange has been my favourite colour. I guess it began with the tangerine in my tuck box but it was enhanced by orange Fruit Gums and orange Fruit Pastilles, orange Chewits, the Orange Maid iced lolly and then later the orange Calippo. I loved oranges so much that at school aged seven I started the Tangy Man Club (you say it tan-ji, as in tangerine). I founded the club, then drew and laminated the membership cards for myself, Raulin Amy and Daniel Hawson. We were an epic trio, having already been members of the Chicken Bombers, which was loosely based on the Chicken Bombers from *The Goodies and the Bean Stalk*. We were worryingly convinced that if we ran and flapped our arms hard enough, we would be able to take off. One Halloween round at Raulin's place, a magnificent old farmhouse called Le Boulivot, we busted into the old barn and ran upstairs. I charged across some rickety floorboards flapping my arms hard and bellowing, 'CHICKENBOMBERS', and promptly disappeared from view, crashing through the old boards and landing winded with a split head on the ground floor in a pile of earth and hardcore. I still have the scar on my forehead – long before Harry Potter made such things cool. I remember Raulin's dad wrote a really funny limerick about the whole head-splitting affair. The Tangy Man Club was a more sedate society, though, and our activities revolved around the cult of the tangerine. We reckoned it was the finest fruit and would unite with our packed lunches and membership

cards to peel our tangerines and share in their secret powers. Years later when Sophie (then my girlfriend, now my wife) was studying in Seville, I found the orange trees that lined the medieval streets utterly hypnotic. I remember gazing up at them, transfixed, and, although at the time Halley's Comet was riding the sky, I couldn't keep my eyes off the real stars, the oranges. And I wanted to do one thing and one thing only: make marmalade.

Seville oranges would bust down our door every year in Jersey and my parents would fetch their large, golden jam pan down from the drinks cabinet where it lived all year round and the kitchen would turn into a marmalade factory for several days. I'm sure Mum and Dad won't mind me outing them as marmalade addicts – they are fanatical about it and guzzle it every morning on their toast. MUM'S MARMALADE is quite runny in consistency but the flavour is impeccable and the dribbly, syrupy consistency is what makes it. Mum once made a jar for the crew filming me on *Saturday Kitchen* and my producer Dave Mynard was so enthralled he wrote a charming letter of thanks and has been known in the family as Marmalade Man ever since. I am seriously thinking of initiating him into the Tangy Man Club . . . In honour of Dave and with thanks to Mum, here's how to make sublime, dribbly, delicious marmalade:

MUM'S MARMALADE

1.8kg Seville oranges

3.6kg sugar (can use 2.7kg sugar which makes the result less sweet, but you then have a smaller yield – approximately 9–10 jars as opposed to 12–13)

1.4 litres water

→ Wash jam jars in hot soapy water, then rinse well. Put them into a preheated oven at 170°C/325°F/Gas 3 until you are ready to use them.

→ Simmer the whole oranges until soft. (In a pressure cooker this will take approximately 15–20 minutes but over a low heat it will take approximately 2 hours.)

→ When soft, cut the oranges into 4 and scrape the pips out. Put these in a separate pan. Now cut the orange segments into fine strips. Get all the family involved with the cutting up – as soon as children can cut up safely, let them join in!

→ Boil the pips in enough water to cover them, for approximately 5–10 minutes. When they have boiled, strain the juice into a pan and make up the liquid to 1.4 litres.

→ Place the oranges into a preserving pan or a large saucepan. Add the sugar and the 1.4 litres of pip water and put on a high heat. Make sure you stir all the time, until the sugar has completely dissolved. Once dissolved, bring the marmalade to a rapid rolling boil and continue to cook for 30–40 minutes, which should be enough to produce a 'set'.

→ When cool enough to handle, pot, label and thoroughly enjoy!

I picked up a wonderful savoury way to enjoy the outrageous orange in a little restaurant in Sicily. I tasted it there and created my own version when I got home. It is super-easy and super-fun to make. SICILIAN ORANGE FARFALLE makes a great quick lunch for two or a light starter before your main meal:

→ Cook the farfalle in plenty of boiling salted water according to the packet instructions.

→ Meanwhile, heat the olive oil in a large frying pan and add the garlic. Fry over a gentle heat for 1 minute until it starts to turn light gold.

→ Pour in the orange juice, turn the heat up and simmer for 5 minutes to let the juice reduce.

→ Sprinkle the flour over the sauce, stir until mixed and simmer until thickened, then take the sauce off the heat. Season with salt and pepper, add the flat-leaf parsley, and toss the drained hot farfalle straight into the frying pan to coat in the sauce.

→ Drizzle with extra virgin oil and then serve.

> What could be finer to match with the zing of this dish than a cool glass of Sicilian Fiano — gorgeous, bright white wine with an aromatic hint that makes a drizzly day feel like the summer solstice.

SICILIAN ORANGE FARFALLE

150g farfalle

2 tablespoons olive oil

2 garlic cloves, crushed

200ml fresh orange juice without bits

½ teaspoon plain flour

handful of fresh flat-leaf parsley, roughly chopped

extra virgin olive oil, for drizzling

salt and freshly ground black pepper

YUMATHON!

BEETROOT, ORANGE, GOAT'S CHEESE AND WALNUT SALAD

This is a British dish that I love when the beetroot in my garden is sweet and young in July but you could still make it when the beetroots have grown to be the size of my head in late August and it would taste great! The citrus orange and bright tangy goat's cheese work brilliantly with the earthy beetroot and crunch of those walnuts. A supersalad that will serve four as a starter.

1 tablespoon grainy mustard

1 tablespoon honey

2 tablespoons orange juice

1 tablespoon white wine vinegar

3 tablespoons rapeseed oil

200g cooked beetroot, cut into wedges

2 oranges, peeled and segmented

75g walnut halves

2 heads chicory, cut lengthways and leaves separated

200g Slipcote soft goat's cheese (or any other soft rindless goat's cheese)

salt and freshly ground black pepper

→ Place the grainy mustard, honey, orange juice and vinegar into a bowl, and whisk together. Whisk in the rapeseed oil, then season with salt and pepper.

→ Toss the beetroot in a little of the dressing and leave to marinate for 30 minutes, if possible.

→ Lift the beetroot from the dressing into a clean bowl and toss with the orange segments, walnut halves, chicory and a little more of the dressing.

→ Place on to individual serving plates and dot with the goat's cheese. Finish with a drizzle of the remaining dressing.

Beetroot can be a tricky flavour to match with wine — Pinot Noir is a decent red to try, but for the summery nature of this dish, I'm seizing the chance to sit in the garden and grab a glass of English rosé. Cheers!

Orange is still my favourite colour. I just feel happy at the sight of oranges – especially if they are accompanied by lemons and limes. The vivid brightness of them, the zip of their juice, their fleshy segments, their aromatic peel, the pectin in their pips for thickening jam – it all makes them multi-dimensional flavour bombs, ready to turn a dish with a twist, or theme a dish with their singing citrus power. I wish I could grow them in my garden. I had an old friend called Hugh who managed to grow a lemon tree on a south-facing wall. He was a magical gent, full of stories about how he was descended from Lord Nelson, and how he'd accidentally chopped his finger off, and he kept a book on the pests and rodents he'd captured and dispatched, like an almanac of execution. But the thing I remember most about him is looking into his papery old hand and seeing the glowing perfection of a home-grown lemon. Citrus will always make me smile.●

AROMATIC

Aromatic is a magical dimension; it's the flavour that I imagine Gandalf and Dumbledore must ponder during their monthly wizard-dinners-à-deux. It is a wide world of flavour, encapsulating everything from liquorice to lychee, Thai basil to cardamom, so to make aromatic more accessible, I'm scrutinizing it under three different headings – Herbage, A Lick of Garlic, and Fragrant Asian. But where did my love for all things aromatic begin?

Aniseed balls are awesome. As a child, they were my favourite sweets. I used to dream of owning a whole jar. These days I have to stop myself buying them by the bag in my local sweet shop in Lewes or I would probably turn into one. I love their bullet hard exterior and their fragrant crumbly centre with the tiny, chewy dot of sheer aniseed. As a more civilized version of the gobstopper (size really isn't everything in a gobstopper) the aniseed ball is a treasure of aromatic intensity that repays investment. If you're patient and allow the sweet to divest itself of all its secrets as you read your book/ski down the mountain/await the results of your first presidential campaign, the final flourish of the aniseed ball is a moment of aromatic ecstasy.

In my early drinking years, I was quick to discover the ultimate anise pleasure of pastis. I distinctly remember a Pernod cinema campaign that caught my imagination when I was small, which had a golden elixir morphing into (I think) a 33" record with a blaring saxophone and the slogan 'Free the Spirit'. It must have run for ages because I became mildly obsessed by Freeing the Spirit – I'm still not entirely convinced that the spirit has been unleashed . . . I've hunted on YouTube but there only seems to be a later lurid version with a punching disco beat. Less sophisticated than the original. But I remain a huge fan of the flavour of aniseed in drinks whether it's pastis, ouzo or sambuca. Although these are generally domineering flavours of nuclear potency, they can be great fun to experiment with in blending bonkers cocktails such as the lunatic French Perroquet, which is bright green and involves blending pastis with mint syrup, or Ernest Hemingway's famous 'Death in the Afternoon', which is pastis sloshed into a glass of Champagne. Less is usually more in these blends and, fun aside, I'm not convinced they are superior to the pure anise hit of a traditional pastis with water. In cooking, a slug of pastis is sublime when added to a sauce based on fish stock for serving with, for example, sea bass. Think of fennel and that vegetable's affinity with fish – same goes for pastis. But the flavour aromatic is not just aniseed . . .

Aromatic is a much wider riddle. Aromatic is a catch-all. Aromatic can be fragrant or bitter, pungent or subtle. Take drinks. In wine, Gewürztraminer is the Emperor of Aromatics and can smell of a whole bunch of stuff but most commonly it is scented with rose, elderflower and sometimes orange blossom niffs. It is perfumed, spicy, and its aromatic fragrance is a real divider – some love it, some hate it. For me, Gewürztraminer has always been my Christopher Biggins wine – fragrant, flamboyant and unmistakable. I was a huge fan of Biggins as a child and one panto season I waited with the family outside a frosty stage door in Southampton to catch a glimpse of His Biggness. I remember he was playing Widow Twanky that night and he was half in costume when he came to the stage door, which was mildly terrifying. Biggins was extremely kind and signed my newspaper programme for me and I have never forgotten it. Biggins wine – Gewürztraminer – is found in Alsace but if you're after something a bit less perfumed and full-on you can hunt out a Gewürztraminer from northern Italy or New Zealand. For a long time, Gewürztraminer was thought to only really work as a match for Indian curries and spicy cooking. But it doesn't cover all bases in spice, especially with the rising elegance and finesse of chefs such as Atul Kochhar, Cyrus Todiwala and Vivek Singh. While, in fact, Gewürztraminer can work with something traditionally spice-less like roast pork or even a pungent cheese soufflé. Try it with a cheese board (for example alongside a slice of powerful Munster) and serve it in small glasses (often it's the large quantities of aromatic elixirs that can put off your guests, but a little nip of something unusual can go a long way).

There are stacks of aromatic white wines to chase and purchase, but opposite are a couple of ideas to get you started on your quest . . .

Refreshment is a unique area to consider in aromatic, and is usually edged with pungency. Take Campari – it's an aromatic bitters drink which can give people the fear, but try your guests on a shot of Campari topped up with ice and San Pellegrino sparkling *limonata*. As a summer drink in the garden, it's hard to beat. Think of it as Pimm's with an edge. Aperol is another Italian aromatic drink that isn't a million miles off Campari. They are both massively popular in Italy where you'll see Aperol and prosecco, or Aperol and white wine, Campari and soda, or Campari and orange juice sipped merrily on every street corner. They are unique aromatic drinks with a bitter tang a bit like orange peel.

There's an established tradition of Brits loving this kind of flavour in drinks – our ales are often hopped to give a bitter grapefruity kick, and James Bond is a great martini guzzler – but we don't seem to go for the full-on aromatic head-rush as often as we once did. And yet, we love aromatic herbs and spices in our drinks, such as mint in Pimm's and cloves in mulled wine . . . Context seems to be important. If it feels unfamiliar it can put people off –

One aromatic white wine that I think is massively underrated is Riesling Spätlese from Germany. Spätlese is a style that is off-dry which means it is late harvested and offers a wealth of exotic flavours along with brisk, refreshing acidity. Off-dry wines may not be fashionable but this type of wine is unique, often lower in alcohol than other wines, with subtle enticing floral aromatics and ripe generous flavours. It is gorgeous with goose, epic with roast pork and cinnamony apple sauce, and I love a dose of German Riesling Spätlese as an aperitif.

Viognier and Condrieu (which is Viognier from the appellation of Condrieu in France and wafts of peach and honeysuckle) are generally mildly aromatic with an apricot-infused touch. Sometimes Viognier can taste like peaches and cream, and it works a treat alongside mildly sweet veg such as parsnips, squash and pumpkin — especially when they are served with a Sunday roast chicken!

Argentinean Torrontes can be super-heady and an aromatic escapade in a glass. Think floral and lemony (in fact, sometimes it can be a touch like lemon Turkish delight). I really love it when it's bright and zingy with the aromatics and lemon-curd character under control. It is marvellous with cardamom-dominated dishes and can also work a treat with simple fish dishes, especially if they are spicy or aromatic.

Off the beaten track, Irsai Oliver is a white wine from Hungary that tends to have a similar orangey, aromatic aroma to Muscat, and Narince from Turkey (sounds like Narinja), which is somewhere between Verdelho and Viognier, is also seriously refreshing.

IF YOUR WINE DOESN'T QUITE HAVE THE AROMATIC EDGE YOU CRAVE, CUSTOMIZE IT WITH CORDIALS, FROM ROSE TO ROSEMARY. AROMATICS UNLEASHED!

but that's the very thing about aromatic cooking that is so appealing! I remember as a child we never ate Thai food and an Indian curry was a special treat. These days, the whole country is in love with aromatic-infused cooking from as far afield as Indonesia, Japan, China, North Africa and Mexico – witness the rising popularity of MasterChef winner Tommi Miers and her Mexican restaurant Wahaca. Aromatic cooking adds depth to dishes and drinks. The very scent of aromatic herbs, such as coriander and cardamom, crackling away in a pan is enough to get your juices flowing. And sprigs of rosemary slow-roasting in the oven over chopped Mediterranean vegetables that have been tossed into a roasting dish with some olive oil are the simple touches that make humble dishes great. When I'm roasting lamb studded with garlic, anchovies and rosemary, the scent of the charring rosemary fills the house and tickles every nose like incense on a holy day. Add the sound of the papers rustling, kids larking and Barney my border terrier snoring merrily and you've got the ultimate day off! (Blimey, sorry to cut into your reading but, as I type, I am being besieged by a Rick Astley iTunes stealth attack. Resistance is futile, 'Together Forever' grips me like a mind-ray and I am twitching like an animatronic robot version of myself. Help!)●

ROCK SHANDY

A gloriously invigorating, mildly aromatic drink that offers the ultimate refreshment. South African winemaking legend Ken Forrester introduced me to the Rock Shandy during a meeting at Kleine Zalze. It's genius and couldn't be simpler to make. Thanks for the intro, Ken!

Tip 5 OR 6 ICE CUBES into a pint glass. Add SEVERAL DASHES OF ANGOSTURA BITTERS. Top up with equal quantities of SODA WATER and LEMONADE.

It's a glorious pinky colour and has a dry, aromatic edge that quenches like nothing else on a roasting hot day. Try it with Peppadew sweet peppers stuffed with cream cheese for an alfresco summer snack. Awesome.

HERBAGE

I love Greece. The very air is laden with heady, aromatic herbs drying in the bright blue Aegean blaze. Sophie and I spent our first-ever holiday together as students camping around the Greek islands when we were nineteen years old and I have returned to a different part of Greece every year ever since. Tinos, Amorgos, Naxos, the Mani – we romped as far as our £300 budget would take us. Ferries, mopeds, hiking – all our outdoor travel was accompanied by a pot of taramasalata, a shot of *sketo* coffee and air infused with pine, thyme, oregano and the briny blue sea beyond (Phew – Rick has subsided like a stormy tide finally conceding victory to the beach. It was a close-run thing – that Rick Astley has powers like He-Man. Does that make me Skeletor?). The thing about Greece that really rocks my world, though, is how astonishingly diverse the landscape and flavours are. From the mountain plateau of Amyndeo with the world's finest vegetables that you've never tasted, to the oak forests of Kavala where you might still spot a naked centaur and feast on *Soupies Krasates* (cuttlefish with red wine). The rose-petal jam prepared each year by the monks of the Taxiarhon, the fizzy *tzitzi bira* (ginger beer) of Corfu and the sun-dried roe of Messolonghi. The sparkling wines in Zitsa, the fat juicy Amfissa olives near Delphi, the *laiki* (travelling farmer's markets), the spices, herbs, meat and fish of Athens Agora, the tomato *keftedes* of Santorini (which you can find in my Salty chapter), *sardeles pastes* (the sardines caught in the morning, salted on the boat and served that night), *horta* (the super-healthy winter and spring greens that grow wild by the side of every road in the country), the *psistaria* grill houses of Vari, the goat meat of Sifnos cooked in a clay pot, the *loukaniko* sausages of Naxos, rabbit *stifado*, and more than three hundred indigenous grape varieties making wines of untold glory, not to mention more fish dishes than Poseidon himself could ever finish munching – octopus, swordfish, sea urchins…

OK, I think I've made my point. I rather like Greece. I can smell the thyme just thinking about it – and it's not like the thyme we grow here or the pale flaccid stuff we find in the supermarkets. Greek thyme grows in thorny, spiky, squat bushes and the aroma (somewhere between mint and rosemary) fills the warm, breezy hillsides and draws your senses deep into the countryside. I remember fishing once with my Greek chum Krisna who was living in Sitia on Crete. I had managed to catch a rather splendid 'fagri' (red porgy a.k.a *Pagrus pagrus* – don't you love Latin names that repeat themselves. It's all a bit nudge nudge, aye aye, oi oi. And in birds *Turdus turdus* refers to the thrush family. So there). So, there we are with our fishylicious haul on a rocky outcrop with the wind stirring the thyme across the hot hillside. We strode manfully back to our rented Daewoo Matiz and realized that Krisna had splendidly left the radio on. And the battery was flat. And we were in the middle of nowhere. Balls. We strolled down a track and managed to find a handy military base where the men with guns were initially a bit prickly but then they thought we were a couple of hilarious incompetents and generously helped us with a ride in their jeep and some military jump leads. We shared our haul – which included an octopus – with the local café when we got back and then returned to Krisna's little flat to pan-fry the 'fagri' with a sprinkling of wild hillside thyme. It tasted amazing in lashings of local olive oil with a glass of chilled white Sitian wine (a crisp and mildly herby blend of Vilana and Thrapsathire which tickled the thyme perfectly) as the sun lazily clocked off for the night and seeped down the planetary plughole. It was one of those magical days where in my head a flugelhorn plays on the soundtrack, crooning gently as the adventure unwinds. A bit like the very relaxing flugelhorn solo played by a splendid soloist called Eddie Blair on the soundtrack of *For Your Eyes Only*. 'Take Me Home' – I recommend listening to it in the bath after a long, hard day. Thanks Eddie!

It's impossible to recreate the full, fresh thyme blast of the Greek island hillsides, but there are ways to preserve it – dried herbs, herbs in oil or in dressing. Here's my favourite THYME DRESSING, which manages to capture the aromatic edge of thyme as well as tap into a bright, sunny, zinging flavour:

Get a small jar and toss in 6-10 sprigs of fresh thyme. Pour in 2 tablespoons cider vinegar and 2 tablespoons Greek extra virgin olive oil. Add 1 tablespoon lemon juice, 1 small, finely chopped garlic clove, 3 teaspoons runny Greek honey and a sprinkle of sea salt and some freshly ground black pepper. Seal the lid and shake! Serve with a teaspoon in the jar and re-shake before each serving. (Hang on, I could never be Skeletor. Can I be Battle Cat? Or Orco? No, wait! Castle Greyskull itself.)

Dressings are a bit of an obsession of mine and I am always collecting small jars and bottles to keep my library of dressings in. A dressing can be complex in its own right and wrap a cloak of stimulation around leaf salads, bean salads and crusty bread or even add a lively streak of magic to a stew or a bowl of soup when drizzled over the top. An alternative aromatic take on dressings is this BALSAMIC VINAIGRETTE. It has a touch of heat and a three-way funfest of tarragon, cumin and coriander seeds. Aromatic attack! It works a treat with salads that have some punch to them – perhaps something that has a sliced radish bite, the kick of rocket or even comes with slices of orange:

Fill a small jar three-quarters full with half extra virgin olive oil and half balsamic vinegar (the thick, rich and treacly sort). Sprinkle in some salt and freshly ground black pepper, 2 finely sliced garlic cloves, 10 coriander seeds and a sprinkle of dried chilli flakes to taste. Squeeze in the juice of a whole lime, a drizzle of honey, a pinch of ground cumin and a fresh sprig of tarragon. Shake!

SUMMER SALAD

This is a super-simple dish for a summery light lunch or for an impromptu visit from a pal. Made with store cupboard ingredients and a handful of mint from your garden or window box, it'll serve two:

Combine 1 TIN MIXED BEANS AND PULSES, drained and rinsed, with 1 TIN TUNA in brine, drained, and ½ CHOPPED RED APPLE. Season with salt and freshly ground black pepper. Pour over some Thyme Dressing (see opposite) and sprinkle with GENEROUS AMOUNTS OF FRESH CHOPPED MINT.

SUMMERAMA!

During my island hopping holiday around Greece with Sophie, I remember being transfixed by the deep blue sky competing with the Aegean Sea to see which could be the bluest. With the scent of pine trees wafting in the hot breezes, we scooted around islands on rickety mopeds from rocky beach to craggy monastery, playing endless games of backgammon over a handful of drachmae and a cloudy glass or two of chilled ouzo. We became ouzo aficionados and particularly enjoyed sloshing a few slurps of ouzo into a split watermelon and feasting greedily on the contents. On one particular occasion, we were given a giant watermelon by a shopkeeper who refused to accept payment as we boarded the bus to head to the airport and home. It was vast, took both of us to carry it and we had the greatest fortune to be delayed so we had plenty of time to indulge and munch every last juicy mouthful. The ultimate melon!

OUZO IS WIDELY FOUND IN GREECE, BUT SOME OF THE BEST COMES FROM LESVOS AND IS WELL WORTH HUNTING DOWN. IF YOU LIKE LIQUORICE, YOU'LL LOVE OUZO!

Ouzo's aniseed tang is closely linked in my mind to fennel. There's a refreshing aromatic character to fennel and it works beautifully in salads such as this FENNEL SLAW:

Slice 2 carrots into ribbons with a potato peeler and very finely slice 2-3 heads fennel and 1 red onion. Tip everything into a bowl. Whisk together 125g mayonnaise and the juice of 1 lemon. Pour this over the veg and toss to coat lightly. Season with salt and freshly ground black pepper.

Greece still has a wealth of little-known local wines. The opportunities to taste them are increasing and often the best places to try them are in restaurants there where you can find terrific value that'll encourage a spot of risk-taking. There are hundreds of local Greek grape varieties for wine fans to get their chops around and some of them have some interesting aromatic qualities that work spectacularly with the local, sun-kissed fresh herbs and olives.

SOME AROMATIC GREEK GRAPE VARIETIES

Malagousia is a white grape variety that nearly became extinct in Greece and was saved by Evangelos Gerovassiliou. If you're a fan of Viognier you'll love Malagousia; it is peachy and brisk and, when well made, is a beautiful crisp aperitif.

Moschofilero is found in the AOC region of Mantinia, in the Peloponnese, and has a pinky skin, which produces white wine that is tinged with floral aromatics — think rose and violet. If you're a fan of Gewürztraminer, Moschofilero is one to hunt.

Savatiano is the grape formerly of Retsina fame but winemakers such as Vassilis Papagiannakos, who insist on careful production and lower yields, are making interesting white wines with subtle mellow aromatic tinges.

A LICK OF GARLIC

I'm good mates with TV producer James Winter, a serious foodie and feaster. We've worked together on a few shows but *Saturday Kitchen* is probably the best known. Whenever we go out, whether it's together or with chef buddies like Stuart Gillies, Theo Randall, Atul Kochhar or the great James Martin himself, we always end up discussing the virtue of garlic. Garlic adds dimension to dishes. Depending on when you add it to a dish and how finely you chop it, it can have a hugely different impact. For example, crushed garlic added late is the most intense manifestation because it has the greatest surface area and shortest cooking time. If you add bigger pieces earlier in the cooking process it has less of an impact on the overall dish, just contributing a subtle garlic tinge. My writer pal Mark Huckerby is a passionate allotment guru and home cook and he has insisted for years that nothing sets the appetite going as much as garlic. I love roasting whole bulbs alongside any roast meats and squeezing the garlic out of the papery cloves like toothpaste to mix with mash, enrich gravy or as an awesome mouthful of glory in its own right. But for the discovery of one particular use of garlic I have to hand it to my buddy Sarah Weal. Living in London years ago, I remember Sarah prepared a stunning Sunday roast in her tiny kitchen and the thing that blew my mind was her GARLIC CARROTS. It couldn't be simpler:

Boil your carrots as you would normally (I like mine to be very firm, not soggy), drain them and then toss in a knob or two of butter and 1 or 2 crushed garlic cloves, depending on how many carrots you've cooked (1 clove is good for 4–6 portions of carrots).

They are amazing. The carrots have a beautiful sheen because of the butter, and the garlic adds an extra dimension of aromatic enhancement. Genius, simple and scrummy.

Garlic tends to be a wine-crushing flavour but for dishes that contain a lot of it, such as aioli, Italian Verdicchio works with its nutty, mellow, round character — it envelops the intense garlic quite successfully. For a more intense flavour, rosé from Provence can be a sublime ally. With Sarah's Garlic Carrots, it all depends on what you're serving them with — they work particularly well with roast lamb or lamb chops and I'd serve a red Rioja or a Tempranillo from Spain's Ribera del Duero to link up with the lamb and shoulder the garlic.

One night at home when we were totally out of supplies after a particularly hectic few days, Sophie whipped up this CRUNCHY CABBAGE and it was a meal in itself. Completely delicious with a sweet, aromatic flavour thanks to the garlic-ginger combo. Hurrah for Sophie! And hurrah for the aromatic duo garlic and ginger! These quantities serve 2:

→ Cut the cabbage into narrow strips. Meanwhile, heat a glug of sesame oil in a large pan or wok.

→ When the oil is hot, fry the sliced garlic, chopped ginger and sliced spring onions. Add the sliced cabbage and stir-fry. Add a dash of Tabasco.

→ When the cabbage is cooked but still crunchy, turn off the heat, add the lemon and lime juice, and a pinch of salt and stir. Serve!

Alongside this dish, we sipped a Roussanne from southern France and it worked a treat with its mellow honeysuckle touch that picked up beautifully on the gingery-garlic combo. Have it!

CRUNCHY CABBAGE

½ cabbage (you can use most types except Savoy, go for the crunchiest you can find)

glug of sesame oil

2 garlic cloves, sliced

knob fresh ginger, diced

2 large spring onions, sliced

dash of Tabasco

squeeze of lemon juice

squeeze of lime juice

salt

FRAGRANT ASIAN

When I was nineteen I spent several months working as an English teacher at UNJA, the University of Jambi, in Sumatra, Indonesia. In terms of flavour, it was a world away from my day-to-day feasting habits in the UK. Aromatic flavours play a big part in Indonesian cooking, with the wealth of spices and herbs available. The Indonesian archipelago has an amazing diversity of cookery traditions, fused from all sorts of different cultural emphases – too many to include here, though certainly enough to fill another book! One of the common themes I found in Indonesian cooking was garlic. It is amazing how so many of the world's great cooking cultures prize the unique aromatic dimension that garlic brings to a dish – France and Italy love the stuff and it seems wherever I travel in the world, it's the one ingredient that never quite disappears.

I always used to sip a cold Bintang beer with Nasi Goreng on my travels — a cool crisp lager to refresh the body after the heat of the day and a dusty day's travel. Depending on how you customize the dish, choose your wine accordingly. A rosé for a summery day with prawns and spice, or a Sauvignon Blanc for a zesty shellfish-inspired incarnation. If you decide to customize the dish with beef, though, you could try a light-bodied red from the Gamay grape, a Sicilian Nero-D'Avola or perhaps a fruity Aussie Grenache — and you could even experiment with chilling it down in an ice bucket for ten minutes to bring out the flavour of the fruit.

NASI GORENG is a cracking dish that I used to gorge on all over Indonesia. It varied according to where I was (shellfish beside the shore, beef inland). You can adjust the recipe and replace the prawns with pork, beef or chicken, or add sweetcorn, fish, tofu or bacon and a host of other veg – stir-fried carrots, broccoli or mushrooms etc. Be creative! This version is all about the aromatic qualities of garlic, anchovies and spices, which wreath around the other flavours to bind the dish up into a lightly spicy meal that is simple to cook and even easier to eat. This will serve 4:

→ Beat the egg with the groundnut oil and set aside.

→ Grind the shallot to a paste or chop very finely and fry it with the garlic, anchovies and spices in the sesame oil until golden and the anchovies have started to dissolve (around 4–5 minutes).

→ Add the prawns and peas and fry for a further 3 minutes. Tip in the cooked rice and stir.

→ Move the mixture to one side of the pan, pour the egg and groundnut oil mixture on to the cleared side of the pan and after about 20 seconds stir with the wrong end of a wooden spoon to break it up. Now, stir this into the rice and splash in some ketchup manis or soy.

→ Serve garnished with the fried spring onion and cucumber, and some sambal (see page 162).

NASI GORENG

1 egg

1 tablespoon groundnut oil

1 shallot, finely sliced

2 garlic cloves, crushed

2 anchovy fillets

½ teaspoon saffron

½ teaspoon turmeric

½ teaspoon dried chilli flakes

2 tablespoons toasted sesame oil

50g fresh prawns, chopped into morsels

50g fresh or frozen peas

150g plain rice, cooked according to the packet instructions, drained and set aside

1/2 teaspoon or more ketchup manis or soy sauce, to taste

sprinkle of fried, sliced spring onion (to garnish)

scattering of finely sliced cucumber batons (to garnish)

Another aromatic rice dish that has been inspired by my travels in Indonesia is my JUMBO JAMBI RICE. It is a great treat but, since it's made with leftovers, it couldn't be simpler. These quantities serve 2 hungry people but you can make as much or as little as you need. It's utterly delicious and you could also replace the rice with noodles, if you prefer:

Grab a wok or big frying pan. Take 1 large or 2 small carrots, cut into very fine batons, 1 large shallot or 1 small onion, diced, and fry in a mixture of 1 tablespoon each vegetable oil, groundnut oil and sesame oil for 3–4 minutes. Add 4 big broccoli florets quartered lengthways and then chopped roughly, 2 garlic cloves, diced, a thumbnail-sized cube of ginger, finely diced, or 1 teaspoon ginger paste and the juice of 1/2 lime for 4–5 minutes. Stir in 150g cooked peas and fry for another 3–4 minutes. Add 150g cooked basmati rice and sprinkle 1/2 teaspoon dried chilli flakes (or a ¼ teaspoon if you don't want it too spicy), a pinch of ground cumin and 1/2 teaspoon ground coriander over the top and stir. Meanwhile, finely chop and fry 2 spring onions until crisp. Finish by drizzling the juice of 1/2 lime over the top with 1/2 tablespoon ketchup manis and mix in well. Garnish with the crispy spring onions and a drizzle of soy sauce. I love this for the fresh crunchy veg infused with zesty lime, the spicy kick and the aromatic layers of flavour. Gorgeous!

A simple South African Chenin Blanc, chilled down for optimum refreshment, with its mild aromatic edges is the ticket for this Jumbo Jambi Rice. Ideally sipped and feasted on outdoors with the summery sounds of grasshoppers, cicadas and crickets chirping merrily beneath the sunset.

I came across a wonderful aromatic fish dish at a beach-side stall in Lombok – as I was munching, a shark washed ashore at my feet! Sadly it was dead but it was sufficiently huge and so impressively jawed it stuck in my mind nonetheless. The dish, called IKAN BAKAR (which translates literally as 'baked fish'), is simple and absolutely gorgeous. You could also cook it with a whole fish, such as bass, and then barbecue it after marinating. This will serve 2:

→ Blitz the shallots, garlic, nuts, palm sugar, tamarind water, groundnut oil and salt into a coarse paste. Marinate the fish in these spices for ½ hour.

→ Place the fillets on some foil under a medium grill for 10–12 minutes, depending on the size of the fillets. Turn them over halfway through and baste with the marinade while they cook.

→ The marinade should become a gorgeous coating on the fish so make sure you spoon up as much as you can from the foil to coat the fish again before feasting with plain rice and a wedge of lime.

The tamarind paste is what gives this dish its zesty, bright, aromatic character. On that beach in Lombok, I sipped a cold beer with this and it was exceedingly good! If you're after some wine, I'd go for a glass of refreshing, chilled Sauvignon Blanc from New Zealand — preferably one full of passion fruit, tropical flavours to match the bright aromatics in the dish.

IKAN BAKAR

3 shallots, finely diced

3 garlic cloves, finely chopped

50g macadamia nuts, finely chopped

30g palm sugar

1 tablespoon tamarind paste, diluted with 60ml water

2 tablespoons groundnut oil

2 x 250g haddock fillets, skinless (whole sea bass also works a treat but you can experiment with a wide range of white-fleshed sea fish from gurnard to pollock. You could even try it with chicken – *ayam bakar*)

salt, to taste

BOOST THE MARINADE WITH CHILLI IF YOU WANT TO AMP UP THE SPICE!

And while chilled aromatic whites are superbly satisfying, you can create warm concoctions that have an awesome aromatic kick by mulling! Try OLLY'S MULLED WHITE WINE:

Pour 1 bottle leftover, fruity white wine into a pan and add freshly chopped pineapple, a few lemon wedges, honey and 1 cinnamon stick. When warm, strain and serve with a slice of lemon (to garnish). You could give it an extra kick by adding a dose of brandy or vodka, or even Cointreau to give it an orangey tang.

Red grapes tend not to be overtly aromatic; instead they are more floral, spicy or smoky, but there is one sure-fire way to encourage aromatics in a red and that's to create OLLY'S MASSIVE MULLED WINE. It is a simple drink to make and you can easily customize this version to concoct your own. The key is not to boil the wine, just keep it warm:

Pour 1 bottle red wine into a pan and add 1-2 glugs orange juice, a splosh of brandy and sugar to taste. Tip in 1-2 cloves, a knob of fresh ginger and 1 cinnamon stick and load it with orange, lemon and lime slices (or try using fresh mango for a tropical twist). The rule of thumb is keep tasting until it's right – and don't overdo the cloves or it'll be bitter. For another flavour boost, try adding some Port. It's a wonderful drink for when the weather turns frosty.

I love skiing with my mates Sean and Cath in La Tania. We adopt nicknames for the duration of the holiday (Sean is 'Badger', Cath is 'Big Poppa', Sophie is 'Laser Lady' and I am 'Sir Roger'). On a chilly slope at sub-zero temperatures, there's nothing like stopping for a quick *vin chaud*. Here's my version – OLLY'S WARMING GLORY, which serves 6:

Gently warm 1 bottle fruity red wine in a pan but do not boil. Add 1 cinnamon stick, 1 star anise, 1 vanilla pod and 2 slices of lemon, and then drizzle in runny honey until optimum sweetness is reached. Serve in glass mugs, paper cups, or egg cups for a quick nip.

FILL YER
BOOTS

BELTING BHAJI WITH ROCKING RAITA

Toss SLICED RED ONION with SEASONED GRAM FLOUR and TOASTED, CRUSHED CUMIN SEEDS, add A LITTLE WATER and LIME JUICE to form a light batter. Deep-fry and then serve with YOGHURT mixed with CRUSHED GARLIC, GROUND CUMIN and LOTS OF CHOPPED MINT.

This dish is simple to make and so a simple quaffing wine is required. But the crucial thing to remember is that it has to stand up to the aromatic cumin and garlic and the fresh, razzle-dazzle, high-kicking mint. Grape varieties such as Marsanne and Roussanne work delightfully with aromatic spices – they tend to be peachy and bright without being too acidic and they have a floral complexity that brings the dish to life. You could also consider Chenin Blanc, which is a bit of a chameleon – in the Loire Valley it produces wines that are dry, sparkling, sweet and everything in between. South Africa is capable of producing outstanding Chenin Blanc – look for winemakers such as Ken Forrester and Bruwer Raats, both big characters and both make sublime wines.

RAZZLE DAZZLE!

Aromatic is a flavour thread that singles out a dish with its uniquely distinctive, fragrant or herbal twinge. As a flavour group it is surprisingly diverse, embracing everything from jasmine tea to Turkish delight, with cloves tagged along the way. When deployed in dishes, it usually requires a wine with a similar aromatic quality to match with it – and there's a plethora of styles out there to choose from. My rule of thumb is to go with an exotic white wine, but light-bodied reds are always worth experimenting with on your quest for aromatic excellence. For me, the aniseed ball is a wondrous delicacy that encapsulates the sweeter side of aromatic but I urge you to enquire further into the bitter edges of Campari, and Aperol along with some of the bonkers aromatic wines – all drinks that dazzle! Served in the spirit of experimentation and exploration, they feel to me as though someone is shining a summertime flashlight directly on to my soul.●

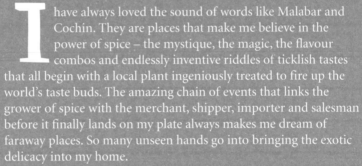

I have always loved the sound of words like Malabar and Cochin. They are places that make me believe in the power of spice – the mystique, the magic, the flavour combos and endlessly inventive riddles of ticklish tastes that all begin with a local plant ingeniously treated to fire up the world's taste buds. The amazing chain of events that links the grower of spice with the merchant, shipper, importer and salesman before it finally lands on my plate always makes me dream of faraway places. So many unseen hands go into bringing the exotic delicacy into my home.

Spice adds an extra dimension to a dish. It's like the percussion in a band – it can be a loud marching beat, leading everyone to a climax, or a subtler offbeat echo in the background. Spice can operate in two distinct ways – high-impact heat or, more subtly, layers of aromatic spice that offer depth of flavour and elegant, expansive qualities to a dish. It's the difference between adding a chilli or a stick of cinnamon to your curry. They both have a spicy character but in completely different ways. Now that curry is officially Britain's best-loved dish, the realm of spice deserves closer attention.

Spice in food can knacker your taste buds, when it comes to wanting something to drink with it. Generally a chunky red will magnify hot spice in a dish, whereas an off-dry white will taste zingier. Definitely avoid very crisp, dry whites as they will turn into darting, dazzling laser bolts that bounce off your taste buds – spice makes wine taste zingier. So, stick to the off-dry whites, such as Ken Forrester's FMC Chenin Blanc from South Africa which, year in year out, seems a winner with mild, spicy dishes, from prawns with a sweet chilli dip, through to a toasted sesame stir-fry. If it's a red you're after, though, go for low tannin with a good fruity flavour. I've had luck with fruity Grenache from Australia, especially with curried game such as partridge. With more aromatic spicy dishes, you can go for Gewürztraminer, but I often find its intense floral character and unctuous texture overpowers subtle spice, like a bear strangling a mouse. When the spice in your dish comes from flavours such as cardamom, cinnamon, ginger and coriander seeds, I would go for Viognier, Chenin Blanc or lesser known varieties such as Marsanne and Roussanne. All of these have subtle aromatic qualities and, when they have been intelligently oaked, they offer a richness of texture and a superb springboard for a spicy dish.

Of course, there's no denying that a cold beer is hugely popular with spicy dishes but, rather than go for an everyday lager, I would urge you to sample some of Britain's outstanding India Pale Ale. Two that I regularly sip are Timothy Taylor's Landlord and Deuchars IPA. Both have compelling aromatic aromas and rich flavours, with a spank of tangy hops that breaks just after you sip it, like an echo of dynamite in a quarry. Sensational! And if you find yourself in my neck of the woods in the Sussex town of Lewes, a pint of Harveys Best Bitter is hard to beat – a great accompaniment to many spicy dishes thanks to its balance of fruity flavour and pungent hops. I could bathe in the stuff! And did you know that Belgian white beers often have a dose of spice in them, such as coriander? True – next time you sample one, give it a good sniff and you'll notice the coriander lifting the whole aromatic profile, like a forklift truck hoicking a massive treasure chest hoarded with jewels.●

AROMATIC SPICE

Spice is cooking out loud; as it toasts and turns in the pan, it takes us globe-trotting in search of Iranian saffron, Sri Lankan cardamom and the horseradish that grows along the rivers and streams in the Sussex town where I live. I've marched through a cinnamon forest in Indonesia, munching on sweet young stems as I passed the wild trees and thought I had arrived in Rivendell, home of Elrond the Elf Lord.

Ooooh trivia fact for you: in Peter Jackson's *Lord of the Rings*, Elrond was played by Aussie acting star from *Priscilla Queen of the Desert* Hugo Weaving – he's my mum's cousin. For real! How cool is that? The family were so proud when Hugo played evil agent Smith in *The Matrix* – Smith! That's my name! Kung-fu! Genius. I made sure to congratulate him at my brother's recent wedding where Hugo sported the most magnificent pair of sideburns ever grown by a human man.

Babies could have swung from them. I salute face furniture and urge all men to sprout forth at once in as inventive a manner as possible. Have a look at www.worldbeardchampionships.com. It is a world of astonishment and the website opens with the words, 'Like many things having to do with the World Beard and Moustache Championships, the history of the event is shrouded in controversy.' There you go – perfect for Dan-Brown-type novelization. Get scribbling! Do it for me!

Throughout my stay in Indonesia, the scent of cloves filled my nostrils 24/7 – the smell is abundant across the Indonesian archipelago thanks to the popularity of Kretek cigarettes (tobacco laced with cloves). I remember touching down in the middle of the night after my long-haul flight and wondering what the sweet smell that followed me everywhere could possibly be. I started to think that jetlag had a distorting effect on smell as well as on time. It took me weeks to work out the Christmassy niff was wafting from the local cigs! The clove is a very pervasive and powerful spice, best in small doses. I have found that it can work magnificently in cocktails to give them a trademark festive spice, as in THE OLIGARCH which I invented one evening with my friend Sean for pure jollies:

Bung 1-2cm square of orange peel, 1 crushed clove (again use a pestle and mortar or crush between two spoons),

½ teaspoon sugar and 1 measure Grey Goose vodka into a jam jar. Shake for a minute or 2, and then pour through a tea strainer or muslin into a Champagne flute. Top up with chilled Champagne, cava or sparkling wine (leaving room in the glass for the grenadine). Using a syringe or a straw (suck the liquid up into the straw, cover the end with your finger and then release into the glass), inject just over 1 measure grenadine into the bottom of the glass. The grenadine sits at the bottom and the drink has a beautiful pink colour gradation. And, amazingly, it smells like Christmas!

Or alternatively, try this SIBERIAN SUNRISE. It's a belter and was invented the same evening as a variation on the vodka/clove/spicy cocktail theme. It's a cracking drink for when the weather gets moody – guaranteed to give you a comforting warm glow:

Pour 1 measure vodka into a jam jar and infuse with 1 crushed clove (use a pestle and mortar or crush between two spoons), a slice of red chilli (fingernail size, lightly crushed with the base of a teaspoon) and ½ teaspoon sugar. Shake together and then pour into a long glass through a tea strainer. Add 150ml fresh, chilled orange juice (no bits). Using the same method as for The Oligarch, inject 1 measure grenadine into the bottom of the glass. I absolutely love it – and it doesn't even taste of booze!

As a student in Edinburgh I was knocked out by the inventive use of spice in the vodkas sold in Bar Kohl. It's still there on George IV Bridge, though I haven't been in years. The vodkas came in all sorts of incarnations, from chilli-flavoured to cumin-infused. There's a rich history of blending spices into drinks – gin is a great example with its infusion of liquorice, orris root, coriander and various fruit peels. The monasteries of Europe have strong traditions in the realm of spicy drinks, too – Chartreuse is still reported to be the only spirit in the world that is naturally green. Only two Chartreuse monks guard the identity of the 130 plants that go into making it, and the technique of how to blend and distil them. I'd love to see a renaissance of these kinds of drinks, with layer upon layer of flavour to savour, contemplate and revel in. The approach requires patience and a willingness to experiment with infusions that work in harmony – a bit like a tagine. That's it! Eureka! We need to think of our spicy drinks recipes more along the lines of tagines.

CORIANDER SEEDS SPRINKLED WHOLE ON TO A LEAF SALAD, OR A BEAN AND PULSE SALAD, GIVE LITTLE BURSTS OF FRAGRANCE WITH THEIR BLOOMING FLAVOUR. LOVE IT!

SPICY MOROCCAN LAMB

I was first inspired by tagines after a chat with a teacher/cigarette salesman/orange smuggler in Morocco one summer train journey in the late 1990s. He was basically a rogue of many trades, but his tagine tips were unsurpassed. And, if memory serves, he was a huge fan of Pink Floyd and we ended up hooting 'Comfortably Numb' at one another across the carriage – much to the delight of our fellow passengers. His main point (in terms of tagines) was that when you slow-cook lamb, you need to deploy equal quantities of ground cumin, ground coriander, ground turmeric and ground cinnamon. A year later, on a wine-hunting trip to South Africa, my good pal Rozy Gunn shared with me this recipe, which uses the same principle of equal spice. Rozy's kitchen is always packed with the scent of something awesome cooking and has a bright colourful glow from fresh fruit and veg gleaming in every nook. The options with this dish are endless – depending on the ratio of meat, beans, vegetables and stock that you use, this can swing from a soup to a stew. (The beans in this recipe can come from a tin – Rozy does her own because they keep their form better during the cooking process and she's a bit fanatical about unnecessarily using preserved stuff.) It is fantastic served with brown meal rotis and a cup of Greek yoghurt spiked with chopped mint.

Serves 4

8–10 chunks lamb on the bone (e.g. neck chops), trimmed of all fat

2 tablespoons olive oil

3 onions, chopped into chunks

1 stick celery, finely sliced

3 garlic cloves, crushed

4 large carrots, peeled and cut into generous slices

1 teaspoon ground cumin

1 teaspoon ground coriander

→ Preheat the oven to 160°C/312°F/Gas 2–3.

→ Brown the meat in the olive oil in a cast-iron casserole dish. Remove and set aside.

→ Using the same pot, very gently fry the onions, celery, garlic and carrots, as well as all the spices, for about 5 minutes, taking care not to let the spices burn. Add a few tablespoons of water, if necessary.

→ Put the browned lamb back in the pot; add the tin of tomatoes, the sugar, the chickpeas, the beans and the dried lentils. Finally add the fresh herbs and then pour over as much stock or water as you wish. (You do need a basic minimum to allow the lentils enough liquid to cook.)

→ Put the lid on and bake in the oven for 2–3 hours, or until tender and all the individual ingredients have come together but before they've lost their identity completely.

A glass of modern fruity Rioja or Grenache from Australia will more than hold its own with this fragrant and succulent dish!

1 teaspoon ground turmeric

1 teaspoon ground cinnamon

1 bay leaf

1 x 410g tin tomatoes, roughly chopped, plus the juice

1–2 teaspoons sugar

1 cup chickpeas, soaked overnight and boiled on a low heat until cooked

½ cup any other dried bean of your choice, soaked overnight and boiled on low heat until cooked

large handful lentils

handful fresh oregano, thyme or parsley (whatever you have on hand)

750ml–1.5 litres stock or plain water (quantity depends on whether you want a stew or a soup)

salt and freshly ground black pepper

GINGER PARKIN

225g self-raising flour

1 tablespoon ground ginger

½ teaspoon ground nutmeg

½ teaspoon mixed spice

125g medium oatmeal

zest of 1 lemon

pinch of salt

100g unsalted butter

125g dark muscavado brown sugar

75ml treacle

75ml Golden Syrup

25ml stem ginger syrup

75g stem ginger, finely diced

50ml milk

1 egg, beaten

½ teaspoon bicarbonate of soda

Ginger is a unique spice that has the double dimension of heat and aromatic appeal. My first memory of ginger was in parkin – one of Britain's finest spicy, sweet traditions. I was born in Darlington and we lived in the Northeast for the first few years of my life. My uncle and aunt and cousins still live in Newcastle. Aunty Anne is a Yorkshire lass and, apart from making world-class Yorkshire puddings, I have fond childhood memories of her outstanding custard. In fact, I must ask her for the recipe . . . In my next book, I will do my best to include the recipe for Aunty Anne's custard! I loved living in Witton-Le-Weir, a village near Crook in County Durham. Will and I used to romp across the fields on long adventures pretending to be Batman and Robin, James Bond, cowboys and spacemen. All in the same field. And parkin featured quite a lot. I think Mum had a recipe from the local WI but I've since tinkered with it and I always serve my own version with a bonus mincemeat frosty sidekick. GINGER PARKIN with QUICK MINCEMEAT ICE CREAM – a bit like Batman and Robin but more edible. The parkin will serve 10 or more, depending on how indulgent you're feeling!

→ Preheat the oven to 170°C/325°F/Gas 3 and butter a deep, 20cm square cake tin and line the base with baking paper.

→ Sift the flour and spices into a bowl, then stir in the oatmeal and lemon zest and add a pinch of salt.

→ Place the butter, sugar, treacle, Golden Syrup and ginger syrup into a saucepan and heat until totally melted. Pour this mixture on to the dry ingredients and stir well.

→ Add the diced stem ginger, milk and egg, and mix once more.

→ Finally, add the bicarbonate of soda, mix well then pour into the baking tin, smoothing to the edges. Place in the oven and bake for 45 minutes – check with a skewer to see if it is cooked through (the skewer should come out clean). If it does, remove from the oven; if not, bake for a further 10 minutes, and then check once more.

→ Remove from the oven and cool in the tin before turning out and cutting into squares.

→ Keep in an airtight container for up to 2 weeks – the longer the parkin is kept, the stickier it gets!

And if you fancy some QUICK MINCEMEAT ICE CREAM (I always do) as an accompaniment to the parkin, here's how to make it:

Place 300ml/½ pint double cream into a bowl with 50ml stem ginger syrup and 2 tablespoons honey, and whisk until soft peaks are formed. Fold 125g Greek yoghurt into the cream, until fully mixed. Stir in 150g luxury cranberry mincemeat so it is marbled through the cream. Place in the freezer and freeze for 3–4 hours until solid. Remove from the freezer 10–20 minutes before serving to soften slightly. Luxuriant and spice-tastic!

Aromatic spice crosses the boundaries of sweet and savoury. Hot spice can do that, too, for example in the case of chilli-infused dark chocolate which I adore. But, generally, where heat spice is concerned, you're up for a more savoury ride. Buckle up – this is where the rubber meets the road!

Now, you could absolutely match a sweet wine with this parkin, but a sweet chai latte with its ginger, clove, cinnamon and cardamom joy would be sublime. For a quick recipe that'll give you 2 cups, pour 2 mugs' worth of full-fat milk into a pan. Add a cardamom pod, 2 cloves, ½ teaspoon ground cinnamon, ½ teaspoon ground ginger and 3 teaspoons caster sugar. Stir and bring to a simmer, then take off the heat and add 2 teaspoons Assam tea. Stir. Leave for 2 minutes. Stir again. Carefully pour into mugs through a fine tea strainer and enjoy. Watch out for the gingery kick, though! Power spice! And you can use the same spices to create chai porridge, the ultimate insulation against a snap frost.

HEAT SPICE

When I was working in Indonesia, there was a splendid café along the street where I lived called Kantin Telanai (I was living in the district of Telanaipura) and I used to spend hours watching the guys preparing the two chilli pastes that were a staple of most cafés but which were particularly excellent in Kantin Telanai. It helped that we shared a love of Queen's *Greatest Hits* and I remember once, during a tropical storm, listening to 'Bohemian Rhapsody' while the guys showed me how to grind the paste with their ENORMOUS pestle and mortar. Seriously, the giant in Jack and the Beanstalk could have used it as a toothpick, it was that big. The pestle was almost as tall as me and made of rock – super-heavy but fantastic at grinding the paste to the perfect texture. When you make this TANGY SPICY SUMATRAN SAMBAL CHILLI PASTE, you can use a pestle and mortar or blitz the paste in a blender, depending on how smooth you like it to be. Either way, it keeps for weeks if you cover it in a layer of oil and refrigerate. Use any type of chilli you like, depending on how hot you want it, and include the seeds to pump the heat or remove the seeds to tame it. You can use green or red chillies, again depending on your preference. The green chillies are less ripe and offer a milder flavour, whereas the red chillies give you that full-on, turbo-charged, hairdryer-in-the-trousers hot spice effect:

Put 50g chillies, chopped and deseeded, 3 garlic cloves, chopped, 1 small shallot, very finely chopped, 1 teaspoon caster sugar, the juice of 1 lemon (or you can use a big lime or about 2 tablespoons vinegar), 1-2 drops sunflower oil (to make it slithery and mashable), a pinch of salt and a drizzle of water (if necessary to make the sambal a bit looser) into a pestle and mortar, or a blender, and mash, or blitz, until combined.

Add more sugar to tone down the spice, if you need to. You could also add other layers of flavour such as ginger, coriander, thyme, mint, or whatever herb or spice you like. Choose something that will funk it up and match it to your main course. I used to eat my sambal with everything from salads to curries and savoury *martabak* (pancake parcels – yummy!). This particular sambal works beautifully with cold roast beef sandwiches in place of horseradish.

That said, there is nothing like a dose of real horseradish for a bit of spicy action! I make my own by digging up fresh horseradish (they look a bit like the mandrake plants in *Harry Potter and the Chamber of Secrets*), peeling the root and grating it finely into crème fraîche, or sour cream, then adding a sprinkle of sugar, salt and lemon juice to taste. You can also experiment and customize by adding a bit of Dijon mustard and mayonnaise to the mix.

OLLY'S NOT HORSERADISH

If you've run out of horseradish or you can't face the eye-watering experience of grating it (I have been known to don my mask and snorkel!) then there's only one thing for it — cheat! This is a bulletproof replacement and it's made with stuff that's usually lurking in the fridge and store cupboard. It is a spice bomb of a recipe:

Combine **4 TABLESPOONS PLAIN YOGHURT, 2 TABLESPOONS DIJON MUSTARD, A PINCH OF DRIED CHILLI FLAKES** and **1 DESSERTSPOON CIDER VINEGAR**. Season with some salt and freshly ground black pepper. Magic!

WEAR A SWIMMING MASK WHEN GRATING HORSERADISH TO PROTECT YOUR EYES (SNORKEL OPTIONAL).

Hot sauces are a worldwide phenomenon. We all seem to love a dose of heat with our nosh whether it's wasabi with sushi, sweet chilli sauce with our stir-fry or mustard with our bangers. I've already dealt you my recipe for Indonesian sambal, but when I went on my first wine-tasting adventure in Chile, I discovered the South American equivalent – *pebre*. It's a really simple salsa that you'll find on every table in Chile and is just beautiful to dip plain, warm white crusty bread into. I call my version OLLY'S GRINGO-CHILEAN PEBRE:

Combine **4-5 tomatoes**, skinned, deseeded and finely chopped, with **1 shallot**, finely chopped, **1-3 red chillies**, deseeded and finely chopped (you control the spice volume here), **a few sprigs of fresh coriander**, finely chopped (to taste), the **juice of ½ lemon** and **2-3 garlic cloves**, crushed (depending on how much you're in the mood for). Mulch everything together, adding more lemon juice if required to get a good consistency. Taste and doctor the recipe according to your fancy. Leave to infuse for an hour or so, and then devour with the best warm, buttered, crusty white bread you can lay your hands on.

The heat of chillies is fiery, but the heat of black pepper has a more aromatic quality to it, and it can be used beautifully to bring out other flavours – such as sweet things. A grade-A flavour trophy is a hard item to find, and often appears in the most unlikely combinations. For example, a mind-blowing companion to black pepper spice is the succulent strawberry! Wahey! Some people who enjoy drinking posh Bordeaux wine from Margaux say that it pairs well with strawberries. Other people say that they marry up well with a slick dose of aged balsamic vinegar (the treacly unctuous kind that sticks to everything like tar). But I say strawberries are the knackers with a twist of black pepper! It emphasizes their fruitiness and the pepper character comes through with more subtlety than you'd expect.

In this STRAWBERRY, CHILLI AND BLACK PEPPER SALAD, I've unleashed even more spice with the help of a crushed chipotle chilli. Growing chillies is very simple – you don't need a lot of space (window boxes and pots are fine) and you can do all sorts to them – dry them, pickle them, create inventive herb and chilli oils or use them fresh. Chillies range so widely in heat and flavour that it's well worth doing – chilli-tastic!

→ Place the strawberries into a bowl.

→ Put the sugar and water into a saucepan and heat until melted.

→ Add the chipotle chilli, peppercorns and lemon zest and stir well. Pour this mixture over the strawberries and toss to coat.

→ Set aside for at least 1 hour to macerate.

→ Just before you're ready to eat, toss the strawberries with the mint leaves and then serve them with a large dollop of crème fraîche.

STRAWBERRY,
CHILLI AND
BLACK PEPPER

400g strawberries,
hulled and halved if
large

3 tablespoons caster
sugar

3 tablespoons water

½ teaspoon chipotle
chilli, crushed

¼ teaspoon black
peppercorns, crushed

zest of ½ lemon

1 tablespoon mint
leaves, finely shredded
(Vietnamese mint
leaves if you can get
them)

Champagne with strawberries is a classic – but with the spice in this dish, try a glass of fruitier and more generously flavoured Demi-Sec Champagne. Its fruitier fullness would be the perfect partner to this salad. Remember, you need balance in your wine matches. I would love to see Roger Federer face Big Daddy on the tennis court – highly entertaining on one level, but it would be rubbish tennis. The better balanced game would be Federer versus Nadal. SERVICE!

From chilli in sweet dishes, we can easily hop to the ingredient that always shrieks 'holiday' to me. Chorizo! For a ridiculously easy and delicious spicy treat, try this CHILLI PEPPER SQUID AND CHORIZO SALAD:

Pan-fry some chorizo and then add some squid. Crush some salt and Szechwan black pepper together and then add it to the pan with a squeeze of lemon juice. Serve the salad tossed through with a little chopped red onion and flat-leaf parsley. Yummo!

Like the black pepper strawberries, the kumquat chutney is the point where Sweet meets Heat. But the masters of this dimension are my spice-loving chums Jan Coles and her husband Mighty John. They're an astonishingly adventurous couple who have lived across the world with a glorious sense of flair. I recently went on a night out feasting with them and they are top tippling partners as well, who never say no to a sharpener or two. Splendid! After travelling the world sailing yachts, piloting helicopters and preaching their unique 'whisky way' to son-in-law Nick (their 'whisky way' is pretty much 'stop whimpering and get it down you'), John and Jan finally settled on top of the Pyrenees, where I have always imagined them as eagles living in a giant eyrie. Feathers or not, they are experts in the art of growing, feasting and sharing food. Huzzah! Jan has divulged her top-secret, spicy recipe DINAH'S HOT PEPPER JELLY for us all to share and enjoy and I am hugely grateful. She has kept it under wraps for decades and I am chuffed to bits to reveal the details here:

DINAH'S HOT PEPPER JELLY

6 Scotch bonnets deseeded and roughly chopped

3 red peppers, deseeded and chopped

300ml/½ pint vinegar

1.1kg Confisuc/preserving sugar

→ Wash some jam jars in hot soapy water, then rinse well. Put them into a preheated oven at 170°C/325°F/Gas 3 until you are ready to use them.

→ Blitz all the peppers in a processor with a pinch or two of the sugar and a little of the vinegar.

→ Put the rest of the sugar and vinegar in a large pot and start warming it.

→ Add the peppers from the processor to the sugar and vinegar and bring to a fast boil (a boil that you cannot stop when stirring). Boil for 3 minutes, stirring all the time. Put a little on a saucer and into the fridge to make sure it will set. If not, another few minutes of boiling are necessary.

→ Remove from the heat and leave to stand for 5 minutes. Pour into the sterilized jars and seal.

→ Serve with goat's cheese on crackers for a moment of sublime revelation. It will send your tongue, tonsils and toes tingling for several minutes of sheer delight. Big thanks Jan!

CHECK OUT THE EXCELLENT SOUTH DEVON CHILLI FARM WHO SUPPLY TERRIFIC CHILLIES OF ALL DIFFERENT STRENGTHS – WWW.SOUTHDEVON CHILLIFARM.CO.UK

SOME COOKING TIPS

- Use a large pot as it will bubble up.
- If you stir throughout the cooking time you will not get a scum on top.
- Wear gloves when cutting up the Scotch bonnets.

DEPTH-CHARGED DUCK

WITH FIERY KUMQUAT CHUTNEY

Pork is amazing in its ability to wrestle with paprika, garlic, salt and spice, and still come out on top with the victory that is chorizo. Duck is another meat that I think we need to be more brazen with – spice it up, it can take it!

Serves 4

4 boneless duck breasts

1 tablespoon vegetable oil

1 onion, diced

1 red chilli, deseeded and finely chopped

2 garlic cloves, finely chopped

1 cinnamon stick, broken in half

½ teaspoon ground mixed spice

1 teaspoon ground cumin

1 teaspoon turmeric

250g cooked puy lentils

1 x 400g tin cooked chickpeas, drained

400ml chicken stock

juice of 1 lemon

3 tablespoons coriander root and leaves, roughly chopped

salt and freshly ground black pepper

→ Preheat the oven to 220°C/425°F/Gas 7.

→ Place the duck breasts, skin side down, in an ovenproof frying pan and set over a low heat. Cook gently until most of the fat has rendered out from under the skin – 8–10 minutes. Turn the duck breasts over and then place the frying pan in the oven and cook for 5–8 minutes until medium rare/medium. Remove from the oven and rest for 5 minutes.

→ Meanwhile, heat a sauté pan until hot and add the vegetable oil, onion and chilli and sweat for 2–3 minutes until just softened. Add the garlic, cinnamon, mixed spice, cumin and turmeric and fry for 1 minute. Add the lentils and tinned chickpeas and stir to coat well.

→ Pour over the chicken stock and bring to the boil. Reduce the heat and simmer for 5–10 minutes, until the liquid has reduced by half.

→ While the lentils and chickpeas are cooking, to make the chutney, heat a sauté pan until hot and then add the vegetable oil and shallot. Fry for 2–3 minutes until just softened. Add the chillies, mustard seeds and spices, and fry for a further 2 minutes. Add the kumquats and cook for 3–4 minutes until they are just softened. Add the brown sugar and vinegar and bring to the boil. Cover and simmer for 8 minutes until the kumquats are softened fully, then remove the lid and continue to cook for a further 5–8 minutes until the juices have thickened.

→ Just before serving, stir the lemon juice and coriander into the lentils and chickpeas, and season with salt and pepper.

→ Carve the duck into thick slices and serve on a bed of lentils with the chutney alongside. Have at you! Duck-tacular!

In general, Pinot Noir rules the roost with game birds. But here, the flavours have an aromatic depth with the cinnamon, cumin and also the spice-thrust of the chillies and mustard seeds. With this in mind, Pinot Noir from cool northern European climates would be too lean and would suffer a bit of a walloping. Californian Pinot Noir tends to be bigger, fruitier and bolder than its European cousins and with its extra dose of fruit, it's ready to take the plunge alongside this depth-charged duck!

For the chutney

1 tablespoon vegetable oil

1 shallot, finely diced

½ teaspoon dried crushed chillies

½ teaspoon black mustard seed

½ teaspoon ground cumin

½ teaspoon turmeric

1 cinnamon stick, broken in half

500g kumquats, sliced in half lengthways

65g brown sugar

120ml malt vinegar

IF YOU WANT TO KEEP ANY OF THE LEFTOVER CHUTNEY FOR A RAINY DAY, YOU'LL NEED STERILIZED JAM JARS. SEE PAGE 22 TO FIND OUT HOW TO DO THIS.

1 tablespoon vegetable
oil

55g onion, finely
chopped

1 dessertspoon curry
powder

1 teaspoon tomato
purée

1 glass red wine

¾ glass water

1 bay leaf

pinch of sugar

juice of ½ lemon

425ml mayonnaise

1–2 tablespoons apricot
jam

2–3 tablespoons cream,
lightly whipped

salt and freshly ground
black pepper

When Sweet meets Heat you can also play with texture. GABRIELLE'S CREAM OF CURRY SAUCE embraces apricot jam, wraps it up in spice and then revels in a luxuriant creamy texture. It's an amazing all-rounder that goes with so many dishes, from cold meats to a bowl of plain rice, and it was given to my mum by her pal Gabrielle a few years back. It's a top base for coronation chicken but is also rather gorgeous to dip chips into! It is also sensational with lobster in an open sandwich or as an accompaniment to a crab salad:

→ Heat the oil in a frying pan, add the onion and cook for 3–4 minutes.

→ Add the curry powder and cook for a further 1–2 minutes.

→ Stir in the purée; pour in the wine and water, and add the bay leaf. Bring to the boil and season with salt and pepper, the pinch of sugar and the lemon juice. Simmer with the pan uncovered for 5–10 minutes.

→ Strain into a bowl and leave to cool.

→ Add the mayonnaise and apricot jam, a little at a time, to taste. Season again and add more lemon juice, if required. Finally, stir in the whipped cream.

The most humane way to dispatch a lobster is to leave it in the fridge for two hours and then hold the lobster firmly in one hand so it is flat on the table. Aim the blade of a very sharp kitchen knife an inch towards the tail. Push the point of the knife hard and firm down through the lobster's head until the knife hits the board and bring the rest of the knife down to cut firmly between the eyes.

The simplest way to cook lobster is to boil them in sea water, or add a tablespoon of salt for every litre of tap water, to make your own.

BEEF RENDANG

One dish I used to guzzle with my spicy sambal was Beef Rendang – rich, fragrant, spicy and with awesome layers of flavour, like a rolling storm of glory. I guess it's the equivalent of our roast beef with horseradish sauce. Thunder-food! Rendang is widely available across the Indonesian archipelago and it fuelled my passion for spicy beefy treats.

Serves 4–6

groundnut oil, for frying

1kg beef, sliced into chunks (stewing beef is fine)

2 tins coconut milk

spring onion, chopped and crisply fried (to garnish)

For the curry paste

1 chunk (about 4cm wide and deep) galanga (or ginger), chopped

1 stick lemongrass

4 shallots, peeled and roughly chopped

6 garlic cloves

1 teaspoon ground coriander

1 teaspoon turmeric

1 teaspoon ground ginger

1 red chilli, deseeded and finely chopped

pinch of salt

pinch of sugar

→ Blitz or finely chop all the curry paste ingredients (use another chilli or include the seeds if you like it hot!) and then fry over a low heat in a splodge of groundnut oil until the aromas are released and the sauce has softened up.

→ Add the meat and brown on both sides. Stir in the coconut milk and leave to simmer gently, uncovered, until the liquid has reduced completely. All that should be left is a frothing, bubbling oil that has separated out from the coconut milk (this can take anything up to 1 hour or more, so it's wise to allow plenty of time – you can even prepare it the night before and reheat when required). Drain off most of this oil but don't lose any of the delicious caramelized dry spices that will be at the bottom of the pan – they are seriously delicious.

→ Scrape the meat and all the spicy goodies from the pan and serve on bowls of plain rice, garnished with a few rings of crispy fried spring onion, and alongside a good dose of sambal.

Choose a butch, dark, fruity red such as Touriga Nacional from Portugal or Shiraz from Chile to drink alongside this and revel in the bigness of it all!

MI GORENG

Mi Goreng is one of those glorious recipes that is super easy to customize to your own taste. The basic rule is to boil some egg noodles (which take just a couple of minutes) and stir fry some fresh veg (such as finely chopped shallots, garlic and perhaps some fresh peas) with anything from prawns to chicken, beef or pork. Finally, sprinkle with some freshly chopped chillies and perhaps even some ginger. But for me, simplicity is best and this Monday Night Mi Goreng is simple to prepare after a hard day back at work and is always delish!

Serves 2

150g good-quality egg noodles

2 shallots, finely chopped

2 cloves garlic, finely chopped

2 tablespoons toasted sesame oil, plus extra for drizzling

1 tablespoon groundnut oil (optional)

2 thumbnail-sized chunks ginger, finely chopped (or 1 teaspoon ginger paste)

fresh red chilli, to taste, finely chopped

50g fresh prawns, chopped into thirds

1 or 2 splashes soy sauce

juice and finely grated zest of ½ lime

handful of fresh coriander leaf, chopped

→ Boil the egg noodles until done (they cook in minutes; check the packet). Put them to one side.

→ Pour the sesame oil into a wok and put over a high heat. (If you need more oil, you can add a further tablespoon of groundnut oil.) Add the shallots and the garlic and stir fry for a minute.

→ Add the ginger and fresh red chilli (use more chilli to amp up the heat, less to tone it down). Then tip in the prawns and cook for a minute or two max (don't overdo them!). Add the cooked noodles and turn off the heat.

→ Splash with soy sauce, pour over the lime juice and zest, then stir well until the noodles are nicely coated and glossy.

→ Serve in two bowls with a touch more sesame oil drizzled over the top and a wedge of lime on the side. Sprinkle with fresh coriander and deliver to the table!

One final option is to serve this with a fried egg on top, which is how I was always had it in Indonesia – along with an ice cold Bintang beer. Cheers!

WHISKY

A planet of spice – from smoky, peaty Islay malts to the more fragrant Highland examples – in some ways, whisky is the ultimate fusion of spice. You can find all sorts of spicy treasures just by smelling it – liquorice, pepper, vanilla, medicinal herbs and so forth. It's a journey of discovery and one that all Brits should embark on! How you take your whisky, though, is a personal matter. Personally, I take mine with a dash or two of water to bring out the flavour. If you're new to whisky, try it equal parts whisky to water, in order to tame it a touch, then take it from there. Ice in a long whisky drink can work but with a malt, I find it mutes the flavour rather than enhances it. Diverse and awesome, whisky, like spice, is a world in itself. I'll drink to that!

GROW YOUR OWN SPICE! CHILLIES ARE SIMPLE TO GROW AND VARY HUGELY IN THEIR SPICINESS. GARDENING WITH A BANG!

Spice unites the world. A bit like football. Except with less chanting. It's hard to find anyone these days who doesn't enjoy spicy food – even if it's just a creamy korma or someone with a penchant for cheese and pickle sandwiches. Haggis is another classic example – jacked up on black pepper, it works superbly with an accompanying glass of potent whisky. I am a huge fan of black pepper and wish that more of us used a generous crunch of it in our dishes. It's like miniature dynamite, shocking and lifting other ingredients up higher, reaching upwards and outwards, expanding dishes that would otherwise remain comfortable. And it's not just about heat. Consider the mellow aromatic edge of cardamom, the warmth of cinnamon, the spark of ginger . . . Spicy flavours are poetic, unmistakable and highly charged. In some ways they feel cleansing, in others, regenerative. Above all, they inspire curiosity. Like the fleeting, floating feeling of jumping off a high dive. What would life be if we never went for the splash?●

SALTY

Saturday Kitchen has given me the opportunity to work alongside some of the world's greatest chefs on a show that I love to be part of. It's a fantastic team, with James Martin leading the charge each week in front of the camera, but behind the scenes there's a crack team of passionate foodies making it all happen. Amanda Ross is our chief, James Winter is our series producer, and then you've got the team I work with – producer Andy Clarke (who could power the national grid with his persistent singing and disco passion), Dave Mynard, lovely Emma Welch and our sensational home economist Janet Brinkworth, who thinks in cooking. James Cook is the cameraman who I work with. He was there on my first-ever *Saturday Kitchen* shoot and we've now been on the road for many years together having adventures up and down the UK. Here are some highlights:

DRIVING BERGERAC'S CAR IN JERSEY I used to live in Jersey so it was a complete hoot to snaffle Jim Bergerac's wheels for the day. James was sitting on the passenger side filming me, while we were driving at a fair old lick. His door flew open as we rounded a corner and, were it not for me grabbing him by his belt, James would have been mincemeat! Also, we sort of broke it. Well, it broke down anyway. But we had a magnificent day driving along St Ouen's Five Mile Road singing the *Bergerac* theme at the tops of our voices.

SCALING THE TOWER OF ROMSEY ABBEY Wow. What a view. The verger took us up and it became very narrow as we got higher. I remember thinking how amazing the history of our land is when I got to the top. The hands that built the tower are long gone, but the view will never fade.

RIDING THE WORLD'S SMALLEST MOTORBIKE FOR THE HAIRY BIKERS! The Bikers are pals of mine and whenever they're on the show, there's always a rumpus. We usually try and get a mode of transport into my wine shoot in homage to Si and Dave's roaring bikes. In Southampton I drove a tiny motorbike, which I seem to remember had been imported from New Zealand. It was such a sunny, special day and I'll never forget cruising in the sunshine thinking how lucky I am to be doing a job I love. Another gig we did for the Bikers involved me riding an actual racehorse, which very nearly bucked me off! What larks!

THE BIKERS RULE!

STRIDING THE BRIDGE OF A CROSS-CHANNEL FERRY IN THE CAPTAIN'S HAT That was on our Mission to Calais and I fulfilled a lifetime's ambition to wear a captain's hat and peer through binoculars at the French coast. Wine ahoy!

PERCHING ON THE ROOF OF MARKS & SPENCER IN GLASGOW A glorious golden view of the city . . . then I dressed up as a genie and skipped down Buchanan Street. Well, it was Christmas!

James Cook has been with me on almost all my adventures and he's known as 'The Captain' on the wine shoots. In fact, I always give nicknames to anyone who comes on our shoots. Dave Mynard is known as 'Lord Mynard', Sophie Alcock is 'The Princess', Kirsty Dougall is 'Duchess Dougall', Ben Harris became 'Bomber Harris', Tom Melia earned the title 'Master Melia'. And me? I am 'The Earl' due to the little-known fact that I'm related to Thomas Lennard, who was the Earl of Sussex during the reign of Charles II. Apparently Thomas Lennard was one of cricket's earliest fans – something which I have definitely inherited!

Being part of *Saturday Kitchen* is awesome. But perhaps the biggest thing I have learned from belonging to that team is how to season food – properly. Every chef that comes on our show, whether it's awesome Angela Hartnett, genius Jun Tanaka, affable Atul Kochhar, the one and only Theo Randall or sensational Stuart Gillies, praises the virtue of tasting to make sure that the seasoning in a dish is sufficient. Salt is vital for creating balance in our daily diet and when deployed correctly can transform something bland into something with serious potential. And salt doesn't just come from seasoning – think of briny shellfish, green olives, even smoky chorizo – they are all salty in their different ways.

Salt works with crisp, zinging drinks – wines such as Sauvignon Blanc or long drinks such as gin and tonic are a good place to start. A glass of Champagne with a salty snack is a treat that invigorates the palate with bright, uplifting, cleansing flavours. Fino sherry with green olives or bone-dry Muscadet with briny oysters are also champion matches. But salt also works when balanced with a squirt of sweetness, as in the case of salted almonds and Tawny Port. Scrummy! Generally when it comes to wine, you want to watch chunky reds – salt can make them taste bitter so, if you're picking a red, go for lighter wines from grapes such as Gamay, Pinot Noir or Nero D'Avola.

The question of which type of salt to use is one I have asked many chefs and the consensus seems to be Cornish, Welsh or Maldon sea salt, rather than table salt. Smoked salt is a luxury but there are all sorts of other salts, too – I once tried a volcanic salt from Hawaii. And don't forget the library of salty infusers in your kitchen, such as anchovies and soy sauce. Salternatives are one thing, but once you've discovered that a decent dose of salt enhances rather than dominates your dishes, your cooking will flourish.

Salt can be used in a variety of ways to change a dish: instantly by seasoning it; or more gradually, as in the case of curing meat or fish. LET'S LAUNCH THE SALT ASSAULT!●

TEQUILA GRAPEFRUIT GRANITA

Possibly the most salt-influenced drink is the Tequila slammer. You gulp the Tequila down and follow it with a lick of salt and a bite of lime wedge. We've all been there, but I am delighted to see that Tequila is being taken more seriously. Distilled from the blue agave, it has a fantastic heritage and comes in all sorts of shapes and sizes – fresh, aged, oak aged, unoaked – and is well worth getting your chops around. It can also work magnificently in desserts, such as this granita. It follows the same principles as the Tequila slammer but offers a sweet contrast to the salty/citrus combination and is a tongue-spankingly fresh dessert!

Serves 4

350ml pink grapefruit juice

juice of ½ lemon

125g caster sugar

1 teaspoon sea salt, crushed

65ml Tequila

→ Place the grapefruit and lemon juice, caster sugar and salt into a saucepan and bring to the boil, stirring to dissolve the sugar.

→ Remove from the heat and allow to cool to room temperature.

→ Stir in the Tequila – taste and check the balance of salty/sweet.

→ Pour into a shallow, freezeable container and place in the freezer for at least 3 hours until frozen solid.

→ Remove from the freezer 20 minutes before serving.

→ Scrape a spoon across the top of the granita and pile it into small glasses – it should be like small shards of ice.

Hic!

SALT ASSAULT

PURPLE PULPO!

Salt Assault is salty in its most immediate form. Like taking a deep breath of sea air, it's instantly invigorating – refreshing, tangy and inviting. Here's an example: bring together olives and the seaside and you've got two similar takes on a salty theme. Throw in some octopus and you've got a rich texture, too. Suddenly you're eating a dish that I munched in a Peruvian café in South America, which felt like a curious cross between Italian and Thai, but was, ultimately, uniquely Peruvian: PULPO CON OLIVAS Y TAPENADE CREMA. It's a simple dish to prepare and this will serve 2 people:

Sauté 100g octopus in a splash of olive oil until golden. Coat the octopus in a blended mixture of 2 teaspoons tapenade and 20ml cream. Stir in 6 black olives, sliced, and squeeze over ½ lime. Yum!

The luxuriant texture of the creamy tapenade echoes the dense octopus flesh, while the salt and savoury olives combine with the unctuousness of the cream to give it a marvellous richness. A great salty starter to serve in small bowls with crusty bread.

The sea is full of noble sea beasts. As a keen fisherman, I love discovering new fish dishes to prepare. I remember the first time I hauled a red gurnard out of the sea – I half wondered whether I'd caught a magical red flying fish! At the time I was filming with John Wright, the Champion Forager from River Cottage. John is a top fellow and his challenge when we were filming was to produce unusual items of rare culinary appeal for me to match wines to. I will never forget the moment when he pulled several giant oysters out of his bag – freshly caught from somewhere in Poole harbour. To my eyes, they were bigger than a human foot. Seriously, their shells were the size of guinea pigs! John showed me his technique for shucking them, which felt a bit like busting into Fort Knox, but the oysters inside were SENSATIONAL – packed with briny flavour and with an amazing underlying sweetness! They were so massive it was impossible to shuck and eat them whole so we had to slice them into manageable proportions – which gave me the idea for this recipe. CRISPY OYSTERS WITH SHALLOT DRESSING is another way to cook morsels of giant fresh oyster. But you can use individual regular-sized oysters, too:

IF YOU DON'T HAVE A DEEP-FAT FRYER, YOU CAN SHALLOW-FRY THESE INSTEAD. JUST MAKE SURE THEY'RE GOLDEN BROWN AND CRISPY ALL THE WAY ROUND.

→ Heat a deep-fat fryer to 180°C.

→ Place the flour, polenta, celery salt, pepper, lemon zest and parsley into a bowl and mix together thoroughly.

→ Drop a few oysters at a time into the mixture and toss to coat. Set aside and repeat until all the oysters have been covered.

→ Drop the oysters into the deep-fat fryer a few at a time and cook for 2 minutes until crispy. Drain on to kitchen paper.

→ Meanwhile, to make the dressing, place the shallots in a bowl and whisk in all the other ingredients. Season lightly, and serve with the crispy oysters and a squeeze of lemon juice.

Champagne is a classic match with fresh oysters and it would be lovely with this dish — but you could also try a New World Chardonnay or Chenin Blanc. Or, if you're feeling posh and flush, a glass of Puligny-Montrachet from Burgundy would be a rocker!

Always add a little salt at a time when you cook; you can build salt in but it is hard to take away once it's been added to a dish. You can try the trick of adding a raw potato to soak up the salt if you have overdone it, but if you taste the dish as you go, you should avoid this situation. Another trick is to balance the salt with sweetness. Think about adding sugar, honey, Golden Syrup, cranberry jelly, or whatever will work in your dish, to balance the flavours. The key is to think of salt like the frame around a picture — it should enhance the overall experience, never dominate.

CRISPY OYSTERS WITH SHALLOT DRESSING

100g plain flour

100g quick-cook polenta

½ teaspoon celery salt

¼ teaspoon freshly ground black pepper

zest of ½ lemon

2 tablespoons flat-leaf parsley, finely chopped

24 oysters, shucked and juices reserved

vegetable oil, for frying

2 lemons, for squeezing

For the shallot dressing

2 shallots, finely chopped

½ teaspoon Dijon mustard

1 teaspoon red wine vinegar

2 tablespoons reserved oyster juices

2 tablespoons extra virgin olive oil

LEMON SOLE ROLL

The breezy tang of the sea is found in most fish and shellfish, however subtle their salty glory. This will serve 4.

Preheat the oven to 200°C/400°F/Gas 6. Mix 375G WHITE AND BROWN CRAB MEAT with 2 TEASPOONS CURRY POWDER and THE JUICE OF 1 LEMON together in a bowl. Fold in 75ML DOUBLE CREAM, lightly whipped, and then season with salt and freshly ground black pepper. Place 8 SKINLESS LEMON SOLE FILLETS on to a board and spread the crab mixture on top – to about 5mm thick. Starting at one end, roll each one up into a pinwheel. Place on a baking tray, seam side down, and drizzle over A LITTLE OLIVE OIL. Place in the oven and roast for 12–15 minutes, until cooked through. Meanwhile, heat a frying pan until hot, add 2 TABLESPOONS OLIVE OIL and 600G POTATO, peeled and cut into 1cm dice, and fry over a medium heat for 5–8 minutes, until golden brown and tender. Add 250G BABY SPINACH LEAVES to the pan and toss through until wilted. Season with salt and freshly ground black pepper and serve 2 lemon sole rolls each with a pile of potatoes.

A safe bet with this dish is a Chardonnay. However, Albariño is underrated with fish and it is a glorious grape – imagine the energetic zing of Freddie Mercury singing into your face, with a fleshy, exotic squeeze of peach flesh. Galicia in northwest Spain is the heartland of Albariño and it's a green, lush, windswept land. Albariño is a top aperitif generally and is awesome with shellfish – oysters, prawns and mussels. Think Chablis with a touch of Thai aromatics.

EATING OYSTERS AND DRINKING OYSTER STOUT WORKS BRILLIANTLY THANKS TO THE RICH, SALTY, SEA-BREEZE EDGE TO THE DRINK – TRY MARSTONS OYSTER STOUT FOR THE ULTIMATE BEER-OYSTER HI-FIVE!

Oceans aside, salty is often a major component in cheese. By itself, cheese can be an intense journey, like pushing your face deep into a salt mine, but it is often much more palatable when broken up into manageable quantities and served alongside contrasting ingredients.

One dish that changes every single time I have eaten it is GREEK SALAD. It's the easiest dish in the world to prepare as there is no cooking involved. It's just a marvellous jumble of fresh ingredients and herbs with salty feta cheese as the headline act. Feta is a brined curd cheese made from sheep's milk and it has a fantastic salty tang and dense crumbly texture – perfect for breaking into chunks for salads. A traditional Greek salad contains:

Roughly chopped tomatoes, green peppers, red onion, black olives (I like the vinegary purple kind), peeled cucumber slices, dried oregano, a slug of extra virgin olive oil and possibly some capers and vinegar, depending on which bit of Greece you find yourself in. You can, of course, beef it out with lettuce and add all sorts of other things, from fresh anchovies to roasted vegetables, but I love it simple. There's a wonderful summery purity to it – refreshing, crunchy cucumber contrasting with the salty feta. Play with the quantities until you've perfected your own version and embrace the spirit of salt!

A sharp hit of chilled Sauvignon Blanc is fab with feta but, if you want to go all out, a Greek Assyrtiko from Santorini, with its salty mineral edge, is a beauty. Otherwise a crisp lager with proper hops served ice cold will match the salty tang of feta and do the job nicely.

TOMATO KEFTEDES

This is a recipe I picked up on my travels through the Greek islands. Heading south from Mykonos to Santorini, where some of the world's most intensely flavoured cherry tomatoes are found ripening over the roasting volcanic soil, I first came across these *keftedes* in a taverna in Pyrgos thanks to my mate Steve.

Makes about 10

20 cherry vine tomatoes (as ripe and sweet as possible)

125g plain flour

approximately 190ml chilled sparkling water

1 packet fresh mint, finely chopped

1 packet fresh dill, finely chopped

1 packet flat-leaf parsley, finely chopped

1 packet chives, finely chopped

1 bunch spring onions, finely chopped

1 teaspoon capers, rinsed and finely chopped

1 tablespoon tomato paste

groundnut oil, for frying

salt and freshly ground black pepper

→ Preheat the oven to 50°C/120°F/Gas 1.

→ Chop the tomatoes in half and scatter over a baking tray. Sprinkle with salt and place in the oven for about 3 hours, until most of the liquid has been removed. You do not want brown or fully dried tomatoes, though. (You can cheat and buy *demi cuit* – not sun-dried – tomatoes from a deli or supermarket.) Chop finely.

→ Meanwhile, sift the flour into a mixing bowl and pour in the water, beating all the time to make a smooth, thick and creamy batter. (You might need more or less water.) Put in the fridge until you are ready to use it.

→ Tip the herbs, spring onions, capers and tomato paste into a bowl with the cooked cherry tomatoes. Season with salt and pepper. (You can add more herbs or onions to suit your taste.) Stir in the batter mix.

→ Meanwhile, heat about 1cm of groundnut oil in a high-sided frying or sauté pan, or use a deep-fat fryer.

→ Using a dessertspoon, scoop up some of the batter mix and add to the hot oil. Do not move or touch the *keftedes* until you see that it is setting. Flip over very gently once it is solid and fry on the other side until nicely browned. Drain on kitchen paper. Continue with the rest of the batter mix.

→ Serve the *keftedes* with tzatziki (see page 58).

```
The saltiness of this dish works well with a
local white wine known as Thalassitis, which
means 'from the sea'. The white grapes
are irrigated by the salty sea dew which
gives the wine an exceedingly dry edge —
chill it down and sip the salt!
```

SANTORINA
A.K.A. TOMATOLAND

For an alternative take on a Greek salad, check this bad boy out – GRILLED HALLOUMI SALAD. Here we have crunchy, fresh leaves imbued with salty cheese. This will serve 4:

Halve 2 heads little gem lettuce and separate out the leaves into a bowl. Halve 12 baby plum tomatoes lengthways and add these to the lettuce. Cut ½ cucumber in half lengthways and then slice it thickly – add these to the lettuce and the tomatoes and then tip in 16 pitted Kalamata olives. To make a dressing, whisk 1 tablespoon red wine vinegar and 3 tablespoons extra virgin olive oil with ½ teaspoon dried oregano. Toss the salad in the dressing and then divide between 4 plates. Heat a griddle pan until hot. Meanwhile, cut 400g halloumi cheese into thick slices. Griddle the cheese, a few slices at a time, until it is marked on both sides. Place straight on to the salad and serve immediately.

THE TANG OF A TOMATOEY PIZZA WORKS BRILLIANTLY WITH THE ITALIAN BARBERA GRAPE.

PRONTO PUFF PIZZAS

Gather together some SMOKED SALMON, CREAM CHEESE, CAPERS, TAPENADE, SERRANO HAM, MANCHEGO CHEESE, ROASTED ONIONS and GRUYÈRE CHEESE. Roll out some PUFF PASTRY, cut into discs and then top with ingredient teams – cream cheese, smoked salmon and capers; tapenade, serrano ham and Manchego cheese; sliced roasted onions and grated Gruyère. Bake in a hot oven until crispy and golden.

There's no tomato here so you could experiment with a refreshing Italian white, such as Gavi, to pick up on the ping of the capers and seduce the salmon. Fiano from Sicily is also worth checking out – along with other little-known Italian grape varieties, such as Falanghina, Verdicchio and Grillo. They are all crisp, dry whites that work by refreshing the pizza's saltiness.

One of the saltiest of all the cheeses is Stilton. Why is it that we only grab Stilton at Christmas or on special occasions? It is a magnificent ingredient and we should deploy it more frequently and less formally – as in these POTTED STILTON SNACKS:

Bring some Stilton to room temperature and then crumble it into a bowl. Add some softened butter; a little Port – the key is to make the texture rich not runny so only use a splash – and some crumbled walnuts. Make sure you smash the walnuts quite fine – I put mine in a freezer bag and then wallop them on the kitchen counter with a rolling pin. Mix everything together well then press into a serving dish. Serve with toasted sourdough bread. Tangy salty glory!

PORT! With Stilton you could go for a sweet Hungarian Tokaji, but with the dark, tangy walnuts in this dish, it has to be Port. There are some awesome treats and bargains to be had. For an inexpensive Port, buy LBV — Late Bottled Vintage — which is a step down from traditional vintage Port but far better value for money and easier to drink. Alternatively, try a chilled Tawny Port; it's like licking the armpits of Hercules — powerful and an honour to taste. If you'd prefer a non-fortified wine, experiment with Portuguese reds made from grapes such as Touriga Nacional. Or hunt for wines from hot places — big fruit with a touch of sweetness is what you want to offset the salt-o-rama of the Stilton. Otherwise, grab a rich, dark, malty ale and give it a whirl!

I'm a porridge fanatic. I really got into it when I started looking into slow-release foods after reading the work of Michel Montignac. In the winter months, it is my breakfast of choice every possible day. Porridge gives you power! It keeps you nourished for a long time and doesn't flood your bloodstream with sugars all at once. Impeccable. I love my porridge made with milk, or made with part milk and part water, with dried fruit sliced into it, such as apricots or figs, with a slug of cream if I've really been working hard at the gym, with a drizzle of honey, or with a special treat of Golden Syrup. But made with milk and just a pinch of salt, it's perfect. Oats seem to come alive when you add a jot of salt. It gives them a nutty sweetness and that's the secret behind these gorgeous CHEDDAR OATCAKES:

CHEDDAR OATCAKES

100g medium oatmeal

100g wholemeal flour

½ teaspoon bicarbonate of soda

generous pinch of sea salt

25g lard, chopped into small dice

100g mature Cheddar cheese, finely grated

4 tablespoons boiling water to mix

→ Preheat the oven to 200°C/400°F/Gas 6.

→ Place the oatmeal, flour, bicarbonate of soda and salt into a bowl and mix well.

→ Add the lard and cheese and rub together. Add the water a tablespoon at a time to form a stiffish dough.

→ Roll the dough to about 2–3mm thick then stamp out into rounds.

→ Place on a baking tray and bake in the oven for about 10 minutes until the edges start to go golden brown.

→ Remove and cool before eating with a good cheese.

And it's not just oats that seem to take beautifully to a sprinkle of salt. MY MUM'S SCONES work a treat with salt. When you smear on the cream and jam, you create a 3D flavour and texture matrix that has me diving for the next scone before I've even eaten the first. Greedy!

MY MUM'S SCONES

225g self-raising flour

pinch or two of sea salt

55g butter, cut into cubes

55g caster sugar

55g sultanas or currants (optional)

approximately 140ml milk

→ Preheat the oven to 220°C/425°F/Gas 7.

→ Tip the flour into a large bowl with the salt and add the butter. Rub together with your fingertips until it resembles crumbs.

→ Stir in the sugar and the fruit, if using.

→ Pour in the milk, a little at a time, and combine to make a dough.

→ Scatter some flour on the work surface and roll out the dough until it is approximately 1cm thick. Using a 6cm cutter, cut into rounds.

→ Place the rounds on a baking tray and bake in the middle of the oven for 10–12 minutes – be careful they don't burn!

Sprinkle some salt on your next Crunchie and live the dream. The surprising contrast gives a punchy, mouth-watering, dynamite thrust. Try this SALTY CARAMEL POPCORN, too – it'll make enough for a family to snack on while watching a film. How about *Up*? It's a brilliant, family film – I took Ruby to see it at the cinema. I remember leaving the theatre with Ruby grinning and doing impersonations of Kevin the bird, when it struck me how wonderful it is that Pixar created a movie that a four-year-old and a thirty-five-year-old can watch together and unanimously agree is fabulous. Magical! And like a tip-top dish, it's a creative moment in time that unites, inspires and gives us pause for thought. I wish we could all get together with a bowl of popcorn and watch *Up* right now!

→ Place the popping corn into the microwave and cook according to the instructions on the packet.

→ Open carefully, making sure no more corn pops out. Set aside to cool slightly in a large bowl.

→ Place the water and sugar into a saucepan over a medium heat and cook until a light golden caramel forms.

→ Whisk in the butter and salt, and mix well.

→ Pour over the popped corn and toss to coat all the pieces – take care as the caramel is very hot. Allow to cool slightly before devouring!

SALTY CARAMEL POPCORN

100g salted microwave popping corn

2 tablespoons water

100g caster sugar

40g butter

1½ teaspoons sea salt, crushed

SALT AND CHOCOLATE, OR SALT AND CARAMEL ROCKS!

BAKALA FISH PIE

Bakala is a top example of how to preserve fish in salt. There are stacks of recipes for salted cod, perhaps because it is oddly un-fishy and firm in texture and takes well to a variety of processes and ingredients. This is my take on fish pie, using the glorious texture of salt cod to make a truly stunning dish.

Serves 4

500g salt cod, soaked overnight in cold water and refreshed several times over

750ml milk

1 bay leaf

80g butter

1 onion, finely sliced

1 garlic clove, finely chopped

60g plain flour

500g waxy potatoes, peeled and cut into small dice

2 tablespoons flat-leaf parsley

80g dried breadcrumbs

60g Manchego or Portuguese firm cheese, finely grated

salt and freshly ground black pepper

→ Preheat the oven to 180°C/350°F/Gas 4.

→ Place the cod into a saucepan with the milk and bay leaf. Place on the heat and bring to the boil. Simmer for 10 minutes until just cooked through.

→ Strain off the milk and reserve, then flake the fish into a bowl.

→ Heat 60g of the butter in a large sauté pan until foaming, then add the onion and cook for 10 minutes until tender and golden brown.

→ Add the garlic and cook for 1 minute more.

→ Add the flour and cook for 1–2 minutes, until lightly toasted.

→ Add the reserved milk, a little at a time, stirring continuously, until all the milk has been added.

→ Bring to the boil, and then simmer for 5–7 minutes until thickened.

→ Meanwhile, heat the remaining butter in a separate frying pan until hot, and then add the diced potatoes. Cook, stirring occasionally, for 4–5 minutes until golden brown and nearly cooked through.

→ Add the flaked salt cod and the cooked potatoes to the onion mixture and mix really well. Taste and season with a little salt and plenty of pepper, then add the parsley.

→ Spoon into a buttered oven proof dish and smooth the top over. Mix the breadcrumbs and cheese together and sprinkle over the top.

→ Place in the oven and bake for 30–40 minutes until golden and bubbling.

→ Serve with a crisp green salad.

The creamy texture of this dish works with a wine of similar richness, such as Pinot Gris from Alsace. Or, for sheer refreshment against the salty edge, a crisp, chilled Italian white would be charming.

SALTING WITH PRIDE

Infusing and curing ingredients not only gives them a salty dimension which brings out flavour, but it can also have a dramatic effect on texture. Cured meats have a fantastic density and an oily character. But salt can also be used to insulate food while it's cooking in order to preserve tenderness and freshness – as in the case of roasting salt-crusted fish.

Sticking with my seaside theme, one of my favourite ingredients for adding a salty stratum to a dish is the anchovy. They taste so beautifully of the ocean when they are fresh but when salted in brine and preserved they develop an unparalleled salty intensity. They are amazing when added to the base of a tomato sauce for pasta. Dissolve them whole in some olive oil in the pan and watch them as you stir – they melt! And they do just the same thing if you stud them into a joint of lamb before roasting. They are magical salty miracles and I hereby offer praise and thanksgiving for the small might of the humble anchovy.

Try this GARLIC ANCHOVY LINGUINE, which is my offering to the temple of anchovies:

→ Heat a large sauté pan until medium hot, add the olive oil and anchovies and cook over a gentle heat for 2–3 minutes, stirring all the time so that the anchovies dissolve into the oil.

→ Add the garlic, dried chilli flakes, lemon zest and capers, and cook for another 1 minute. Turn off the heat and allow the flavours to infuse.

→ Bring a pan of salted water to the boil and cook the pasta according to the packet instructions. Drain and toss the pasta straight into the sauce. Return to the heat to heat through.

→ Add the parsley and season well with a touch of salt and plenty of pepper. Serve topped with the grated Parmesan.

GARLIC ANCHOVY LINGUINE

8 tablespoons extra virgin olive oil

8 tinned anchovies

2 garlic cloves, crushed

½ teaspoon dried chilli flakes

zest of 1 lemon

2 tablespoons fine capers, drained and rinsed

400g linguine pasta (dried or fresh)

3 tablespoons flat-leaf parsley, roughly chopped

3–4 tablespoons Parmesan cheese, finely grated, to taste

salt and freshly ground black pepper

Salt is one of cooking's most valuable flavours. It is unique. It can be edgy, thrilling, tangy, supportive, thirst-making, or all of those things rolled into one. It can shore up or collapse the strata of flavour in a dish. One of the saltiest spontaneous moments of my life came on my first day of hosting The F-Word Live. Stuart Gillies rocked up to the roar of the festival crowd as I strutted my stuff, bigging up the dish he was about to cook, revving the audience and getting everyone whizzed into a frenzy of cooking excitement. And that's when Stuart and I realized we had no gas on stage. No heat. No way to cook. And a packed house of paying customers hungry for a demo. That's what I call a salty moment – a sudden realization that changes everything. Stuart is a chef of great invention and we promptly turned the demo into a sashimi masterclass, embracing the freshness of fish and saltiness of pickles, and capitalizing on the joy of live cooking and the spontaneity of a chef who is 100 per cent worth his salt.●

EARTHY

Earthy cooking is not musty or tired – earthy ingredients are vibrant! Think of beetroot, celeriac and radishes. All earthy in their own way, but with different emphases – beetroot has a sweetness lurking within its deep purple sphere, celeriac has a pungent earthy intensity (as well as looking like a scarecrow's brain), and radishes have a pink hue and an earthy, peppery kick – marvellous sliced into a salad! Apart from these and other root veg, there are stacks of leaves, such as chard, which have an earthy tang, as well as an abundance of mushrooms to consider. Certain river fish have an earthy flavour, too. Something that makes them unmistakably 'rivery'. I think of earthy as dividing into two – things that grow underground, and things that grow overground.

In wine, earthy aromas can be found in older vintages of classy, top-notch kit. In fine, old, red Pinot Noir from Burgundy, for example, it's common to smell a leafy forest floor. In Barolo there can be truffly notes and in red Bordeaux the woody scent of a cigar box is a common descriptor. As a result, aged wine can be a winner with earthy flavours in dishes, especially when you're in the mood for something deep, unusual and engaging – like slow dancing with a grandfather clock while dressed up as a giant leek. However, earthy notes in wine can indicate that a wine is dirty (when it smells off and, trust me, you'll know) but, in older vintages, earthy notes are positively admired.

Wine tastes have changed a lot in the past few years. Up until quite recently, fine wine was made to take home and hibernate in the bottle until it had softened up and released its aromas and flavours but, increasingly, we want to slap down our cash, nip home and crack open the bottle there and then. If you are keen to age your wine, though, you'll need a cool, dark place with a constant temperature of around 13°C to keep the wine slowly developing like a very slow negative in a photo lab. And if you're into earthy flavours, the result is worth waiting for. If you're keen to taste aged wine but don't have anywhere appropriate to store it, help is at hand. You can buy wine *En Primeur* – before it has even been bottled – for a bit of a bargain price and it is then stored for you in pristine order for around a tenner per year. Many companies offer this service, but I would urge caution. Only buy wine from wineries you know you like and only place orders with well-established companies, such as Berry Bros and Rudd, Armit, Corney and Barrow, Bibendum Wine or Farr Vintners. There are others you can trust but you want to make sure you know what costs are involved on top of storage, such as VAT, duty and insurance. If you read a wide range of reviews and pick wineries well, your path to the world of earthy, aged wine is opening before you. You can also buy wines that are ready-aged but they tend to be pricey. Some of the best-value, aged red wine comes from Rioja where, in the case of Gran Reservas, the wine has had at least two years in oak casks and three in the bottle. Well worth knowing if you're a fan of aged wines but not their price tag!●

RED WINES THAT AGE WITH EARTHY GLORY
Barolo, Pinot Noir from Burgundy and Bordeaux reds. But look to the New World — there's some movement on wines that age and it's a place to keep a close eye on .

EARTHY THINGS THAT GROW ABOVE THE EARTH

Fava are amazing beans. Everywhere in the world, fava beans are what we in the UK refer to as broad beans – the beans that Hannibal Lecter so memorably matched with a human liver and 'a nice Chianti'. Not my taste! But in Greece, fava are split yellow peas. And when they come from Santorini, their aromatic, sweet, earthy edge is intense and wonderful. Santorini is famous for many things – black sand beaches, amazing tiny tomatoes packed with intense flavour and, of course, these fava beans. My mate Steve is a fanatic about all things Santorini – he even has a house which overlooks the caldera of the old volcano. When I was there, he cooked up some SANTORINI FAVA for me. According to Steve, there are many ways to serve them. Traditionally they are topped with chopped spring onions and olive oil, and presented alongside some lemon wedges and good, crusty white bread. They are great served with seared scallops or octopus stewed with tomatoes and *vin santo* (a sweet wine from Santorini that is made with sun-dried grapes). For a more sophisticated purée, though, you can add a few drops of white truffle oil. Or you could sprinkle fried pistachio or almonds over the top. Wahey! These quantities will serve 6:

SANTORINI FAVA

250g fava beans (yellow split peas) – ideally from Santorini!

1 garlic clove, peeled but left whole

1 small red onion, peeled and sliced in half

1 bay leaf

1 small bunch fresh thyme, tied together

75ml olive oil (a good, fruity Greek variety)

lemon juice, to taste (optional)

sea salt and freshly ground black pepper

→ Rinse the fava in a sieve, taking out any grit. Put the beans in a medium saucepan and cover with cold water.

→ Add the garlic, onion, bay leaf and thyme, and bring to the boil – skim as much scum as you can from the top. (Do not add any salt at this stage or the beans will not soften.) Simmer for approximately 45 minutes, or until the fava are soft and most of the liquid has evaporated.

→ Drain the beans, discarding the herbs and onion. Blitz the beans and garlic together, drizzling in the oil while the blender is running, until you have a very smooth purée. Season with plenty of salt and pepper and blitz again.

The other thing that Santorini is famous for
is wine — particularly the zinging white wine
known as Santorini. It is produced from
vineyards on volcanic soil that are supposed
to have been there since Homeric times. The
headline grape in these fantastic white
wines is Assyrtiko and it has a superbly
bright, dazzling intensity. If you're a
fan of intense crisp white, get your
chops around a glass of Assyrtiko pronto!

As a contrast to Steve's recipe here's a spiced-up BLACK
LENTIL DAHL recipe. Talk about layers of flavour, this is
stratum upon stratum of stimulation:

→ Rinse the lentils well then place in a saucepan and cover with
cold water. Add the ground cumin and turmeric and bring to
the boil. Turn the heat down to a simmer and cook for 20
minutes until tender. Drain and set aside.

→ Heat a deep frying pan until hot, add the butter and heat until
foaming. Add the ground coriander, chilli and salt and fry for
30 seconds.

→ Add the onion and cook over a medium heat for 5 minutes
until softened and just starting to colour.

→ Stir in the garlic and chillies and fry for another 2 minutes.

→ Add the drained lentils, stock and lemon juice, and mix well
then simmer for 5 minutes.

→ Add the garam masala and fresh coriander. Taste and adjust the
seasoning if needed.

→ Serve with some warm naan bread.

BLACK LENTIL DAHL

250g split black lentils

½ teaspoon ground cumin

½ teaspoon turmeric

40g butter

½ teaspoon ground coriander

½ teaspoon chilli powder

¼ teaspoon salt

1 onion, finely chopped

2 garlic cloves, finely chopped

2 green chillies, finely chopped

150ml vegetable or chicken stock

juice of ½ lemon

½ teaspoon garam masala

2 tablespoons coriander leaves, roughly chopped

I suppose I have always had a fixation with beans. I once wrote to 'Mr Heinz' at the Heinz factory early in childhood to congratulate him on his excellent baked beans and received a bunch of posters and bumf by return. I have never forgotten it and for years I believed that Mr Heinz had personally written back to me. Wow. I still love his beans. Now I love growing all sorts of beans every summer. They can do anything – whole in salads, mashed into fluff-mountains, or deployed to the front line in a glorious soup. Every time I make this BRILLIANT BEAN SOUP, it vanishes in moments. The soup fairies seem to love it – as soon as my back is turned, it is hoovered up by unseen mouths! These quantities will serve 2:

Finely chop ½ onion and sauté with 10 lardons in a saucepan in a splash of olive oil until golden. Rinse and drain 1 tin mixed beans/pulses and ½ tin lentils and add these to the pan. Cut 1 carrot into thin wands (about 1½cm long) and add to the pan, along with ½ glass white wine, 2 glasses water, ½ vegetable stock cube, 1 bay leaf, 3 sprigs of thyme, 8 coriander seeds, a generous pinch of ground cinnamon, a pinch of dried chilli flakes, a pinch of ground cumin, 1 teaspoon wholegrain mustard and the juice of ½ lemon. Season with sea salt and freshly ground black pepper to taste. Simmer everything together and when you're ready to eat, grate some Parmesan over the top and sprinkle with fresh thyme leaves. Serve with crusty bread in big bowls. An earthly earthy delight!

BACON AND ARTICHOKE HEARTS
Wrap ARTICHOKE HEARTS in DRY-CURED BACON and secure with a wooden toothpick. Sizzle in the pan with some SLICES OF GARLIC and OLIVE OIL. Serve as a warm, earthy, salty aperitif. Pig it up!

With rustic dishes like this bean soup, go
for wild wines that glug easily, are made to
drink now and offer a simple dose of fun.
Places in France like Minervois, Fitou and
Corbières offer good-value, uncomplicated
reds with character and flourishes of spice
that would match with this dish. Because of
its herby notes, I also love finding wines
from southwest France, which are infused with
a subtle, herby character from the hillsides
known as 'garrigue' (think wild thyme and
rosemary). Sometimes wines get imbued with
the flavours that surround them, you see. One
hotly debated topic is whether or not the
earthy, minty aromas in some wines come from
eucalyptus trees planted near the vineyards
in countries such as Australia and Chile. The
theory is that the oils from the trees blow
on to the grapes and infuse the wine with a
eucalyptus-style character. I've spoken to
winemakers who absolutely believe this and
others who believe the flavour is caused by
other things, such as the grapes not being
ripe. Whatever the cause, there's no doubt
it's there. And, interestingly, in Chile
there are also claims that the local
Boldo trees, which have a similar
aromatic freshness, are infiltrating
wines by the same method. Flavour by
stealth!

BIG UP
THE BEAN!

I've always thought of aubergines as being a bit like giant beans. I find them fascinating. Amazing things. They are so smooth and satisfying in their shape and depth of colour, and they are amazingly versatile, too – they can go into dips (think of Greek *Melanzana Salata* or Egyptian *Baba Ghanoush*), they can be smoked, grilled, sautéed, or finely chopped and added to ratatouille. However, I had never thought of serving aubergines with eggs until I strolled into a southern Spanish tapas bar and ordered *Berenjenas Revueltas al Estilo de Tia Luz* – which more or less translates as AUNTY LUZ'S FRIED AUBERGINES. I ordered them out of curiosity and when I got home I had to have a go at making them myself. I know it sounds a weird match but the similar texture unites them and the sweetness of the olive oil in the recipe brings out the vegetable's subtle savoury, sweet and earthy character:

Thinly slice 1 aubergine and fry the slices in olive oil. Set aside. Whisk 2 eggs and fry in batches to make thin omelettes. Stack these with the aubergine slices. Think of it as an outsized Liquorice Allsort. Season with salt and freshly ground black pepper, and drizzle with extra virgin olive oil. You can stack it haphazardly for a rustic look or be more precise and cut the layers with a kitchen ring for more finesse. Either way, it's outstanding. You can vary it by adding your choice of fresh herbs but I prefer it simple. Dive in for a squidgy mouthful. Yummo!

My mum was always exchanging recipes with her pals. Gabrielle was one of them. She once took me out for the day from my boarding school, King's College Choir School, when I must have been around eleven years old. She bought me gooey cakes and squidgy buns, and I remember having great fun. Until the time came to go back. I landed Gabrielle in it by shouting loudly in Robert Sayle department store, 'Don't take me back to that terrible place!' Poor Gabrielle was intensely embarrassed, which only fuelled my theatrics as we passed the perfume counter and scurried out into the damp November evening. In spite of that sticky situation, Gabrielle has kindly provided me with her recipe for ASPARAGUS MOUSSE, so I guess I'm forgiven:

Dissolve 1 sachet gelatine in 425ml hot chicken stock. Allow to cool, then tip into a blender with 1 bunch fresh asparagus, steamed or boiled until tender (or 1 tin asparagus

THIS MOUSSE IS A GREAT WAY TO PRESERVE FRESH ASPARAGUS AS IT FREEZES WELL AND THERE'S NO FLAVOUR QUITE LIKE IT!

tips, drained) – reserving a few to garnish – and 200ml mayonnaise. Blitz until smooth. Season with salt and freshly ground black pepper, then spoon into individual ramekins or one large mousse dish. Serve with Melba toast.

English asparagus is a special treat for me and while some swear by Sauvignon Blanc as the drink to match, I often find it is too high in acidity — especially if you're serving the asparagus with butter. The wine can feel a touch shrill and piercing for the creamy melted butter. Another all-round winner with asparagus, however, is Grüner Veltliner — it is mildly aromatic but fuller in texture than Sauvignon Blanc (less bite and more body). It's a delicious white wine, a speciality of Austria, generally unoaked and with a glassy, cool polish and a grapefruity twist. It's also got an invigorating white pepper niff that works amazingly well alongside tricky flavours, such as asparagus. And, listen to this: Grüner Veltliner will jet your palate to the peak of Mount Happy if you serve it with scallops!

Names to look out for: Johann Donabaum is my favourite (he's a young dynamic producer who insists that freshness rules) but it is also worth hunting for Bründlmayer, Huber, Tegernseerhof and Heidler. These may sound like a collection of Alpine ski resorts or brand names for chunky power tools, but they are far more fun. After all, you can't drink a power tool.

There are some earthy flavours that come neither from below the earth nor above it, but instead from the water . . . My mum's buddy Selina passed a fantastic WATERCRESS SOUP recipe to the family years back and it's become a staple in the Smith household ever since. It's super-easy and a real testament to the earthy bite of British watercress:

Melt a large knob of butter in a saucepan and then gently fry 150g watercress. When it has softened and is wilted, add about 1 tablespoon flour and cook for a few minutes (add more flour if you want the soup thicker). Pour in 600ml/1 pint water and 1 vegetable stock cube, bring to the boil and simmer until tender. Take off the heat and liquidize until smooth. Add 600ml/1 pint full-fat milk and put back on the heat. Warm through, season and enjoy with a glass of groovy Grüner Veltliner.

There are several moments in my life that I massively rate. Getting married, having children, becoming an uncle and meeting Roger Moore all rank at a fairly solid, high-cruising altitude in terms of delight and revelry. However, I have recently had an experience that unleashed a mighty shuddering gastrogasm deep within my soul. Picture the scene – I am at London's Earls Court Olympia hosting MasterChef Live on stage with John Torode and Gregg Wallace. There I am, warming up the audience, matching wines to the dishes, darting around the crowd with my stick mike, having a hoot and generally leaping about like a goat in a velvet jacket when suddenly all my foodie dreams come true at once – John and Gregg invite me to help judge the dishes with them! It's the final show of our run in London, the great Matt Follas and gifted Derek Johnstone are on stage cooking head to head. Both chicken dishes – Matt with an outstanding, earthy, autumnal mushroom and celeriac concoction, Derek with a sweeter more caramelized tone to his chicken as it is wreathed in gloops of unctuous buttery gravy. Both are awesome dishes that have been cooked live on stage in twenty minutes from scratch from a surprise selection of ingredients. Both kept the audience enraptured and commanded their respect. (Although Derek just squeaked a victory, I urge you to hunt Matt Follas in his eatery The Wild Garlic in Dorset and feast on his tucker.)

I think I am the first person on Planet Earth to infiltrate John and Gregg's judging huddle and I will maintain discretion. Except to say, I wish I could visit that huddle every day for the rest of my life! The good-humoured warmth and huge affection for the chefs, and the massive respect for their cooking pumps it right into my top five experiences of all time. And remember, I have also fondled Anne Robinson's golden orbs on BBC1 – which frankly takes some beating.

Matt's mushroom dish got me thinking, though. Mushrooms are abundant, especially in the autumn months, and my friend John Wright, the mushroom man and general forager at River Cottage, is a profound inspiration. He is a dear man and the first time I met him I was interviewing him for *Food Uncut*. John was a gent and full of superb information, and even came to the studio dressed in a t-shirt with a picture of a mushroom on it. His books are fantastic, too, and his website has a terrific page of warnings and advice on how to hunt for mushrooms prefaced with the words: 'Warning: Eating wild fungi can be a wonderful way of enjoying the fruits of nature, but if you get it wrong you may kill yourself. Before you eat anything please read this.' Brilliant!

SHROOM-
TASTIC!

PAN-FRIED PORTOBELLO MUSHROOMS

WITH TRUFFLE OIL ON CIABATTA

Aside from the risk of death, what could be more glorious than a mushroom? They have a wonderfully unique texture and the range of flavours on offer is astonishing: from apricot-like chanterelles, to meaty-textured chestnut mushrooms and the earthy aromas of the portobello. Boosted with a dose of truffle, this recipe for Pan-fried Portobello Mushrooms with Truffle Oil on Ciabatta is a celebration of the magical mushroom which I dedicate to John. Crikey, I hope he approves!

Serves 4

75g butter

1 banana shallot, finely diced

2 garlic cloves, finely chopped

8 large portobello mushrooms, thickly sliced

100ml white wine

1 squeeze lemon juice

3 tablespoons truffle oil

2 tablespoons flat-leaf parsley, roughly chopped

1 ciabatta loaf, halved lengthways then cut in half widthways

salt and freshly ground black pepper

→ Heat a large frying pan until hot, then add the butter and shallot and cook for 1–2 minutes until just tender.

→ Add the garlic and cook for 1 minute.

→ Add the portobello mushrooms and cook for a further 2–3 minutes.

→ Pour in the wine and bring to the boil. Reduce the heat and simmer for 1–2 minutes until the mushrooms are tender and the liquid reduced.

→ Add the lemon juice and truffle oil, then taste and season with salt and pepper. Stir in the parsley.

→ Meanwhile, heat a griddle pan until hot. Add the ciabatta and cook on each side until lightly charred and hot through.

→ Serve the ciabatta in the centre of the plate, topped with the mushrooms and all the juices poured over.

EARTHY THINGS THAT GROW BENEATH THE EARTH

When you think of mushrooms you mostly think of that classic shape growing above the ground. But move your thoughts underground and the flavours become even more earthy. Truffles are prized by many chefs – I am fortunate enough to have compered a live cooking demo in which Michel Roux Junior prepared the famous *Coeur d'Artichaut 'Lucullus'* from Le Gavroche. It is a base of artichoke and has foie gras, chicken mousse and truffles sculpted around it. Michel laughed as he saw me scurry backstage to tuck in before urging the backstage guys to taste his masterpiece, too. It has become one of my favourite food moments. It was thrilling and uplifting – a thicket of people gathered around the dish, all making appreciative noises that conveyed a joint state of being. All of us loving the harmony of the dish, while mentally being scattered in several directions by the collage of unified flavours. If you have never been, go to Le Gavroche, order this dish and take me with you. It is sublime!

TRUFFLY SCRAMBLED EGGS

Store truffles in a jar with your eggs (still in their shells) – when you use the eggs you'll find their permeable shells have allowed sweet, earthy, truffly notes to infiltrate the eggs within. It's a glorious flavour and takes nothing away from the truffle but does wonders for the eggs! Use them for scrambled eggs, omelettes or even sauces...

Some swear by Champagne and scrambled eggs to start the day but, when there are truffles in the mix, a little more funk than fizz is called for. I would love to match a serious white Burgundy (made from Chardonnay) for a celebration but, for a top-value treat, a Chardonnay from high in the Argentinean Andes or cool coastal Chile will do the trick.

As far as wine goes, artichokes are an enemy, often combining to produce a metallic bitterness that feels like being ping-whipped with the aerial torn from a wrecked car. However, Grüner Veltliner works well with artichokes. You could try experimenting with older vintages of Grand Cru Chablis, which have texture and rounded, savoury notes to link up with the dish. But, for me, this dish was born for a red Burgundy — a savoury, aged, elegant, soft Pinot Noir that's been nestling somewhere and re-inventing itself as an earthy glass of mature resonant glory. Think of the meatiness in the dish — foie gras and chicken mousse as well as the earthy truffles and the reduced jus with its intensity, richness and depth. You need a wine with savoury edges, fine structure (nothing too chunky) and a lightness of touch to move the dish towards its savoury heartland.

The link between truffles and artichokes is fascinating. Both have a similar level of intensity of flavour that stands out and can dominate a dish if it is allowed to romp and run free. But handled carefully, I adore them both. Globe artichokes are a sort of thistle and different to Jerusalem artichokes, which grow as tubers and look a bit like gnarly potatoes. I adore these underground gems and here is a recipe for JERUSALEM ARTICHOKE GRATIN WITH LEMON that brings out the best in them. This will serve 4–6:

→ Preheat the oven to 180°C/350°F/Gas 4.

→ Use half the butter to rub around the inside of a medium gratin dish and then layer the Jerusalem artichokes in the dish. Season with salt, pepper and a little pinch of ground cumin on each layer.

→ Mix the lemon juice and chicken stock together, and then pour over the artichokes, pressing the layers down with your fingers.

→ Dot the top with the remaining butter and season once more.

→ Cover with foil then place in the oven and bake for 45 minutes until the liquid has been absorbed and the artichokes are tender.

→ Remove the foil; turn the temperature up to 200°C/400°F/Gas 6 and cook for a further 15 minutes until the top layer is crispy and golden.

→ Serve with a char-grilled steak and green salad.

JERUSALEM ARTICHOKE GRATIN

50g butter, softened

750g Jerusalem artichokes, peeled and thinly sliced

1 teaspoon ground cumin

juice of 1 lemon

300ml chicken stock

salt and freshly ground black pepper

CHESTNUT AND PARSNIP SOUP

50g butter

1 onion, roughly chopped

3 garlic cloves, finely chopped

2 sprigs oregano, leaves picked and roughly chopped

200g parsnips, peeled and roughly chopped

450g cooked chestnuts, peeled and roughly chopped

725ml chicken or vegetable stock

125ml double cream

2 tablespoons flat-leaf parsley, roughly chopped

4 tablespoons extra virgin olive oil

salt and freshly ground black pepper

Parsnips are fantastic and have a curiously sweet earthy flavour. They can be very dominant in dishes, though, so I like to pair them up with something else. In my CHESTNUT AND PARSNIP SOUP, I've blended them with a dose of chestnuts. They have terrific texture and round, nutty sweetness which complements the parsnips so well it's like He-Man and Battle Cat charging across Eternia to give Skeletor and his cronies a jolly good hiding. Advance! This will serve 6:

→ Heat a large saucepan until hot, add the butter and onion and cook for 2–3 minutes until just softened.

→ Add two of the garlic cloves and the oregano and cook for another minute. Turn the heat up to high, add the parsnips and all but 50g of the cooked chestnuts, and sauté for 3–4 minutes until lightly coloured.

→ Add the stock, bring to the boil, then reduce the heat and simmer for about 20 minutes until the parsnips and chestnuts are tender.

→ Pour into a food blender in batches (or blitz using a stick blender), and whizz to a smooth soup.

→ Place back into a saucepan and reheat. Check the seasoning and add the cream.

→ Combine the reserved chestnuts, garlic and the flat-leaf parsley together and serve on top of the soup with a swirl of extra virgin olive oil.

I grew up in Jersey and will never forget one summer when I got a job picking potatoes. We were a motley crew – me and my mates, a chap called Bee who lived in Nevis and kept bees, and several men who were all called Bob. Bent over, it was tough work picking the new potatoes by hand, but to me it felt like a treasure hunt. The perk of snaffling the occasional bag of spuds to take home was magnificent and, whenever I got transferred to the heat of the greenhouse to pick out carnation shoots, I would look outside at the golden day and think how amazing it is that such a small patch of land, the island of Jersey, can have pumped out two of the world's greatest things: Jersey Royals and Jim Bergerac!

The potato gets a raw deal – always the sidekick, rarely the main draw. We've all felt the warm, buttery squidge of a baked potato – or baked sweet potato – and indulged in its comforting cuddly texture. You can mash 'em, fry 'em, boil 'em, serve 'em hot or cold in a variety of concoctions and use them to thicken recipes, so I think it's high time we hi-fived the potato in all its glory. For a start, I urge you only to peel your potato in extreme circumstances. I love the flavour of the whole thing and it seems bonkers that we diss the skins. I've even been known to shallow-fry potato peelings for a crisp snack. And when you mash them, get creative: blend your potato with dollops of mustard, or some chopped apple, or swede – another earthy hero – celeriac or parsnip. Get in there and embrace the treasure of the tatty!

OLIVE OIL MASH
Place some POTATOES in a pan of salted water and bring to the boil. Reduce the heat and simmer for 12–15 minutes until they are tender. Drain and return to the pan. Put back over the heat for 1 minute to drive off any excess moisture. Mash well then add A GLUG OF OLIVE OIL and beat to form a smooth mash. Season with salt and freshly ground black pepper.

TRY CANAPÉS OF FRIED BEETROOT SLICES SMEARED WITH CREAM CHEESE AND A SLIVER OF SALTY ANCHOVY ON TOP.

Earthy covers such a diverse selection of bounty – underground, overground and wombling free. Some things are born earthy, such as the mighty truffle, and some things take on an earthy mantle as they grow older, such as fine wines. For me, the strata of earthy flavours in cooking are at their best when they take no prisoners. We should embrace our curiosity for mucky things and proudly revel in our filthy fascination. If you've ever wound down your window when passing a farmyard and secretly smiled, you know what I mean.●

Meaty doesn't just refer to meat. We can all agree that something that comes from an animal is meaty but, for me, meaty also means richly textured. Have you ever devoured a chicken of the woods? It's a bracket fungus that grows on trees and, there's no two ways about it, it's MEATY! Think of glorious field mushrooms – they're fleshy. So meaty in my book goes for texture as well as flavour. But it also refers to the flavour of umami (think soy sauce, Bovril, Parmesan cheese – anything mouth-coating that has a deeply savoury dimension). My chef pal John Campbell – a double-Michelin-starred flavour-wizard who, like me, is mad about wine and food matching – once sent me a fantastic piece he'd written about umami. He explained that it is a 3D flavour that works by interacting with other flavours – intensifying salty and sweet, but muting bitter and sour. It's a magnificent way to think about how to use umami in your cooking – which is something you will have already done if you've ever boosted a cheese toasty with a splash of Worcestershire Sauce. David and Anna Kaspian wrote a book called *The Fifth Tastes: Cooking with Umami* (Universe) and in it they have a tasting experiment that is simple to do and absolutely brilliant!●

Prepare the following solutions:

SWEET: 1 cup water with 2 teaspoons sugar

SALTY: 1 cup water with 1 teaspoon salt

SOUR: 1 cup water with: teaspoon cream of tartar (tartaric acid)

BITTER: teaspoon unsweetened baking chocolate — do not mix with water but instead chew and coat the mouth with it

UMAMI: 1 cup water with 1 tablespoon dried shiitake mushrooms — boil it and then let it cool

Taste each solution in turn and rinse your mouth with water between each one. Then taste each solution again but, this time, add a small amount of the umami solution to each one.* As if by magic, you will find that the salt and sweet solutions become more intense, while the sour and bitter sensations are muted or rounded. Behold the power of umami! It really is a meaty flavour booster.

*Remember — only add a small amount of the umami solution; too much will distort the results.

UMAMI

IS NOT A CATCHPHRASE FROM VIC AND BOB...

EAT MEAT!

Meaty flavours are generally packed with highly savoury dimensions, as well as having a more robust texture than other ingredients, so they require drinks with a touch of muscle. I remember once on a skiing holiday in Andorra hitting a restaurant for dinner and, first up, being thrilled that the owners had placed all their spirits on the bar and said, 'There's a delay on your table. Help yourself.' Wow. That was fun. After a happy interlude, I peered at the menu. Greedy Salad peered back up at me from the pages of the menu. What on earth could a Greedy Salad be? I wondered. So I ordered it. Greedy Salad, folks, is basically an Andorran codeword for Meat Blunderbuss. The salad was a single lettuce leaf surrounded by an entire foie gras, gizzards, duck *confit*, cured ham and a roasty, charry piece of porky love. If you could eat meat puddings they would have served it. This place was Meat City, the Capital of Flesh County in the land of Hoof.

FARMER JONATHAN'S FORE RIB

I've always been a fan of sizzling my fore rib for 25 minutes before cooking it more slowly, but my beef-farming mate Jonathan Rees of Welsh Farm Organics has a different take. (Visit www.welshfarmorganics.co.uk for some of Britain's best meat.) Jonathan says that for a fore rib that is 5cm thick, you should stick it on at 50°C for 24 hours and then sizzle it for 25 minutes on a high heat right before resting and serving. The meat is much softer and cooked more evenly than if you sizzle it at the start. Try both!

Argentina is another place where they love their meat… Hang on, what is it with countries that begin with 'A'? Australian barbecues, Andorran gizzards . . . OK I've run out. Phew, I thought there was an alphabetical conspiracy of meat fanatics. Relief all round. Now, where was I? Ah yes, Argentina. I have enjoyed some of the finest steaks in the world in Argentina. And their wineries have run a very successful campaign to champion their signature red grape, Malbec. The chant rose up around the world, 'Meat with Malbec', and it's a good maxim to follow since it really does work a treat. However, in general I would advise grabbing the best red wine you can afford with beef – a royal wine for a kingly dish!

HEARTY BEEF is a dish that I created for my girls Ruby and Lily. They love eating and beef is always a treat whether it's a steak, a roast, stewed or curried. But Daddy's Hearty Beef is the one dish that will always get them going. It does what it says on the tin and is a fantastic dish to power up on. If there's a hint of drizzle in the air, a good dose of Hearty Beef will fuel you up to stride forth and seize the day! This will serve 3 (or 4 if two of you are small girls):

Sauté 1 finely chopped onion until golden, and then add 650g organic minced beef and brown. Add 2 bay leaves, a generous bunch of fresh thyme sprigs, 1 tin tomatoes and a squirt of ketchup. Bring to the boil and simmer for 15 minutes so the sauce can reduce. Add 2 garlic cloves, crushed, while it's simmering – adding them late like this will increase their impact!). Pick out the whole herbs and serve the beef with pasta, rice or alone for the ultimate meaty moment.

VARY THE TRADITIONAL RECIPE FOR A BOLOGNESE SAUCE BY USING EQUAL PARTS BEEF MINCE TO PORK MINCE – A REVELATION IN GORGEOUS FLAVOUR.

Cabernet Sauvignon or Syrah are two of the more muscular red grapes but, for this dish, a herby twist is required — check out southern French reds with their *garrigue* or herby touch. Places like Corbières, Fitou, Minervois and Vin de Pays de Languedoc can offer bold flavours and top value.

STICKY BOURBON BEEF

Now, I know I said that with beef you should go for the best red wine you can afford but with this next recipe we need to focus on the addition of some sticky flavours. Sticky Bourbon Beef has a lift of sweetness in the glaze, is served with sweet potatoes, and gets a robust kick from the bourbon, so you really need to call upon the heft and punch of Shiraz – and not one from Europe, which will almost certainly be a leaner, streamlined and elegant incarnation. Ripe fruit is what you need in abundance. You could look to Australia, the Barossa Valley produces some leathery lovelies, or Chile, which has some stonkers – Elqui Valley is producing some ace work – or you could delve into the wonders of South African Syrah. This will serve 4:

Serves 4

2kg beef fore ribs

1 litre apple juice

1 onion, roughly chopped

1 red chilli, roughly chopped

2 bay leaves

4 sweet potatoes

2 tablespoons olive oil

½ teaspoon Maldon sea salt

½ teaspoon crushed black peppercorns

¼ teaspoon ground cinnamon

100g tomato ketchup

50ml chilli chipotle ketchup

150g dark brown sugar

110ml dark soy sauce

4 tablespoons bourbon

1 teaspoon hot chilli powder

→ Place the ribs into a saucepan with the apple juice, onion, chilli and bay leaves and add enough water to just cover.

→ Bring to the boil, then reduce the heat and simmer for 2 hours until the ribs are very tender. Drain the ribs and place in a roasting tin.

→ Meanwhile, preheat the oven to 200°C/400°F/Gas 6. While the ribs are boiling, clean the sweet potatoes and then rub them with the olive oil, salt, pepper and a little ground cinnamon. Place them on a roasting tray in the oven for 1 hour – until crispy on the outside and tender when pierced with a knife.

→ While the sweet potatoes are cooking, place the tomato and chilli ketchups into a pan with the brown sugar, soy sauce, bourbon and chilli powder, and heat through until the sugar has dissolved. Pour over the ribs, toss to coat and then place in the oven to roast for 30–45 minutes, turning occasionally, until sticky and caramelized.

→ To serve, place a potato on each plate, cut open and dollop some butter on top (or you could use Apple Butter if you've got any, see page 48), then pile some ribs alongside.

Generally with beef, a fabulous red wine will do the trick – Malbec from Argentina for its deep fruit and dark oomph, a classic red from Bordeaux for its savoury style, Barolo from Italy for its glorious tea and rose aromas and sack-loads of structure. I'm a big fan of South African and Argentinean Cabernet Franc. When they're good, they're great and with their svelte fruit and lithe structure, they'd be a perfect match for this juicy BEEF STROGANOFF. I don't know where I got this recipe from or who gave it to me, but it's 'very tasty, Harry!' This will serve 4:

→ Remove all the fat from the meat and cut into 2.5cm strips. Toss in the seasoned flour.

→ Melt half the butter in a large frying pan and cook the onion and mushrooms over a medium heat until soft and transparent.

→ Melt the remaining butter in another pan and brown the meat all over. Add to the vegetables and stir in the tomato purée, Worcestershire sauce and a good squeeze of lemon juice. Allow to cook gently for 5 minutes.

→ Season with salt and pepper, stir in the yoghurt and allow to heat thoroughly.

→ Serve immediately!

I'm passionate about where meat comes from and salute Hugh Fearnley-Whittingstall's ongoing campaign for better quality meat from animals that come from a less intensive farming system. I've had the pleasure of working with His Hughness a couple of times and it was he who inspired me to keep my own pigs. In fact, when my first seven weaners arrived and I showed a photo of them to Hugh, he immediately exclaimed, 'Aha! They look like a cross between Saddleback and Middlewhite.' Top marks – Hugh was bang on!

BEEF STROGANOFF

450g lean fillet or rump steak

25g seasoned flour

55g butter

1 onion, sliced

115g mushrooms, sliced

3 tablespoons tomato purée

1 tablespoon Worcestershire sauce

juice of ½ lemon

140g natural yoghurt

salt and freshly ground black pepper

A cracking pork recipe for getting friends over and dishing up a communal and convivial meal that sets people at ease and gets them diving in for second helpings is THE PULSE OF THE BANGER. It is an awesome pan dish perfect for a frosty evening. Feel the pulse of the big bang!

Put 12 bangers under the grill (or more if you want more than 2 bangers each!) and then get going with the base of the dish – these quantities will serve 6. In a deep pan, sauté 170g pancetta cubes and 8 chunky lardons, chopped up, on a high heat for 4–5 minutes until crispy. Add 2 big red onions, finely chopped, and cook for 2 minutes. Meanwhile, par-boil 4 carrots cut into 1.5cm thick wands for 2–3 minutes. Add the carrot wands, 2 crushed garlic cloves, 4 bay leaves and 12 thyme sprigs to the pan and cook for 2–3 more minutes. Drain and rinse 3 tins lentils and 1 tin mixed beans and pulses, and then tip them all into the pan. Pour in 1 glass good red wine and stir in 1 first-rate vegetable stock cube and a glass of water if it looks too dry. Bring to a simmer and cook for 5–10 minutes (keep tasting and judge the point of perfection!). When you're ready, spoon the mixture into big individual bowls and place two bangers on the top of each. Add a good grinding of pepper and a sprig or two of fresh thyme.

> The ultimate drink to match would be a smoky and fragrant Crozes-Hermitages or a top New World Syrah — and the night is all yours!

But some of the meatiest meat dishes don't want a red wine to be served alongside them at all – the offally, unctuous pâtés of the world are absolutely at their best when there's something sweet in your glass . . . It's a weird wine match – on so many levels you might assume meat and sweet are a no-no, but this kind of flavour match is very common: think tagine, stuffing, chutneys, pickles, even pork and apple sauce.

I am a huge fan of wines from the Tokaji region of Hungary (see page 28 for some more Tokaji information) and if you're into foie gras – and you can source the non-force-fed ethical foie gras – it's worth catching a bus to Hungary and eating their entire stock in one sitting. I tasted some amazing stuff and it goes magnificently with Tokaji. The rich texture complements the pâté, but the acidity cuts through and elevates the entire munch-fest to a new level of indulgence. If you're not into foie gras but still want a pâté treat, then make GRANNY PIP'S CHICKEN LIVER PÂTÉ to go with your Tokaji instead. It's been a family staple for as long as I can remember – unbelievably simple and utterly delicious.

→ Place the bacon in a hot pan and cook covered for 1 minute.

→ Add the livers, garlic and three-quarters of the butter, and stir.

→ Add the herbs and season with salt and pepper. Cover and cook for 5 minutes, stirring halfway through.

→ Pour in the sherry or brandy and then liquidize in a food processor. Meanwhile, melt the remaining butter in a small saucepan.

→ Spoon the mixture into a serving dish or individual ramekins and cover with the melted butter. Leave to rest before serving.

GRANNY PIP'S CHICKEN LIVER PÂTÉ

4 rashers streaky bacon, finely chopped

225g chicken livers, chopped

1 garlic clove, crushed

225g butter

½ tablespoon tarragon

½ tablespoon basil

1 tablespoon dry sherry or brandy

salt and freshly ground black pepper

THIS IS A GOOD RECIPE TO FREEZE!

One of the great bonuses of keeping your own animals is the different cuts that you are rewarded with. Getting my first trotters was a fantastic moment. One hind, one forward. My pal Mark was round for dinner and we'd both seen chefs boning trotters and were big fans of trotters in all their glorious incarnations. But we opted for POTTED PIGS' TROTTERS, which is a straightforward cooking approach. I can warmly recommend it if it's your first time tackling a trotter. The downside with this recipe is that you sacrifice the gelatinous texture of a lot of trotter dishes, but you gain a gorgeous pâté that is super-simple to make and 100 per cent meatylicious!

YOU CAN VARY THIS PIGGY DELIGHT AS YOU SEE FIT BY ADDING WHEN YOU BLITZ SOME FRESH GINGER OR GARLIC OR SMOKED PAPRIKA OR ANYTHING YOU FANCY TO GIVE THE MEATY TREAT AN EXTRA DIMENSION!

Toss 2 trotters into a large pan with 1 bay leaf, several sprigs of fresh thyme, and 1 stick of celery and 1 carrot, chopped. Season with salt and freshly ground black pepper and then pour equal quantities of rosé wine and water over the trotters until they are covered. Finally throw in a few black peppercorns. Bring to the boil and then simmer covered for 2–3 hours, depending on the size of the trotters and how quickly they become tender. When they are tender, hoist them out (reserving any remaining liquor for stock or to use as the base for a soup) and strip the meat from the bones. Leave aside the skin and bones (you can use the skin as casings for rustic sausages if you manage to peel it off in large enough pieces). Blitz the meat in a food processor and add the juice of 1 lime, some more salt and pepper, and a jot of decent Cognac. Scoop into ramekins (it should fill 4–6) and serve with toast as a thrifty pâté.

> With this dish, I'd love a hearty dose of warming Cognac to take on the rich texture of the potted trotters but you could also try a whisky for a glowingly potent alternative.

Fino sherry is a must for any foodie to get into and it works impeccably well with any kind of cured ham, especially *pata negra* – black pigs that are fed on acorns to increase their oily, moist deliciousness. *Pata negra* is the easiest dish in the world to prepare: buy it, unwrap it and let it breathe for an hour, then eat it. Hamtastic. And my kids love it. Family fun. Back to fino, though: it is a fantastic dry tangy wine with a nutty edge. Tio Pepe, Harveys Fino, Lustau Fino are all good but don't be afraid to try some supermarket own-label fino. Try it with *jamón ibérico*, green olives or just a bowl of salted almonds. If you want an even drier version that has a salty streak, try manzanilla. La Gitana manzanila is widely available and stunning (it's the one with the Spanish gipsy-girl on the label since La Gitana means the Gipsy Girl!).

On my first trip to the Tokaji region I stopped off in Budapest first and had a bath with a hundred naked Hungarian men (long story) While I was there, though, I popped into the spa town of Eger where the famous Bull's Blood wine comes from. The story goes that in 1552, 2,000 men of Eger stoked themselves up by drinking many barrels of red wine before going out to face a siege of 150,000 Turks. With red wine splashed on their beards and armour, the rumour spread that the Hungarians had been drinking bull's blood. Apparently, it freaked the visiting Turkish army out so much they broke ranks and fled. If this story is true, then the ultimate weapon in a siege is fine red wine. My kind of military tactic! Eger is also a centre for game and I'll never forget my first dinner there. It was in a small hostelry that had pretty much every single edible game animal you can think of peering down from the walls. Deciding what to drink was interesting – with game birds, Pinot Noir is sublime, while Zinfandel works a treat with more muscular game, like boar and venison. Or should I stoke up on a dose of Bull's Blood which is mainly made from the Kékfrankos grape and is sublime with grand game dishes? I went for venison with Bull's Blood!

AS WELL AS MEAT, HUNGARY HAS MANY WILD DRINKS TO EXPLORE. TRY UNICUM. IT'S INSANE. SERVED ICE CHILLED, IT'S DEEP, BLACK AND MEDICINAL – THINK PEPPERMINTS FUSED WITH NUCLEAR-POWERED TREACLE

HUNGARIAN VENISON GOULASH

Some of the best venison I have ever tasted comes from Hungary and here's a recipe for Hungarian Venison Goulash that puts the arty back into hearty – a rustic masterpiece.

Serves 4

2 tablespoons vegetable oil

2 onions, finely sliced

3 garlic cloves, finely chopped

2 tablespoons paprika

1 tablespoon smoked sweet paprika

1kg boneless venison shoulder, trimmed and cut into 3cm chunks

2 tablespoons tomato purée

1 teaspoon ground caraway seeds

3 large carrots, peeled and cut into large chunks

250g potatoes, peeled and cut into small cubes

1 teaspoon chicken stock powder

water to cover

2 tablespoons flat-leaf parsley, roughly chopped

salt and freshly ground black pepper

→ Heat a large casserole pan until hot, add the vegetable oil and onions, and cook for 10–15 minutes until very soft and lightly coloured. Then add the garlic and paprika, and cook for 1 more minute.

→ Tip in the venison and cook for 2–3 minutes to lightly brown. Then add the tomato purée, caraway seeds, carrots and potatoes and mix well. Add the stock powder and enough water to cover by 2cm, season with salt and pepper, and then bring to the boil.

→ Reduce the heat, cover and simmer for at least 2 hours. Check to see if the meat is tender and the liquid thickened; if it is, stir well, check the seasoning and add the parsley. If not, return to the heat for another 20 minutes and then taste once more – repeat until the meat is as tender as you like and the sauce is nice and thick.

Of course, meat doesn't just mean red meat. There's superb white meat to be had from pork and chicken, so let's swing the compass and set sail for the paler shores of Meat Island. For a start, try these CRUNCHY CHICKEN FILLETS WITH LEMONY POTATOES. This will serve 2:

Bash 2 boneless skinless chicken fillets until they are 3mm thick, dust with a little seasoned flour, and then dip in beaten egg and finally dried breadcrumbs. Shallow fry over a low heat in Mazola oil until golden, crispy and cooked through. Meanwhile, boil 250g waxy new potatoes in their skins until tender, drain, cool slightly and then skin. While they are still warm, slice thickly and then toss with 2 tablespoons olive oil, juice of ½ lemon, 1 finely chopped shallot and 1 tablespoon snipped chives. Season with salt and freshly ground black pepper and then serve with the crispy chicken fillets.

A nutty, lemony South African or Australian Semillon, layered with zing and a creamy texture, is just the job for this dish. It would pick up on the lemon, the meaty chicken and the crunchy texture. Joyful wine!

CUSTOMIZE THIS DISH BY ADDING PEPPERS, PEELED AND CHOPPED CARROTS, CELERY OR ANY OTHER LEFTOVER AND ROASTABLE VEGETABLE. YOU COULD EVEN TOSS IN A WEDGE OR TWO OF LEMON TO ADD A BRIGHT NOTE TO THE JUICES.

For a final foray into chicken dishes, my mum always used to make this PEASANT CHICKEN. The recipe was never the same twice! The general idea, though, to serve 4 people is:

Preheat the oven to 200°C/400°F/Gas 6. Toss 4 chicken leg portions into a roasting tray along with a handful of garlic cloves in their skins, some potatoes chopped into bite-sized chunks and a couple of onions, peeled and cut into four. Season the lot with salt and freshly ground black pepper and drizzle a generous few slugs of olive oil over the top. Roast in the oven for 1 hour (keep checking to make sure it doesn't burn).

For me, it's all about the garlic, which you can squeeze out of the skins in a glorious sweet paste. Fabulous and super-simple. Plus the house becomes scented with heady niffs of charring meat – guaranteed to get your juices going!

MONKFISH TAMARIND CURRY

Meaty fish offer a great opportunity to match lightly textured red wines and defy the traditional logic of white wine with fish. Swordfish, tuna and monkfish can all work with light reds, from grapes such as Gamay, Pinot Noir and even Grenache. One of my favourite ways of cooking meaty fish, though, is in a curry and with a zing of lime juice and an aromatic combo of coriander, cumin and tamarind. I'd grab a mildly aromatic white such as Chenin Blanc, Marsanne or Roussanne and slurp for all you're worth!

Serves 6

800g monkfish fillet

2 tablespoons vegetable oil

½ teaspoon mustard seeds

8 curry leaves

1 onion, finely chopped

2 garlic cloves, crushed

3cm piece ginger, finely chopped

½ teaspoon hot chilli powder

1 teaspoon ground coriander

1 teaspoon ground cumin

½ teaspoon Maldon sea salt

¼ teaspoon freshly ground black pepper

½ teaspoon turmeric

3 tablespoons tamarind paste

325ml coconut milk

juice of 1 lime

3 tablespoons coriander leaves, roughly chopped

For the marinade

1 garlic clove, crushed

1 teaspoon ground cumin

1 tablespoon tamarind paste

→ Fully trim the monkfish fillet and cut into 4cm chunks.

→ To make the marinade, mix the garlic, cumin and tamarind together to form a paste, then add the monkfish and toss to coat. Leave to marinate for just 10–15 minutes.

→ Meanwhile, heat a sauté pan or wok until hot, add the vegetable oil, mustard seeds and curry leaves, and fry for 20 seconds until the mustard seeds start to pop.

→ Add the onion, garlic and ginger and stir-fry over a high heat for 2–3 minutes until just starting to brown. Stir in all the spices and the tamarind then fry for 2 minutes.

→ Add the marinated monkfish and stir-fry for a further 2 minutes.

→ Pour in the coconut milk, bring to the boil, then turn the heat down and simmer for 10 minutes until the fish is cooked through and the sauce reduced slightly. Stir in the lime juice and coriander leaves, check the seasoning and cook for another minute.

→ Serve with steamed basmati rice.

MEATYLICIOUS!

And now for the meatiness that isn't even meat. Mushrooms can be meaty, red wine can be meaty, and meat-meat can even get a meaty boost from umami (in a mushroom ketchup for instance). The joy of mushrooms is how diverse their flavours can be – the mushroom kingdom is truly a world within a world when you consider the fragrance of chanterelles and the earthy depth of morels. The rule of thumb if you're eating mushrooms for their own flavour is to cook them simply in a knob of butter – perhaps with a sliver of garlic. However, the mushrooms that we often see on supermarket shelves can be a touch bland and, if you find yourself with a glut of them, chop them roughly, add them to a pan that has a glug of olive oil and a knob of butter melting in the bottom. Splash in some Worcestershire sauce and reduce until they are a deep brown with toasty edges. Serve on hot buttered toast. Scrum-tastic!

Meaty is a concept, an idea beyond flesh. It offers nourishing, hearty, robust fare, fantastic texture as well as a wide range of flavours to match with drinks. I believe in the value of well-reared, well-treated meat and the importance of respecting the animal by using every part of it. If my dog Barney chases and bags a rabbit on a country walk, I gut it in the field, take it home and cook it. Why leave it for the crows? Like Hugh Fearnley-Whittingstall, I respect those who don't eat meat but, if you do decide to eat it, sourcing meat that is properly reared is a crucial, exciting and thrilling journey to embark on. The meat I get from my own pigs is the best pork that I have ever tasted – full of flavour and juicy richness. But, more than that, I know that they have had an amazing life outdoors with plenty of space and stimulation. Of course, it was a big day when I took the pigs to slaughter with Chris and Jane my pig partners, but I came away feeling we'd accomplished what we'd set out to achieve – rearing and looking after our own livestock to ensure top-quality meat. Wonderful creatures – and undeniably delicious.●

NEVER WASH MUSHROOMS – THEY SOAK UP FLUID AND WILL BECOME DILUTE. BRUSH THEM GENTLY WITH A TEA-TOWEL TO CLEAN THEM.

SMOKY

Smoky is a champion flavour. Unmistakable, transformative and often very powerful. The point of smoky flavours is to work your appetite – think of summer when you've smelt a barbecue on the breeze: it makes you hungry! On the taste buds it acts as a flavour enhancer and booster adding its own tantalizing tang. Fresh salmon has a wonderful flavour, but smoke it and think of the impact – richer and utterly moreish. So smoke changes everything in a dish. While steamed chicken is a pure and mild flavour, smoked chicken is intense, dark and altogether more complex. In wine, smoke is found in aromas and flavours – in fact, there is quite often a smoky character to Syrah/Shiraz. Pinotage from South Africa can also have a deep smokiness, and these wines work well with barbecued food – partly because they are smoky, but more because they are often intensely flavoured so they can cope with the power of smoky food. The key is to match the intensity of the smokiness with the intensity of the wine. You can also experiment with contrasting flavours; for example lightly smoked pork works well with an off-dry German Riesling – the sweet edge acts as a counterbalance to the mildly salty, smoky pork (similar to why the sweetness and saltiness of honey-roast ham works so well). White wines can be smoky, too – Pouilly-Fumé is a French Sauvignon Blanc that can sometimes have a subtle smoky aroma and it works well with smoked oily fish. Smoky notes can also arrive in the wine from the barrels that it has been stored in – they are often toasted (low, medium and high toast) to impart a smoky flavour to the final wine. Try experimenting with whiskies from the Scottish island of Islay, as well. They have a smoky, peaty tinge to them. Indulge in the glory of its distilleries – Caol Ila, Laphroaig, Bruichladdich, Ardbeg, Lagavulin, Bunnahabhain and Bowmore – as you experiment with matching drinks to smoky food.●

CHECK OUT THE SMOKY DELIGHTS OF A CUP OF LAPSANG SOUCHONG TEA MATCHED WITH A SMOKY BACON AND PEANUT BUTTER SANDWICH!

FLAME, SIZZLE AND CHAR
OR WREATHED IN A BILLOW

Aaaah, the open fire, the joy of cooking under an open sky. I am a maker of home barbecues.

They are easy to create and give awesome results, year in year out. And, once cooking is finished, there is no greater pleasure than perching around the warm glow of smoking embers, toasting marshmallows and deciding whether to toss on some more charcoal and dive in for meat feast number two. The smokiness of your food is what cooking outdoors is all about. You can get glimpses of that smoky character from griddling a sirloin steak on the hob. Here's how I make my BEST INDOOR STEAK:

TAP INTO A SMOKY SEAM BY SEASONING DISHES IMAGINATIVELY – SMOKED PAPRIKA IS AN INGREDIENT THAT, ONCE DISCOVERED, SOON BECOMES THE SIRE OF THE SPICE RACK!

Make sure your griddle is as hot as hell. Oil the steak on both sides (I use groundnut oil for its high smoke point) and place on the griddle for 2–3 minutes on each side. Let the meat rest for 10 minutes while you prepare a superb salad to serve alongside. Season the steak generously with salt and freshly ground black pepper, and, as a final flourish, drizzle a touch of extra virgin olive oil over the meat, as well as any meaty juices left in the pan. Char-mazing!

If you're a fan of smoky flavours, but want them from more than just your barbecue, then home smoking your meat or veg is well worth the effort – and it isn't even particularly hard to do. The easiest way is to hang the object to be smoked over some smoking logs – but make sure you use hardwood (oak is the very best, in my view). This is known as hot smoking and, if you haven't got a fireplace at home, an open fire outdoors works just as well. This method will work with fish, meat and veg. Chicken is one of my favourites and smoking adds a superb complexity to the meat, which I love to cook and deploy in chicken salads. Cold smoking is slightly different. With cold smoking you are curing the meat for longer at a lower temperature so you can eat it directly rather than having to cook it – for example, smoked salmon. You want to aim for a temperature of around 27°C. Place a covered metal tray of damp shavings (oak preferably, but any hardwood will do) over the fire and then ideally you want a pipe to carry the smoke it generates into an enclosed space where you hang your meat, fish or veg. It's a specialist area but one you can play with to wreath your taste buds in a billow, if you're feeling that way inclined!

If you love Caesar salad with chicken, you'll love it even more with the smokiness of hot smoked mackerel. SMOKED MACKEREL FILLETS ON A CLASSIC CAESAR SALAD is perfect for a light lunch. This recipe was given to me by Andy Clarke, my charming producer on *Saturday Kitchen*. Thanks Andy! This will serve 2:

Grill 2 smoked mackerel fillets on both sides for approximately 15 minutes or until they are crispy on the outside. Meanwhile, separate the leaves from 1 cos or romaine lettuce but keep them whole. Pan-fry some cubes of ciabatta in olive oil then sprinkle them with salt to make croutons. Combine 1 crushed garlic clove with 2 chopped anchovies from a tin, 2 tablespoons grated Parmesan cheese, 5 tablespoons mayonnaise and 1 tablespoon white wine vinegar to make a dressing. Toss the lettuce in the dressing then top with the croutons, some shavings of Parmesan and the hot mackerel.

Another smoked fish recipe that is utterly delicious and was also given to me by Andy is PEAT-SMOKED SALMON ON SODA BREAD WITH CHIVE CREAM CHEESE. It is perfect as nibbles before dinner, or even as a shared starter. I love the smoked salmon from the Hebridean Smokehouse – check out www.saleshebridean.co.uk. It is superbly peaty and wonderfully smoky – top-quality salmon:

Slice a loaf of soda bread and cut into 2–3cm square pieces. Mix 1 tub cream cheese with 2 tablespoons freshly snipped chives and season with freshly ground black pepper. Place thin slices of peat-smoked salmon on to the bread squares and spoon some of the cheese and chive mixture on top. For a final flourish, cut 2cm lengths of chive and arrange two lengths on top of each cheese dollop in a cross formation. Place on a serving plate with 1 lemon cut into wedges scattered around the edges. Squeeze the lemon over the top immediately before serving.

I've been a fan of smoky flavours since childhood. And not just charry, British barbecue fare – my mum and I used to burn toast on purpose! We'd butter it thickly and top with a piece of smoked haddock. Ahhh, burnt toast and a piece of smoked fish.

THIS WOULD GO BRILLIANTLY WITH CHAMPAGNE!

It may not sound like much, but I love it and when my mum was at boarding school, it was her treat at the end of the holidays, before she was packed off back to school. These days I still love smoked fish and here's a simple breakfast recipe for a DELICIOUS SUNDAY BRUNCH:

Take 1 fillet non-dyed smoked haddock and poach in a saucepan of full-fat milk (enough to cover the fish) and a knob of butter. Season generously. (Remember, it's easy to overcook fish and the fish will keep on cooking once you take it off the heat, so play it safe and take it off when the fish is still nice and pearly – after around 8 minutes.) Serve with poached eggs and a squeeze of lemon. A glorious start to the day.

And, to end the day, here's a top-tastic, smoky cocktail called the SLOPING ROCK FIZZ, created specially for me by Marcis, the barman at Quo Vadis:

Combine 50ml Talisker (Talisker means 'sloping rock' in Gaelic, hence the name), 30ml lemon juice, 15ml sugar syrup and 15ml Pedro Ximenez in a shaker. Strain into a highball glass and top up with soda and garnish with a lemon slice.

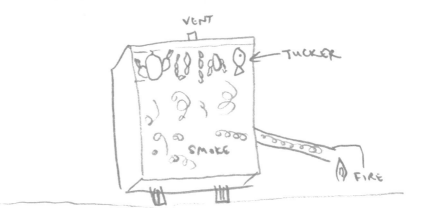

Smoked ingredients, such as the whisky in this cocktail, add superb strata of complexity. An indispensable ingredient in my kitchen is smoked paprika. There is nothing quite like it and it always gives a generous smoky tinge whenever it's unleashed – as in this PIRI-PIRI CHICKEN, which is all about smoky flavours:

→ Place all the ingredients, except the chicken legs, into a small blender and process until smooth.

→ Cut slashes into the chicken legs and then rub the piri-piri all over. Place in the fridge and leave to marinate for at least 1 hour, but preferably overnight.

→ Heat a griddle or barbecue until hot. Place the chicken, skin side down, on to the griddle and cook for 1–2 minutes, then lower the temperature and cook for 6–8 minutes, basting with any left over piri-piri sauce.

→ Turn the chicken over and cook for a further 6–8 minutes until cooked through, basting occasionally. (To check the chicken is cooked, insert a knife next to the bone – if the knife comes out hot and the juices run clear then the chicken is cooked; if not, return to the griddle and cook for a further 5 minutes, then check again.)

→ Serve with a baked potato and some crunchy, homemade coleslaw to contrast with the smoky, chilli chicken.

> And to drink, you can either swing towards
> a fruity young red wine or a refreshing
> glass of white. Either way, I'd stick with
> the piri-piri theme and go Portuguese!

Dave Mynard, my producer on *Saturday Kitchen*, and I have worked together for over two years now. He and I share a love of well-kept British beer and cosy pubs, but I must also credit him

PIRI-PIRI CHICKEN

1 chipotle chilli, soaked, drained and roughly chopped

2 red chillies, roughly chopped

2 garlic cloves

1 tablespoon sweet smoked paprika

1 tablespoon smoked Maldon sea salt

½ teaspoon black pepper

4 tablespoons olive oil

2 tablespoons red wine vinegar

juice of ½ lemon

4 chicken legs

with introducing me to the wonder of Bruce Springsteen. Dave and his family are possibly the world's greatest Bruce fans – Dave recently hosted a tribute band at a birthday party he shared with his dad – and Bruce is their hero. Dave rates Bruce so highly that he has dedicated this top-secret Mynard family recipe to him. Bruce, if you ever read, make and eat this dish, I would love to update future editions of this book with your opinion! The Mynards eat it every Christmas and I've been eating it every day since I first tasted it. Ladies and Gentlemen, I give you: BRUCE SPRINGSTEEN SMOKED MUSSELS – a wonderful treat before lunch and a cracking match with a dry martini:

Open 1 tin smoked mussels (they are amazingly smoky and wonderfully good value!). Gather as many Ritz biscuits (or any other cheese biscuits) together as there are mussels in the tin. Blend 1 tablespoon horseradish with 4 tablespoons plain yoghurt (if you want it hotter, go half and half). Place a dainty dollop on each Ritz biscuit and then top with a smoked mussel. Devour with a DIRTY DRY MARTINI:

1 measure ice-cold gin, a drip of Martini Extra Dry, 1 green olive on a stick and a splash of the brine from the olive tin. It is a cloudy, deliciously dry aperitif to polish your palate and mingle with the mussels.

It isn't just herbs, meat, fish and veg that can be smoked – cheese and garlic are two more ingredients that take on a new spectrum of warm savoury intrigue when wreathed in the magic of smoke. Try these SMOKED CHEESE AND GARLIC CROQUETTES, which make an excellent smoky appetizer:

→ Place the potatoes and smoked garlic into a pan of salted water and bring to the boil. Cook for 12–18 minutes until tender then drain and return to the pan. Place back over the heat and dry well, then mash till smooth.

→ Add the olive oil and season with salt and pepper. Beat well.

→ Take a piece of cheese and mould potato around it, pressing firmly into a sausage shape. Continue until all the cheese and potato has been used up.

SMOKED CHEESE AND GARLIC CROQUETTES

1kg floury potatoes, peeled and cut into chunks

2 smoked garlic cloves

3–4 tablespoons olive oil

100g smoked Cheddar or smoked Wensleydale cheese, cut 3cm x 1cm long

50g plain flour

2 eggs, beaten

100g panko crumbs, or dried breadcrumbs

salt and freshly ground black pepper

→ Roll the potato sausages in the flour, then the egg and then the crumbs. Place in the fridge to set for 30 minutes.

→ Remove the potato sausages from the fridge and shallow-fry in vegetable oil until golden, crispy and gooey inside. Drain on kitchen paper.

And try this CHAR-GRILLED SMOKY PEPPER DIP, to serve alongside the croquettes. A smoky match made in heaven:

→ Preheat the oven to 210°C/425°F/Gas 7.

→ Place the peppers on to a tray in the oven and roast for 25–30 minutes until charred and the pepper has slightly collapsed and softened. Alternatively, place on a cooler part of the barbecue and cook for 15–20 minutes, turning every so often so all sides have charred.

→ Remove from the heat, place in a bowl and cover with cling film. Leave until cool enough to handle, then peel off the skin and discard this along with the seeds.

→ Place the peppers into a food processor with the sugar, paprika, vinegar and olive oil. Blitz to a purée then season.

→ To serve, spoon the dip into a bowl and pile the croquettes alongside.

CHAR-GRILLED SMOKY PEPPER DIP

2 red peppers

1–2 teaspoons caster sugar

1 teaspoon smoked hot paprika

1 tablespoon red wine vinegar

2–3 tablespoons extra virgin olive oil

salt and freshly ground black pepper

With the potency of the peppers, and their spicy, zingy sweetness, and the smokiness of the croquettes, a white could well get lost. Light-bodied reds work really well with smoked cheese but, because of the informal nature of this dish, I'd go for an easy-drinking fruity rosé — perfect for the dynamics of smoke, cheese, crunch and spicy dip.

Duck is awesome when smoked, delivering layer on layer of flavour. And this SMOKED DUCK WITH A WARM CHERRY VINAIGRETTE recipe gives us an excuse to go on a Pinot Noir romp. These quantities will serve 4:

→ Place the orange juice and caster sugar into a saucepan, bring to the boil and simmer for 1 minute.

→ Add the cherries and simmer for a couple of minutes, until the cherries are tender but still hold their shape, and the liquid has reduced slightly.

→ Whisk the red wine vinegar and olive oil into the sauce, then season with a little salt and pepper.

→ Place the toasted sourdough on to individual plates and top with a handful of watercress and the sliced duck. Spoon some cherries over each duck breast then finish with the sauce, spooning over and around each plate.

→ Serve immediately (the duck can be heated up if you wish).

SMOKED DUCK WITH A WARM CHERRY VINAIGARETTE

75ml orange juice

2 tablespoons caster sugar

200g cherries, halved and stoned

1 tablespoon red wine vinegar

2 tablespoons olive oil

4 slices sourdough bread, toasted

125g watercress, leaves picked

4 smoked duck breasts, thinly sliced

salt and freshly ground black pepper

Experiment with New World flavours that are more fruity and intense than their Old World equivalents. They'll cope better with the smoke. California is one option, Syrah from France's Rhône is another, but for me, New Zealand Pinot Noir is an absolute quacker. Sorry, I just couldn't help myself!

The flavours in the recipe opposite are intense and a winning combination. But add a glass of cold, pale, tangy manzanilla sherry to the mix and it will cool down the spice of the horseradish, and cut through the oily fish. It's a classic match for smoky fish. But, if you're not a sherry fan, any bright, zinging, crisp white will be a respectable understudy.

GRILLED SMOKED MACKEREL AND POTATO ROSTI

WITH APPLE, HORSERADISH AND DILL SOUR CREAM

Smoky foods can also work brilliantly with sherry. It's a drink which is an inspiration because of its ability to stand up to powerful flavours.

Serves 4

750g waxy potatoes, peeled

5 tablespoons dill, finely chopped

1 tablespoon olive oil

2 dessert apples

2 tablespoons horseradish sauce

300g sour cream

4 smoked mackerel fillets

salt and freshly ground black pepper

→ Grate the potatoes into a bowl, and then wrap in a tea-towel and squeeze out any excess moisture.

→ Return them to a clean bowl and season with salt and pepper. Add 3 tablespoons of the dill and mix well.

→ Heat a frying pan until medium hot; add the oil then all the potatoes, pressing down to cover the base of the pan. Cook over a really gentle heat for 6–8 minutes until the bottom is crispy and golden brown. Slide the rosti on to a flat plate that is slightly bigger than the frying pan, and then place the frying pan back over the top of the rosti. Holding the frying pan and plate tightly together, turn them both over so the rosti is golden side up back in the frying pan. Return to the heat and cook for a further 6–8 minutes, until the potato is cooked through and golden and crispy on both sides.

→ Meanwhile, grate the apples into a bowl and mix with the horseradish, sour cream and remaining dill. Season.

→ Preheat the grill to high. Place the mackerel under the grill and cook for 2–3 minutes on each side. Remove from the grill, turn flesh side down and peel away the skin and discard.

→ To serve, cut the rosti in quarters and place a piece on each plate. Top with a grilled mackerel and a generous dollop of apple sour cream.

Big smoky flavours need not be confined to savoury dishes. There's nothing finer than charry fruit allied with juicy sweetness twirling on your tongue. Try this CHAR-GRILLED, OAK-SMOKED PEACH ON BRIOCHE – it serves 4 for a delicious pudding:

4 peaches, cut in half and stone removed

small handful of oak chippings

50g butter

1 heaped tablespoon icing sugar

4 slices brioche bread

→ Heat a griddle pan until hot then place the peach halves, flesh side down, on to the griddle. Cook for 1–2 minutes until the peach is just charred, then remove.

→ Place a piece of tin foil into the bottom of an old wok (one you don't mind scarring for life!). Sprinkle the oak chips over the foil, cover with a bamboo steamer or wire rack and then place the peaches, charred side up, on the steamer/rack. Cover with a lid and place on the heat.

→ When you see smoke start to curl out of the edges of the pan, turn the heat off and leave for anything from 2–10 minutes – depending on how smoky you want the peaches to be.

→ Meanwhile, heat a frying pan until hot; add the butter and heat until foaming. Add the icing sugar, stirring well, and cook until dissolved.

→ Add the brioche and cook on each side for 1–2 minutes until golden and crispy.

→ Remove and place on to a serving plate. Top each slice of brioche with 2 halves of smoked peach. I'd serve this with a large dollop of Greek yoghurt and spoonful of honey on top – eat immediately!

Sauternes is a wonderful sweet wine that would match the creamy yoghurt and sweet peach — but with the addition of this recipe's charry dimension, you could amp up the fruity flavour by opting for an Australian Botrytis Semillon, or even have a pop at a South African straw wine, such as Vin de Constance from Klein Constantia.

Smoke in itself is, of course, inedible. But deployed like a spice to bring out other flavours, be they sweet or savoury, it can unlock a whole new dimension of degustation. From burning, charring or sizzling, smoke changes and builds layers of flavour and gives food an even wider spectrum of delight. Smoke at its most basic is evidence that something somewhere is cooking. Remember the next time you catch the scent of a barbecue on the breeze and recognize how your appetite unfolds. You'll need all your strength to hold yourself back from vaulting the garden fences, hunting out the source and grabbing yourself a plate of something smoky with a cheeky wink.●

Welcome to my Cathedral of Shame, the inner sanctum, the confession booth, the place where the kinky secrets, blinding truths and sparks about Flavourland merge into a tantalizing nugget of knowledge. With these facts digested deep, you will never again need to worry about the hidden perils that lurk and growl on the other side of Feast Highway. I guess what I'm trying to say is, here's what you need to protect yourself from the hangover, which I only ever refer to as the Helmet of Thunder.

OLLY'S BIG FAT TIP FOR THE MORNING AFTER

I learned this life-saving technique from my mate Steve while perching on the caldera of the black, boiling volcanic island-blunderbuss that calls itself Santorini. The night before was big. Huge. I am in love with the purity and flavour of white wines from Santorini. And thanks to their delicious dryness, one sip makes you thirsty for another, rather like a glass of fino or a superb, chilled, dirty dry martini. That's a self-fulfilling prophecy in a glass. The dragon that eats its tail! So there I am, the morning after. Dawn stretches out its rosy fingers across the Aegean and tickles the shutters to my room. I bound out of bed like a meteor . . . only to remember that I still have quite a lot of Assyrtiko sloshing around in my ankles . . . and my head feels like it has been inflated with exhaust fumes. I grab the imaginary handles either side of me to keep balance but they prove utterly useless. The tide of my soul recedes and I flop back on to the bed in a squidgy lump laced with neat regret.

Moments later, wearing little more than a pair of Speedos, threads of hope and a veneer of suntan lotion, I drag myself by my lips to the local café where they are playing Tina Turner's 'We Don't Need Another Hero' at a loud enough volume to melt human flesh. The sun is so hot it would make dipping a toe in the volcano feel as frosty as the North Sea. I am in danger of eating in reverse all over the table. Steve calmly orders me a glass of orange juice, a black coffee and an omelette. 'Omelette,' I whimper. 'I couldn't eat a single sturgeon's egg, let alone a giant egg from a Greek chicken.' Steve is firm but polite. I manage a sip of orange but the coffee threatens to set off a chain reaction that I know will result in an eruption from my face that would make the volcano of Santorini weep with shame. The pressure mounts as the stereo emits a pulsing blare of Bryan Adams wailing like a cat with its tail in the mouth of a lion. The omelette arrives. I scoop a sliver and manage to swallow. The moment passes. Another sliver and a few more bites and the tide turns. Within minutes, I am chatting, laughing and planning a hiking trip up to the island's highest point. Thanks to that fresh orange juice, black coffee and the cheeky omelette, I feel like I am already there. A heroic recovery and I can warmly recommend the trilogy of egg, orange juice and black coffee. In that order. Tina Turner, Bryan Adams and semi-dormant volcanoes help but are, of course, entirely optional.

SELF-ESTEEM AND THE HANGOVER

In his book *Everyday Drinking* (Bloomsbury), Kingsley Amis outlines his unique solution to tackling the hangover by dividing it into Physical and Metaphysical. To cure your Physical Hangover, Kingsley recommends telling yourself how lucky you are to be feeling so bloody awful, followed by a bout of vigorous sex and then going up in an aeroplane for half an hour. Once this is accomplished, to cure your Metaphysical Hangover, Kingsley suggests reading *Paradise Lost* Book XII lines 606 to the end, listening to Tchaikovsky's Sixth Symphony and avoiding jazz at all costs – especially the music of John Coltrane, who Kingsley warns 'will suggest to you, in the strongest terms, that life is exactly what you are at present taking it to be: cheap, futile and meaningless'.

Wow!

However, the true key to recovering from a hangover is a) not to get one in the first place and b) flood yourself with water. Drink oceans of the stuff and listen to Bert Kaempfert – he is the ultimate mood enhancer, hangover or no. It is impossible to listen to Bert Kaempfert's 'Tea and Trumpets' without wiggling your toes. Alternatively, an all-out assault on the senses is a good distraction from your misery. Whingeing only increases the pain, so defy your hangover. Play the trumpet at your reflection in the mirror, immerse yourself in *Rambo II* and sit naked in front of the fridge. Within moments you will either realize that a hangover is a winnable battle or you will spot the eggs in the fridge and make yourself an omelette. Either way, your perspective is restored, and soon you will feel like Ming The Merciless, Ruler of the Universe.

Granny Smokey believed in the healing power of ginger wine, but it was Granny Pip and Grandpa who taught me how to drink properly when I was a student at Edinburgh. In spite of my Uncle Tom's kind gift to me of a bottle of Rumola (a defunct rum liqueur) one New Year's Eve when I was a teenager, which prompted my first fitting at the hat shop that only stocks the Helmet of Thunder, I rather loved the flavours of drinks. I'd pop out for lunch to Granny and Grandpa's house in Falkirk and they would show me how to fashion the perfect pink gin, they would explain why Campari and soda goes so well with a game of rugby (because Grandpa was a devoted fan of both) and why a Whisky Mac was the cure for all ills. I loved their quirks, their advice, their sense of exuberance and, most of all, their intimate knowledge of when to stop.

That moment, for this book, is now. Thank you for reading it – and if you would like to continue our chat, you can usually find me hopping around at www.ollysmith.com. Come say hi!

CHEERS!

INDEX

THANKS TO . . .

Jo Roberts-Miller for being the best editor in the known universe, everyone at *Saturday Kitchen*, my agent Gordon Wise for the inspiration behind this idea, the lovely Emma Tait for coming to see me gig at Taste and backing this book so superbly, Janet Brinkworth for so much support and genius behind the hobs, Sir Roger Moore for kindly agreeing to write the foreword and his inspirational work for UNICEF, Gareth Owen for being a big-style champion chum, Jacquie Drewe for being awesome, Jessica Hanscom, Renay Richardson, Natasha Blake, Fran Linke, Mum & Dad, Ruby & Lily, Will, Anne & Leo, Camilla & Mike, Jess Hood, Ellie James, James Martin – you rock!, Gennaro Contaldo for his kindness and passion, Big G & T, Stuart Gillies, James 'Hammerhead' Winter, Amanda & Simon Ross, the Hairy Bikers, Juliet Leith, Matt Wilson, Adam MacDonald, Juliet Leith, Susy Price, Danny Rowlands, Helen Warner, Stuart Cosgrove, Hamish & the team at *IWC* Media, the entire *Iron Chef UK* cast and crew a.k.a 'The League of Awesomeness' with special praise to Nick Nairn, The Chairman, Judy Joo, Martin Blunos, Tom Aikens and Sanjay Dwivedi, Hugh Fearnley-Whittingstall for pig and 'operation goat' advice, Theo Randall, Jon Wright for sharing his delicious guinea-pig-sized oysters with me, Jimmy & Chaela Doherty, Asa, Gerard Greaves, Andrew Davies and the team at *Live Magazine* for the *Mail on Sunday*, everyone who subscribes to www.hotbottle.co.uk, Richard & Judy, Angela Hartnett for teaching me how to make fresh pasta live on stage, Chris Galvin, Fred Sirieix, Atul Kochhar, Raymond Blanc, Jason Atherton and his fantastic flip-flops, Michel Roux Junior for allowing me to steal and devour his *Coeur d'Artichaut Lucullus* not once but twice during MasterChef Live – an official gastrogasm, Jamie Munro, John Torode, Gregg Wallace, Pat Doyle, Paul Kelly, Tommi Miers, Crispin Clover, Tony Murland, Keith Floyd, Tristan Welch, Vivek Singh, Jun Tanaka, Silvena Rowe, everyone at P&O Cruises and especially on board *Azura*, Tina Flintoff, CARA, Sean & Cath Byrne, Nick & Mel, Mark & Anna, Dan Chambers, Digby & Julia 'Jones' Lidstone, Chloë Steele, Steve Daniel & family, Helen, Phillippa, Carly & Helen at Marketing in Partnership, Helen Acosta, Candy, Lady Candy & their Baby Candies, Krisna for sheer amounts of food consumed, Beard for the stir-fries, Jonathan & Sally Rees at Welsh Farm Organics, Jane & Chris Parkinson, Ian Hoey and the Cameo Cinema Clan, Devi Syukur Syafmen for helping with my Indonesian recipes, the choristers of King's College, Cambridge, *Off Licence News*, Dave 'Lord' Mynard, James 'Captain' Cook, Andy 'Applejack' Clarke, Alison Kirkham for the kind words of encouragement early on in my *Saturday Kitchen* career, everyone at Taste Festivals, Fergus 'Lex' Campbell at Channel 4 and his team: Sarah Steel, Harry the Bastard, lovely Rebecca, Charlie Cottrell, Deborah Poulton, Matt Cole, Gareth Rees, Mike Morris, the lovely folk at my official Facebook Fan Club, my Twitter followers, Rob McIntosh, the BBC Good Food Show, Mike and Krisna without whom I would never have got to know the movies of Steven Seagal, The Wine Gang, the IWSC, the IWC, *Decanter Magazine*, *The Drinks Business*, the people of Lewes, the Lewes Arms, Bill Collison for the fab food and words of wisdom, Harveys Brewery for slaking my unquenchable thirst for the UK's finest ale, Sarah Randell, Helena Lang, Kimberley Davenport, Brian & Anne (& Jasper the Prince of Denmark), Dave, Ben & Olly Ingham and lovely Lou who we miss so much, Ben Ward, The Usual Hole, the inmates of the Star Brewery, Fiona Campbell, Jeni Barnett & family, Elaine Bancroft, *Harpers*, the London International Wine & Spirits Fair, the Wine and Spirit Education Trust, the Boathouse Organic Farm Shop near Lewes, Silvio & Lupe Caiozzi, Las Hormigas Asesinas, the monks of Pluscarden Abbey and Phil Balkwill & Harvey Hallsmith – the men who did.●

Granny Smokey's House
39 Sutton Road

Practical Jokes on
Saturday Kitchen

The best Cornish lobster

+ Will,
Swingball Champions

Pretending to be
Sir Roger Moore...

(approx. 60)
4 oz sugar
8 oz. marg or butt
(S.R.)

Flying
feasting